PENGUIN NATURE CLASSICS
Series Editor: Edward Hoagland

THE CLOUD FOREST

Peter Matthiessen was born in New York City in 1927 and had already begun his writing career by the time he graduated from Yale University in 1950. The following year, he was a founder of *The Paris Review*. Besides *At Play in the Fields of the Lord*, which was nominated for the National Book Award, he has published five other novels, including *Killing Mister Watson*. Mr. Matthiessen's unique career as a naturalist and explorer has resulted in numerous and widely acclaimed books of nonfiction, among them *The Tree Where Man Was Born* (with Eliot Porter), which was nominated for the National Book Award, and *The Snow Leopard*, which won it. His other works of nonfiction include *The Cloud Forest* and *Under the Mountain Wall* (which together received an Award of Merit from the National Institute of Arts and Letters), *The Wind Birds*, *Blue Meridian*, *Sand Rivers*, *Indian Country*, *Men's Lives*, *In the Spirit of Crazy Horse*, *African Silences*, and *Wildlife in America*.

D1052552

THE CLOUD FOREST

A Chronicle of the South American Wilderness

PETER MATTHIESSEN

PENGUIN BOOKS

PENGUIN BOOKS
Published by the Penguin Group
Penguin Books USA Inc., 375 Hudson Street,
New York, New York 10014, U.S.A.
Penguin Books Ltd, 27 Wrights Lane, London W8 5TZ, England
Penguin Books Australia Ltd, Ringwood, Victoria, Australia
Penguin Books Canada Ltd, 10 Alcorn Avenue,
Toronto, Ontario, Canada M4V 3B2
Penguin Books (N.Z.) Ltd, 182–190 Wairau Road,
Auckland 10, New Zealand

Penguin Books Ltd, Registered Offices:
Harmondsworth, Middlesex, England

First published in the United States of America by The Viking Press 1961
Published in Penguin Books 1987
This edition published in Penguin Books 1996

10 9 8 7 6 5 4 3

Copyright © Peter Matthiessen, 1961
Copyright renewed Peter Matthiessen, 1989
All rights reserved

Portions of this book originally appeared in *The New Yorker*.

ISBN 0 14 02.5507 9 (pbk.)
CIP data available

Printed in the United States of America
Set in Electra

Except in the United States of America, this book is sold subject to the
condition that it shall not, by way of trade or otherwise, be lent, re-sold,
hired out, or otherwise circulated without the publisher's prior consent in
any form of binding or cover other than that in which it is published and
without a similar condition including this condition being imposed on the
subsequent purchaser.

Nature is our widest home. It includes the oceans that provide our rain, the trees that give us air to breathe, the ancestral habitats we shared with countless kinds of animals that now exist only by our sufferance or under our heel.

Until quite recently, indeed (as such things go), the whole world was a wilderness in which mankind lived as cannily as deer, overmastering with spears or snares even their woodsmanship and that of other creatures, finding a path wherever wildlife could go. Nature was the central theater of life for everybody's ancestors, not a hideaway where people went to rest and recharge after a hard stint in an urban or suburban arena. Many of us still do hike, swim, fish, birdwatch, sleep on the ground or paddle a boat on vacation, and will loll like a lizard in the sun any other chance we have. We can't help grinning for at least a moment at the sight of surf, or sunlight on a river meadow, as if remembering in our mind's eye paleolithic pleasures in a home before memories officially began.

It is a thoughtless grin because nature predates "thought." Aristotle was a naturalist, and nearer to our own time, Darwin made of the close observation of bits of nature a lever to examine life in many ways on a large scale. Yet nature writing, despite its basis in science, usually rings with rhapsody as well—a belief that nature is an expression of God.

In this series we are presenting some nature writers of the past century or so, though leaving out great novelists like Turgenev, Melville, Conrad, and Faulkner, who were masters of natural description, and poets, beginning with Homer (who was perhaps the first nature writer, once his words had been transcribed). Nature writing now combines rhapsody with science and connects science with rhapsody, and for that reason it is a very special and a nourishing genre.

Edward Hoagland

FOR

Andrés Porras Cáceres

my excellent friend and mentor on the Urubamba, whose wiser
head prevailed

AND FOR

Lucha and Alfredo Porras Cáceres

whose kind welcome in Lima and at La Honda, in January,
March, and May, made so much difference

ACKNOWLEDGMENTS

The last month excepted, I traveled through South America alone, but the solitude was broken in the cities by the kindness and hospitality of many people. Most of the introductions I was fortunate enough to have came about, directly or indirectly, through letters written by Mary Lord and by Arturo Ramos, and I should like to thank these good friends first of all.

I am grateful also to Lucha and Alfredo Porras in Lima, who put me up in the beginning and in the end put up with me; to Dorry and Ted Blacque, in La Paz; to Angela and Peter Deane in Buenos Aires; to Jean and Tony Deane in Punta del Este (Uruguay); to Nina and Clayton Templeton in Orizona (Brazil); to Señora and Señor Carlos Menendez Behety in Río Grande (Tierra del Fuego); and to Betsy and Oliver Bridges in Viamonte (Tierra del Fuego), all of whom, for no other reason than their own generosity, cheerfully took me in.

The kind people who gave me supper here and a drink there are too numerous to list, but for kindness, advice and assistance, and incidental hospitality I am especially indebted to the following: Captain Geoffrey Davis, Mr. Deslandes, Brian Starmer, Derek Johnson, and Mike Williamson (M.S.

Venimos); Harry Haddad (Belém); Jack Henderson, Wayne Snell, Joseph Hocking (Yarina Cocha); Andrés Porras, Celeste Allen, Señor Rafael Larco Hoyle, Sir Berkeley and Lady Gage, Madeleine Vuillemin, Anna and John Timoney, Mr. Dum Tweedy, Señor Augusto Benavides, and Elizabeth and Ted Kiendl (Lima); Señora Estelle León de Peralta and her kind family, Señor Benjamín de la Torre, and Colonel Tooey (Cuzco); Peggy Cody (La Paz); Señores Fernando Menendez Behety, Jorge and Francisco Campos Menendez (Punta Arenas); Jaime Speroni, George Blackwell (Río Grande); Capitán Ernesto Campos, Señora and Señor Eduardo Menon (Ushuaia); T. L. Bridges (Viamonte); Peter de Rougemont, Roberto Corte Real (Rio de Janeiro); Otto Austel (Macauba).

And finally, I would like very much to thank Andrés Porras and Wayne Snell, who have been good enough to inspect the finished journal which forms Chapter 6 of this volume for any errors or distortions.

CONTENTS

ILLUSTRATIONS

Beginning opposite

Amazonas
M.S. *Venimos* loading grain meal (Gonaïves Gulf, Haiti)
Pucallpa waterfront, Ucayali River (Peru)
River settlement at Belén, near Iquitos (Peru)
On the Napo River
"Crying God," Tiahuanaco ruins (Bolivia)
Aymara woman (Bolivia)
Quechua Indians of the sierra (Bolivia)
Andean lake (Peru)
Inca ruins at Sacsahuaman (Peru)

Quechua market, Pisac (Peru)
Strait of Magellan and Tierra del Fuego (Chile)
Sheep range, Tierra del Fuego (Argentina)
Beagle Channel and Hoste Island, Tierra del Fuego (Argentina)
Hidden Lake and Lake Fagnano, Tierra del Fuego (Argentina)
Caraja encampment, Araguaia River (Brazil)
Caraja canoes, Araguaia River (Mato Grosso in background)
Caraja boy
Caraja ritual costume

Old woman bathing, Araguaia River

Between pages 152–153

The upper Urubamba, from ruins at Machu Picchu
Hacienda Marquez, on Yanatili River (Black Drunken River)
The cloud forest at El Encuentro
Andrés Porras and his friend Señor Antonio Basagoitia
Ardiles
Epifanio Pereira at Sangianarinchi
Toribio
Construction of balsa raft, Pangoa
Machiguenga campfire
Agostino
Mouth of the Pongo, lower end

Dawn on the Urubamba
Last resting place of the *Happy Days*, Timpia
Machiguenga chief, Timpia
Machiguenga woman, Camisea
Campa woman, Inuya River
Campa hunters and drying arrow shafts
Indian encampment, Inuya River
Quebrada Grasa
César Cruz and author, with *mandíbula*, Mapuya River
Mission Conibos, Ucayali River
The fossil in police yard, Pucallpa

Amazonas

M.S. Venimos *loading grain meal* (Gonaïves Gulf, Haiti)

Pucallpa waterfront, Ucayali River (Peru)

River settlement at Belén, near Iquitos (Peru)

On the Napo River

Aymara woman (Bolivia)

"Crying God," Tiahuanaco ruins (Bolivia)

Quechua Indians of the sierra (Bolivia)

Andean lake (Peru)

Inca ruins at Sacsahuaman (Peru)

Quechua market, Pisac (Peru)

Strait of Magellan and Tierra del Fuego (Chile)

Sheep range, Tierra del Fuego (Argentina)

Beagle Channel and Hoste Island, Tierra del Fuego (Argentina)

Hidden Lake and Lake Fagnano, Tierra del Fuego (Argentina)

Caraja encampment, Araguaia River (Brazil)

Caraja canoes, Araguaia River (Mato Grosso in background)

Caraja boy

Caraja ritual costume

Old woman bathing, Araguaia River

1. SARGASSO SEA AND SOUTHWARD

November 20.

A PALE NOVEMBER SKY, like a sky on the moon. The M.S. *Venimos* is scheduled to sail at three p.m., but freighters rarely leave anywhere on time, and it is 20:32 in the evening by the ship's clock when a stevedore on the Brooklyn pier lets the last hawser slap into the water. "All gone aft," he bawls—incongruously, for he is wearing a fedora—and shoves his hands into his pockets. There is a nine-mile wind out of the northwest, sharp as ice. The man retraces his steps along the darkened pier without glancing at the ship again. She is warped swiftly from her berth by the tug *Isabel A. McAllister*, which remains fastened alongside until the ship has cleared the Erie Basin. To starboard lies Governor's Island, and behind it the bright night walls of Manhattan, soaring up out of the black harbor like the Seven Cities of Cibola.

Now the tug is gone, and there comes a sense of uncertainty, of loss. This is not entirely homesickness; a continuity has been broken with the desertion of that tug, as if life must now start up all over again. On a long journey the first port left behind is the memorable one, and the sense of parting cannot help but be intensified by the scope and light of New York Harbor after dark as seen from the stern of a ship sliding outward toward the Narrows. Nearby a bell buoy rings quietly, the sound strangely penetrating against the night sounds of the city.

Staten Island looms to starboard, and to port the shore parkway flickers along Gravesend Bay. The green, red, and white running lights of harbor craft, and night fires on the Jersey shore. The *Venimos* sounds two blasts of her whistle: a larger ship is overtaking and passes finally to port. In the outer harbor other freighters, anchored, hang suspended on the faint reflections from the shore.

9:45. The lights of Brooklyn widen, fall astern, and the Jersey lights stretch out, marking off great areas of blackness. We are nearing Sandy Hook.

The Narrows, Gravesend, Sandy Hook, the Ambrose Lightship, the Atlantic—wonderful names, sea names. The night sky overcast, and the night wind damp and raw. Even before I fell asleep the ship had commenced that subtle quake which meant that the long swells of the open sea had taken hold of her. She is bound up the Amazon for Peru by way of Bermuda, the Sargasso Sea, the Windward Islands and Barbados, Trinidad, British Guiana, and Brazilian ports along the river. My own destination is less precise—the rain forest and the Andean sierra, Mato Grosso and Tierra del Fuego. The very names evoke so much, and are their own justification for this journey, for one must hurry if one is still to glimpse the earth's last wild terrains. The greatest of these, the oceans and Antarctica excepted, lie not in Africa but within the mysterious continent of South America.

November 21.

At eight this morning, over one hundred miles from land, there were ten herring gulls still with us, and at nine-thirty there were, astonishingly, three times that many. The birds sail forward on the ship's air currents, coast across the cargo booms on the long foredeck, and slide away astern, where they stroke along resignedly in the wake. It interests me that all of them are birds in their second year, not yet in full adult plumage—as if the adults knew when and where to gain their living more easily. Undoubtedly the new birds were attracted to our wake by breakfast slops, but where they could have come from is a mystery, unless we drew them from some passing ship where the pickings had proved lean. I saw no ship, however, and I have been on deck all morning; while a gull's vision is considerably better than my own, it cannot see over the horizon.

The water is turning a deep blue, with an increase in chop though the wind is steady, as if we were entering the Gulf Stream. But there are no signs as yet of the Gulf Stream's floating weed, and the air remains quite cold.

The Venimos rolls smoothly through the chop, by all signs an able ocean-going vessel. She is a small freighter of 1308 gross tons, built in Hamburg in 1956, her registered home port Hamilton, Bermuda. Her length is 265 feet, hull gray, superstructure white. The crew is twenty-five in number—thirteen Brazilian seamen, three Peruvian stewards, a chief engineer who is Welsh, and two Scots engineers (the Malays and Lascars hatching dark, mutinous stratagems in the fo'c'sle may be missing—indeed, the fo'c'sle itself is missing; the crew is quartered below decks in the poop house aft—but surely the Scotsmen in the engine room are in the grand old tradition of British seafaring); the captain, three mates, radio officer (known as "Sparks," of course), and fourth engineer are English. There are two passengers besides myself: a missionary of the New Tribes Mission, returning to the Brazilian interior, and a Lebanese with a Turkish passport, journeying to Belém on business. Both are agreeable companions, though the latter sleeps most of the day. In fair weather he appears now and then on deck, garbed in bazaar blues and yellows and black harem slippers. Truly he is the ageless merchant of the Levant, tired and tireless, homeless and resigned, probing the world on his joyless caravanserai.

The wind has freshened all day long and is now coming out of the southeast at over twenty-five miles per hour. This is a crosswind on the Gulf Stream, which we entered in mid-afternoon, and in consequence the sea has become rough. The sky, dimly overcast all day, with cirrus clouds in heavy ranks on the horizon, is austere and ominous with its signs of changing weather—and weather change at sea is invariably impressive, the ship seeming to shrink in size under the vast engulfing sky. Some of the gulls have dropped away, whether homeward or to another ship one cannot tell. The rest—I count nineteen at dusk—sweep silently up and down the wake or hang on the sky above the taffrail. Now and then they utter high, small, wintry cries, quite unlike the summer yawps so familiar along the coast. Two pelagic birds appear but keep their distance—a swift jaeger and a great skua, hulking along across the gathering waves.

This is only the first day out, with forty left to go, for a radiogram has come, and the freighter has been rerouted: before proceeding to the Windward Islands she must work west again to Haiti, to take on a cargo of grain meal for Barbados.

November 22.

In the Gulf Stream last night it was very rough indeed. Rain in brief fits, and the roar of the sea drowned out for the first time the drum and mutter of the ship. I slept badly, and around three a.m., when the sky grew strangely light, stood at the porthole for a while watching the gray monsters toiling past.

By morning the herring gulls were gone, and true oceanic birds had appeared out of the wastes to take their place. All came quite close in the light rain, and I was able to identify two young kittiwakes with their lovely wing bands, as well as a number of the so-called "sea hawks"—pomarine jaegers and their larger relatives, a pair of great skuas. These flew about the ship for several hours until about mid-morning, when all vanished. We are nearing the southerly limits of the skua and the kittiwake, and it is not likely that these species will appear again. Already, in fact, a single frantic flying fish—the first semi-tropical creature—has skittered off among the Gulf Stream weed patches.

At 3:50 in the afternoon, on the afterdeck, a starling whirled up from astern and landed on the lifeboat davit. Wherever it may have come from, it cannot be less than four hundred miles from shore (the captain was kind enough to estimate our position at 3:50: 35°27′ north by 67°58′ west), and yet when I approached cautiously to photograph it, it flew off immediately to the westward, toward the mainland. It knows where it is bound, apparently, but where it might have come from is a mystery so strange as to be quite disturbing. I can't believe it will ever reach the land. . . .

November 23–24. The Bermudas.

During the night we ran into the fringe of a series of gales which stretch, apparently, from southeast of Bermuda as far north as Iceland, and eastward across Europe. The swells from these storms were huge, and after two a.m. I was thrown about in my berth like a sack of custard. The day, when at last it dawned, was clear, and the great sparkling walls of blue water, some of them thirty feet and more, seemed exhilarating rather than otherwise. (Waves larger than that are awesome, however;

not only are they not exhilarating, they are oppressive, even to the best of sailors. "They soared by us in broad sombre ranges, with hissing white ridges, an inhospitable and subduing sight," as H. M. Tomlinson says in *The Sea and the Jungle*. And: "The mirror of water on the iron surfaces, constantly renewed, reflected and flashed the wild lights in the sky as she rolled and pitched, and somehow these reflections from her polish made the steamer seem more desolate and forlorn." Conrad himself could not put it better than that.)

The starling mystery has been renewed with the sudden appearance of this tireless bird among the cargo hatches early this morning. There is the remote possibility, of course, that two birds arrived yesterday and only one was fool enough to depart, or even that this one arrived separately, but the chances are that yesterday's bird took a good hard look at its situation (and if a bird can be hardheaded, it is certainly the squat, quarrelsome starling) and hastened back to the *Venimos*. In any case, the incumbent seems content to tarry here a while, fluttering busily up and down the ship or diving into a cable drum to rest. It will almost certainly disembark at Bermuda tonight, in quest of food and water. Some of the junior officers have interested themselves in its plight, or interested themselves in my interest—I cannot be sure which seems to them the greater curiosity.

At 10:30 this morning a lone herring gull appeared and as quickly disappeared again, whirled away like a scrap of blown paper. We are now less than one hundred miles from land. I am keeping a weather eye out for the rare cahow, or Bermuda petrel, a bird which was thought extinct for over three hundred years before a few were discovered fifty years ago, still nesting on the islets of Castle Roads. It could appear at any time, but I am not really hopeful.

We arrived at the Bermudas after dark and lay to off the south shore until dawn, when a pilot arrived to take the ship in through the reefs to the town of Saint George's.

Saint George's is a pretty old town, and I was interested to note, at Saint Peter's Church, that the Mr. W. Strachey who supplied a vivid account of the "murtherings" of the then very numerous cahow (in his chronicle of the wreck at the Bermudas of the *Sea Venture*, said to have been the source of inspiration of *The Tempest*) officiated at Bermuda's first wedding in 1609.

We left Bermuda in mid-morning, and I spent several hours on the bridge, scanning the waters, but I saw no cahow; as a matter of fact, I saw no sea bird of any description at Bermuda, though several are known to breed there.

Tomorrow is Thanksgiving.

November 25. Sargasso Sea.

The advantage of this small, slow freighter is that its route encompasses not only the great Amazon but that trackless ocean desert known as the Sargasso Sea—though now we have been rerouted and are bearing southwest to Haiti, so that we shall not traverse the place *in medias res*, as I had hoped, but only its western reaches.

The Sargasso Sea, which we entered late last night, is an amorphous oblong at least 400 by 1000 miles in its dimensions, located approximately in that part of the Atlantic south of Bermuda and south and west of the Azores, or, more precisely, within latitudes 25 to 30 degrees north and longitudes 40 to 70 degrees west. Since it remains strangely isolated, one might almost think of it as a huge island in the mighty ocean rivers which swirl around it—the Gulf Stream to the west and north, the Canaries Current to the east, the Equatorial and the Antilles Currents to the south—all these rivers set in clockwise motion by the earth's rotation and impelled by the prevailing winds. In the north these are the westerlies, and in the south they are those relentless tropic breezes known as the northeast trades.

The sea is named for *Sargassum bacciferum*, brown algae with neat clustered bladders; they collect here, according to old accounts, in quantities sufficient to entrap a sailing ship. Like most old accounts, this one is untrue. The general area is known also as the Horse Latitudes, a name which apparently derives from days when ships becalmed in these blue windless fields would be forced to heave live thirsty cargo over the side; the surface of the sea was allegedly littered at times with the bodies of dead animals.

Virtually everything else one can remark about the Sargasso Sea is still a matter of dispute. Columbus, for example, was the first navigator to report it, but it has been suggested that the original discovery was made by the Phoenicians: the basis for this fascinating theory is still unknown to me. Then the origin of the sargassum weed itself remains uncertain: does it drift here from the coastal waters, or is it an indigenous pelagic plant? (It is generally agreed that *Sargassum bacciferum*, whatever its origins, can reproduce itself in the sea.) The weed, again, is said to swarm with littoral-type life; there is even a species of crab peculiar to it. This view is confirmed by that amazing navigator Captain Joshua Slocum, in his *Sailing Alone around the World*: "Sargasso, scattered over the sea in bunches, or trailed curiously along down the wind in narrow lanes, now gathered together in great fields, strange sea animals, little and big, swimming in and out, the most curious among them being a tiny sea horse which I captured and brought home preserved in a bottle." But marine biologists in general lean toward the opposing view. In their opinion, the area is "dead water," deficient in the nutrient salts which encourage plankton, and therefore incapable of sustaining a flourishing chain of life.

My own experience, which is all but worthless, would tend to bear out the negative point of view. It even supplies some fresh contradictions of its own. The extremities of the Horse Latitudes navigated by my ship, far from threatening to becalm us, were rudely tossed by stiff westerly winds and cresting seas. Furthermore, while sargassum weed was everywhere, it was scarcely more plentiful than in the Gulf Stream, and at no time did I spy a patch more imposing than a good-sized blanket. In a long day spent on deck I saw no animals, big or small, except the ubiquitous flying fish and a single tiny *Velella*, or by-the-wind sailor, a species of sea-going jellyfish which, like its relative *Physalia*, the Portuguese man-of-war, wanders the surface of the ocean by means of an elevated float, a kind of dorsal "sail." The sea birds in evidence farther north had disappeared, and as for horses, I saw none.

My vantage point at the rail of a rolling freighter is scarcely an auspicious one, however, and the only scientific observation I feel qualified to confirm is that the Sargasso Sea is indeed "deep blue"; it is a vibrant, intense blue, depthless as polished stone (a fact which would seem to indicate a relative paucity of plankton communities, in case any reasonable doubt remains in this regard). And if these seas are barren, it is nevertheless true that one of the most unusual of natural histories has its start here. Far below this ship, all breeding adults of the common fresh-water eel of North America, North Africa, and Europe, arriving at unknown rates, by unknown routes, are now convening: by spring, myriad blade-shaped larvae will have hatched from eggs suspended in the murk one hundred fathoms down, and a year later (three years, in the case of the smaller European form) will enter the river mouths, ascend the streams, in the shape of elvers. There they will remain and grow, in the yellow, sluggish phase familiar to Izaak Walton, who was unable to locate their eggs or very young and who, in *The Compleat Angler*, reported doubtfully the opinion that they bred "out of the putrefaction of the earth, and divers other ways," or "of a particular dew, falling in the months of May or June on the banks of some particular ponds or rivers . . . which in a few days are, by the sun's heat, turned into eels." After a period of five to twenty years these yellowish eels will change one autumn to a clean marine silver and, reversing the life process of the salmon, make their way back to the sea, to that vast backwater thousands of submarine miles away upon which now, by the hand of a mustachioed Brazilian seaman, we splash a great pail of nutrient garbage and pass on.

November 26. Bahamas Approaches.

The first fine day, blue and bright, and calm, gleaming seas. At daybreak a few whitecaps still, but these have since disappeared. The Brazilian sailors are putting up sun canvas on the frames of the afterdeck and on the bridge. These men vary in color, but most are intermediates, called *morenos*, and all brandish gigolos' mustaches. They wear G.I. clothes and Levi's as a rule, and one man has the traditional floppy peasant sombrero made of sisal. His companion, however, is rigged out for the tropics in a pair of skier's goggles, worn jauntily on a checked logger's cap, complete with ear flaps.

A Norwegian freighter, the *Margaret Onstad*, comes up on our starboard quarter and crosses close across our bows—outward bound, to judge from her present course, from Jacksonville or Fernandina to South Africa. We are presently several hundred miles due east of northern Florida.

November 27. The Caicos and Inaguas.

The Antilles Current and the Caicos Passage at first light, and a far Caribbean day expanding on the sky, the blue water sharpened by the northeast trades. Way off to the eastward, perhaps twenty miles, the Caicos Islands of the outer Bahamas, vaporish and small, rise on a silver horizon. The Caicos Islands —how many have ever seen them, for they are far off the trade and tourist routes? I savor a faint feeling of discovery.

In the next hour the islands drift forward, ever nearer the bright wake of the sun. First one, then two, as the ship's position changes, and finally three or more—but this is an illusion, the curious mirage effect one often sees at sea. There is only one island visible, Providenciales, with considerable elevation for the Bahamas. The mass floats off mysteriously, semi-transparent in the early light like a puff of wool, and finally, directly beneath the climbing sun, goes up in fire.

No islands visible to the westward, only a huge freighter northward bound, so heavily cargoed that from this distance she appears to ride dangerously down by the head. Our own ship rolls gracefully along in the light swell; at times no other verb describes this motion.

An hour later West Caicos appears off to the eastward, and there is a dark, solitary sail. I can imagine it as if it were nearby, a heavy Bahamian fishing smack built originally, perhaps, at Man-o'-War Key in the Abacos. These ragged craft, trading, transporting, fishing for crawfish and conchs, wander everywhere in the treacherous, windy waters of the Antilles, with neither compass nor a sense of passing time.

To starboard rises the low, barren mass of Little Inagua, and about noon we come riding down upon Great Inagua, that large island north and east of Cuba. Clouds are flying across the sun, and the sea beneath is a dramatic blue-black, the color of a swordfish.

And still no birds.

In the late afternoon, approaching the Windward Passage (a name as beautiful as Tierra del Fuego), a pomarine jaeger, dark and swift, prowled our wake for nearly an hour. During this time two large porpoises of a strange café-au-lait color breached off the port quarter; they were so light that, hundreds of yards away, they were visible even under water. The splash they made was taut in the bright blue—sudden, magnificent, exciting, as if the whole silent sea had come to life. Behind the southern clouds at twilight, Haiti is looming, high and mountainous.

November 28.

At daybreak we arrived off Port-au-Prince. Mountains rose on both sides of the bay, the ridges to the eastward fired by the sun, and a soft mist shrouded the harbor and the town, which lay still in semi-darkness. Against the mist the lateen silhouettes of native sloops wavered and spun, sharp black as Japanese prints in this odd light.

A small launch rushed up out of the mist and honked officiously at the ship. The legend *Capitaine du Port* had been unsteadily inscribed upon its transom, and it fairly swarmed with Haitians, over half of them resplendent in varieties of official dress. A number of these dignitaries came aboard, and after a short exchange of civilities and protocol with Mr. Groen, our dignified chief steward—he may have been taken for the captain—departed once again on their tiny craft, leaving only the port pilot. The pilot conducted us back up the bay, to the float at the end of the long loading chute of the Caribbean Meal Company. Here we are scheduled to take on some four hundred and fifty tons of grain meal, for shipment to Barbados.

With my fellow passengers, an hour later, I was driven in the shipping agent's car along the coast road to Port-au-Prince. On our left rose scrubby foothills, and to our right lay cane-fields and small marshes, fringed by the mangrove border of the bay. Starved, scattered cattle, like survivors of some calamity, wandered aimlessly in the brake, accompanied by the cattle egret, an Old World species which, some thirty years ago, confounded ornithologists by spreading in a few swift decades from its normal haunts in Europe and North Africa to the Americas and even Australia. It has become well established in several of our Southern states, and a few have turned up in Canada and Bermuda.

In the countryside a few species of birds were relatively

plentiful, including several varieties of egrets and herons, yellowlegs, kestrels, and a flock of groove-billed anis. All of these but the ani are common birds of the United States, and even the latter may be found in southern Florida. But in the outskirts of the town is a rich tropic vegetation of palms, coffee trees, hibiscus, poinsettia, flamboyant, and many others, and the only birds seen in an entire day of *tourisme* were a group strung from the barrel of an ancient small-caliber rifle on the ragged shoulder of a native boy, including such morsels as woodpeckers and hawks. The poverty of Port-au-Prince is awe-inspiring and may well account for the scarcity of visible life so striking here.

Port-au-Prince has a certain charm, the sort of charm which is generally described as indefinable, since there doesn't seem much to recommend it. It is a great catch-all of hovels and unassimilated modern architecture, but there is nevertheless a cheerful, rakish air about it, with its pervasive pastels bright against a background of dark volcanic mountain.

November 29. To the Windward Passage.

This morning I got up at six to watch the completion of the loading. This grain meal, or "pollards," is supposed to provide animal feed in Barbados, but I wonder if it isn't really for the natives. . . . Disheartened by this thought, I retired after a while to the afterdeck, where I passed more than an hour observing the tropical fish around the pilings—small delicate blue tangs, yellow-tailed, swaying with the current, the swift blue knife-finned reef fishes, and squadrons of black and yellow striped sergeant majors. Farther out, where garbage from the ship has drifted, a great brown grouper, twenty pounds or more, was feeding hoggishly, like a carp, swirling clumsily on the stagnant surface, and everywhere slid needlefish, blue-tailed, and beaked like ancient marine reptiles; one of these was almost three feet long.

Leaving the pier an hour later, the *Venimos* retraced her inbound course, heading north-northwest up Gonaïves Gulf toward the Windward Passage. Gonave Island like a dead whale to port, and on the starboard side the dark mountainous coasts, crests shrouded in dense cumulus, loomed in oppressive contrast to a soft, slimy sea. Fish were everywhere, their movements chafing the still surface, but birds were all but absent, only an occasional royal tern; and in the distance was another pair of large brown porpoises.

The coast grows wilder as the day moves on, with sharp cliffs and buttes, and forlorn, empty bights and bays. Here and there a sagging sail, and, toward the cape, a rubble of thatch huts set back on small thin mud-gray beaches.

At the cape itself, entering the Passage and turning east again, the wind freshens with startling rapidity, and whitecaps leap up everywhere. A small sloop appears out of the north, making for land and tilting wildly in the unruly gusts. On the bow, where I spent the afternoon, it was difficult to tell the wind's directions: a string held by the fingers flew toward the stern, obeying the ship's passage, but, held below the level of the gunwale, it blew forward, though there seemed to be no following wind.

The north cape of Haiti, at the Windward Passage, must surely be one of the loneliest places in the world, its steep windswept slopes plunging into a deep, dark sea; one jagged rock scar, where the boulder had apparently torn away all the thin cover on its downward rush, is visible miles away.

We pass beneath the cape at sundown. It is nearly-dark now, but in the west the clouds are still touched with violet over Cuba's Sierra Maestra. To the northeast lies the faint silhouette of the old pirate island of Tortuga.

November 30–December 2. Hispaniola, Mona Passage, and the Caribbean.

Another beautiful hot smooth day. We are four or five miles off the Dominican Republic, and Hispaniola here is still extremely mountainous, with one very high peak due southeast at eight a.m. Perfect conditions for sighting whales, porpoises, sea turtles, sharks, and billfish, but there is nothing all day, not even a solitary bird.

During the night the ship entered the Mona Passage between Hispaniola and Puerto Rico, and at daylight the former has already vanished, with Puerto Rico rising off to the north. Now we are actually in the Caribbean, and there are birds this morning, all red-footed boobies so far, but at least a dozen of these, pounding along on deep-crooked wings. A white adult dives on flying fish off to the south, quite like our northern gannet—and of course these birds are tropical members of the gannet family.

During the day the boobies are replaced by a pair of frigate birds, the so-called man-of-war birds, a red-throated male and a white-headed immature. These slide almost disdainfully across the ship, their wings, seven feet in spread, like thin bent blades, and their long tails deeply forked. In their easy, ominous flight they are among the most aerial of birds. They are replaced in their turn by jaegers, six or more, one of them in a very black phase which I have never seen before.

The stars are luminous tonight—great sprawling Orion, and red Betelgeuse, Sirius flashing like an oncoming comet, and above them, nearly overhead, Taurus, Auriga, and the lovely Pleiades.

The second of December, and the weather continues fair. No land in sight today. A few jaegers, and a distant booby. In the afternoon a whale was sighted from the bridge, but I wasn't told of it in time to see it.

December 3. The Windward Islands.

Dominica is the northernmost of the Windward Islands, which also include Saint Lucia, Saint Vincent, and Grenada: the French islands of Guadaloupe and Martinique, which geographically are members of this group, are not considered Windward Islands by the British. Nevertheless, a French heritage is evident here, not only in the pronunciation of the name—the island is called Do-mi-*ni*-ca—but in the prevailing *patois* of the natives, most of whom speak a shy English also.

The Windward Islands were populated originally by peaceful Arawak Indians, but invasions of warlike Caribs from the region of the Amazon apparently dispossessed these people: the Caribs killed off the Arawak males and incorporated the females into their own culture. They were finally displaced in their turn by Spanish, French, and English, though not without a struggle. Dominica, in fact, was so difficult to subdue that it was left virtually alone for nearly two centuries after its discovery by Columbus in 1498. A Carib reservation still exists here, and a few Indians are scattered out among the other islands, but long ago the Caribs mixed freely with the Negro slaves, and the race has all but passed out of existence.

The capital of Dominica is Roseau, a small red-roofed town on the leeward shore, and it is visited infrequently by tourists for these reasons: as in Haiti, there is no decent beach any closer than the far side of the mountains, which are of considerable size (the largest, Mount Diablotin, is named for the nearly extinct black-capped petrel, which is thought to have nested there in the past); modern hotels and facilities are limited-to-totally-wanting—even that humble staple of the tourist, the common postcard, is hard to come by in Roseau—and finally, the tourist willing to accept these drawbacks is rewarded with exorbitant prices. He is expected to pay, it seems, for the thousands of others who have failed to put in an appearance.

All of this is too bad, for Roseau, bright and steepled against a background of deep green valleys and verdant crags—and I use the word verdant because it suits the mood of these broken volcanic summits, which a Poussin or a Watteau would quite appreciate—is a striking place. There are said to be 365 small rivers on the island, and, following one of these inland, one finds oneself in a rich tropic valley where lime, coconut, grapefruit, and banana trees are farmed commercially, and at the head of which, where the black, cloud-shadowed peaks converge, are two high, lovely waterfalls. The vegetation includes a variety of palms, flamboyant, coffee, breadfruit, mango, eucalyptus, banyan, and poincianas—the latter the most magnificent I have ever seen. The island's northern coast is said to be considerably more beautiful, and if this is so, then it is very beautiful indeed. Unfortunately, though the *Venimos* called at all the Windward Islands, one had to be satisfied with brief impressions; among the latter, for what they are worth, is that all four are quite similar geographically, but that Dominica is the most unspoiled (despite this same claim by Saint Vincent on its own behalf) and the most striking. Saint Vincent can claim the first breadfruit tree in the islands, imported from the Pacific by the *Bounty*'s Captain Bligh, as well as what must be the most striking view in the Windwards, obtainable from Fort Charlotte, high above the capital of Kingstown. From this fort, one of many such relics of the faraway European wars, one can see the long line of Grenadine Islands, stretching away southward toward Grenada. And it was the Grenadines, still virtually untouched, which, passing close by one lovely afternoon, most excited my curiosity. Perhaps because we did not stop there—they are largely uninhabited—I felt quite strongly that one day I would go back.

I have warm impressions of the other islands too, of the pretty little ports at Castries (Saint Lucia) and Saint George's (Grenada), of wonderful swimming on long tropic beaches at both these places, of a school of small whales—pilot whales, or blackfish—beneath a swirl of terns and boobies, the latter sparkling white against the mountains of Saint Vincent, and of a sail in a small dinghy off Saint Lucia with my friends the radio officer, the chief engineer, and the third mate.

That these men invited me to go along is a sign of the new atmosphere of relaxation which has prevailed aboard ship since we reached the Caribbean; it may be a symptom of that "wild unbuttoning process" described by Céline as a phenomenon induced by tropic suns. The officers are outfitted in white regulation shorts, not always shipshape, and a good deal of informal rum-drinking takes place in one cabin or another of an afternoon in port.

December 5–7. Barbados.

The island of Barbados, where the ship called for three days after our departure from Saint Lucia and before proceeding to Saint Vincent, lies one hundred miles or so out to the eastward of the Windward Islands. Like Bermuda—and unlike the Windwards, which are peaks of a submerged mountain range—it is a true oceanic island, surrounded by a fringing reef of coral, and more or less unrelated, geologically, to the mainland. Its countryside, patched by canefields, is low and rolling for the most part, with small spare farm communities and pretty churches and roadside trees bent permanently by the trades. When the sea drops out of sight, the landscape brings to mind certain areas in our Plains States, the sugarcane mills standing up out of dry distances like grain elevators in North Dakota, say, on a long, blue afternoon of summer.

December 10. Trinidad.

Arrived in Port-of-Spain last night, coming south from Grenada through the cut between Trinidad and the Paria Peninsula of Venezuela, known as the Dragon's Mouth. A gray day, the first in a long time, and rather welcome. The anchorage is wide, with boats in black silhouette littered out across the dull sheen of it as far as the eye can see. This is not very far today. Laughing gulls, winging up and down.

Its name, Port-of-Spain, is the prettiest aspect of this great dirty town which, according to the port pilot, sees more shipping tonnage come and go than Liverpool. It has a kind of tarnished modernity about it, a fly-by-night air, like an abandoned fair invaded by a pack of gypsies, and it has that terrible sweet smell common to all towns in these latitudes, one which I've found impossible to track down. The smell has now invaded the ship itself, like some sort of pervasive melancholia; it loiters in the vicinity of the galley. I'm told that the island of Trinidad is beautiful and am quite ready to believe it, but I have a very poor impression of its capital. It seems appropriate that, throughout this long listless day, a squadron of vultures swept up and down on the city's damp, stagnant airs.

The name of the place, as I recall from the days when I collected stamps, is actually Trinidad-and-Tobago. The latter is a much smaller island off to the northeast, and, having rounded the cape to the north again, we left it astern at eight a.m. the following morning, headed southeast for Georgetown, British Guiana. We are off the many mouths of the Orinoco, and the water is discolored. A frigate bird, a distant booby, and two black-backed, white-bellied shearwaters, unidentifiable—conceivably the lost diablotin, but in all probability Audubon's shearwater.

December 12. British Guiana.

We are now in green coastal waters, silky and turgid, but the low land is invisible. In midday the screws of the *Venimos* churn up great gouts of brown sand as we ease over a bar, for here the continental shelf, built up by the numerous rivers, is very broad and shallow.

One-thirty p.m., and South America now in sight, a low black line in the sunny mist. Royal terns and laughing gulls, both familiar birds at home, are the first signs of its wildlife. An hour later we enter the Demerara River, with Georgetown to port, its long quays banked with freighters. There is the *Kronos*, a hard-looking rusty craft, black and copper-orange, out of Monrovia, and the green *Ankaka* out of Liverpool, its taffrail crowded with grimy seamen. One old big-backed tub of guts lets fly his spit in our direction; he owns, on closer inspection, the meanest face I have seen in many months, and he has with him the usual thin acolyte, smirking and agitating. Long black skiffs careen up and down the river's muddy chop, powered by outboards, tall raucous Negroes upright in their sterns.

On the warehouse roof perches a bird, bright-yellow-bellied. This is the *bienteveo* tyrant, a large flycatcher—my first wild creature indigenous to South America.

2· AMAZONAS

SURINAM, PARAMARIBO, SINNAMARIE, CAYENNE: small mountains rise behind the flat mud coasts of the Guianas, and small islands fleck a horizon of humid clouds. One of these is the infamous Devil's Island, now a beacon. Off Cayenne, at the edge of Brazilian waters, out of sight of land, a strange lugger drops its sail in signal, and the ship veers sluggishly to investigate. But as we draw near the craft makes off erratically—she has signaled us by mistake. A smuggler, apparently, one of a fleet of midnight traders which serve Brazil's huge appetite for contraband.

Our ship is British, and austerely we pass on. The *Venimos* is nearly a month out, and her cargo is reduced to a small tractor for Belém, oil machinery for Manaus, and shotguns, rifles, and storage batteries for the terminal port of Iquitos in Peru—these in addition to her regular consignment of general goods and foodstuffs, most of which (including a shipment of Christmas trees for the Windward Islands) has now been left behind. She is all but hollow, and she rides high on the olive waters of this forlorn coast, beating southeast against the North Equatorial Current. To the west, just over a dull skyline, lies the wild region of the Araguarí River.

December 18.

The equator is crossed during the night, and at dawn, off the village of Salinas, the pilot comes aboard. Now we are bearing west again, the rising sun directly astern, and ahead a morass of shifting currents, tides—mud, green, gray, and silver—at odds beneath the broken clouds like unmixed paints. The Amazon, and a strange species of tropic tern, strikingly marked across the mantle. Far off, on both sides, small porpoises ease lazily along. A few fishing sloops break the expanse, lateen-rigged, rakish hulls blue beneath rare-colored sails of pink, copper, aquamarine. The jungle, dark, indecipherable patches on the horizon, is too distant to feel as yet, though Marajó Island is rising on the starboard bow, and the river is thickening with sediment. This is the Pará Estuary, the southernmost of the mouths, on which lies the river's important city, A Cidade de Nossa Senhora do Belém do Grão Pará—the Pará of former days, now called Belém, which, in Portuguese, is Bethlehem.

As the morning changes the clouds swell, and a horizon of countless islands and inlets, though still far away, moves forward slowly to surround us. Small settlements rise and sink again into the jungle, and shortly after noon Belém itself appears, gleaming heavily in the hot mist. Ancient river boats and other craft litter its outskirts which, half overgrown, creep out along the river bank, and here the ship anchors for customs inspection, east of the main town.

Customs at Belém is a famous joke, for the town depends on contraband for its economy, and the customs officials themselves expect neither more nor less than their fair share. Agreeable fellows, well turned out, they swarm aboard in numbers and a little while later go away again with the booty of cigarettes, whisky, and others items which have been set aside for them. They move on, gay as birds, to the next ship into port, a freighter which has gained on our slow wake all morning.

Customs takes place out in the anchorage. When the ship ties up at last along the quay the officials happen to be elsewhere, and the crewmen and most of the officers move their wares ashore. One simple mariner has brought from New York four new transistor phonographs; the profit he will make on these will more than match his salary for the voyage.

"In this town," an inhabitant told me later, "everything is against the law and everything is permitted. If a policeman asks you for a license or a paper, ask him for his authority to ask. He hasn't any." We were sitting in a street café, and while this man spoke I absorbed the effect of the cobbled streets and quasi-modern buildings, less like Lisbon than like downtown Madrid. Belém is clean and cheerful, though its waterfront has the seaport complement of paupers and prodigious rats, and everywhere the gray-headed *urubu*, or black vulture, hunching and hopping through the litter on its pale legs, or picking silently at the refuse on the tideline. Across the Pará stand the jungle islands, and one has a deep sense of the smallness of Belém, of the hugeness which lies all around it and beyond.

While in port I paid a visit to the Belém zoo and botanical gardens, a joint establishment which has had the excellent idea of confining itself to the flora and fauna of the Amazon, rather than presenting the usual small-zoo grab-bag of rhesus monkeys, over-age circus animals, and exiled pets. The visit afforded some sort of protection against that flood of misinformation in regard to the Amazon and its wildlife which somehow befits the region's titanic aspects.

Amazonas, as the whole basin is sometimes called, includes large areas of four countries, though the great part of it is in Brazil; in the extent of its unknowns it might be compared to western North America of the early nineteenth century. In places the land behind the river banks is unexplored, and lost cities, lost tribes, and strange animals may still be discovered. This much is true, and exciting enough too, but even so, an immense store of legends has been propagated throughout the centuries, ever since Francisco de Orellana, in 1541, first reported the existence of fierce female warriors in the region of Óbidos. The legends are augmented at every opportunity, not only by the Indians and settlers, but by the adventurers of all nations who drift in and out of the towns on this huge frontier, and by incautious writers like myself who venture within hearing distance.

In four hundred years the river has changed little; its violent wilderness and the potentially lethal elements in its fauna have remained largely intact. The waters of Amazonas harbor large crocodilians of the group known as caimans, the mighty river boa or anaconda, two species of *puraque* or electric eel, sting rays, the notorious piranha, and a sliver-like little fish of wretched bent called the *candiru*, which seeks out even the smallest orifices of the body and lodges itself with its spines; once implanted, it has to be cut out. Land animals include the jaguar and a variety of poisonous snakes, among which the great *sucurucu*, or bushmaster, and the *jararaca*, or fer-de-lance, are perhaps best known; there are also tarantulas, scorpions, and a host of stinging ants and other insects. Biting flies, mosquitoes, and hornets are among the aggressive insects of the air, and this element can boast, as well, the common vampire bat.

Beriberi, malaria, leprosy, and blackwater fever are among the many diseases which do well here, and there are still hostile Indians; to read or listen to most accounts of Amazonas is to conclude that only a maniac would ever set foot out of doors. The truth, which is something else again, is obscured by the fact that, in this country of unknowns, the legends are not only not readily disproved but are even occasionally confirmed. Finally, it is very difficult not to defer to an apparently honest man who has been in the wilderness, when you and your whole gang of pale authorities have not.

In Belém, for example, I fell in with a French Canadian who may as well be called Picquet. He is a lean, neat man, an ex-house-painter and merchant seaman, semi-educated, who carries with him everything he owns—the clothes on his back, a jackknife, a safety razor with a sawed-off handle which fits into a small wood matchbox, and a waterproof packet containing his passport, billfold, and set of worn maps on which he has traced his journeys through South America. When I met him he was weak with recurrent malaria, and broke, but had arranged with one of the contraband boats to take him as far as Paramaribo, in Surinam, where he hoped to find work on a freighter bound for Europe.

Picquet arrived on this continent three years ago, traveling alone and on foot, with a shotgun and two compasses, down through the trackless jungles between the Canal Zone and central Colombia (this is the wild area where a long gap still exists in the Pan-American Highway); since then he has walked, worked, and hitchhiked his way through every country but Paraguay. I could find no flaw in his accounts, nor any real reason to doubt him. ("I don't have to make up stories," he remarked at one point, "because nobody would believe what I actually *have* seen, anyway; I've seen too much." He said this with polite indifference to my opinion, and perhaps that is the charm of the world's Picquets—that catlike and quiet indifference, even to those who, as in my case, were paying for his beer. This trait is a peculiarity of wanderers, so familiar that I felt I must have crossed paths with Picquet before, in the deserts of the West, perhaps, or in Alaska. It's a disturbing quality, and one that induces a certain self-consciousness about one's glasses, say, or the gleam of one's new khaki pants.) For most of what he recounted, consciously or otherwise, he supplied a ready means of checking up on his story and, with a restraint rare in these parts, he actually belittled the dangerous nature of jungle creatures: he admitted that poisonous snakes and other animals were a menace under special circumstances, but, in his opinion, the only one which, unprovoked, might attack and kill a man was the anaconda. I had mixed feelings when he succumbed at last and described a rare striped cat not quite so large as a jaguar and very timid, which is possessed of two very large protruding teeth: this animal, he said, occurs in the mountain jungles of Colombia and Ecuador, and he has glimpsed it once himself. (No such cat is known, of course, but one great asset such stories bear with them is the pathetic eagerness of listeners like myself to rationalize them. Let's suppose, I exulted, that the saber-toothed tiger, like the cougar, had long ago established itself here in a smaller subspecies and had thus survived the Ice Age extinction of its North American ancestor; what are the llama, vicuña, and guanaco, after all, but living descendants of cameloid animals which became extinct on the northern continent? For one wild moment, propped up by my own zoological jargon, I teetered on the brink of great discovery.) I believe Picquet was sincere in his account, however mistaken, though the matter did not seem to concern him much one way or the other. He went on to describe how he and another seaman had fallen overboard from their freighter during World War II, when a deck cargo of lumber shifted in heavy seas off Trinidad —and here again, curiously, he happened to mention the name of the American destroyer which retrieved him eight hours later, so that this story, like most of the rest, could readily be traced. He believes he has a charmed life, and has since put it to the test all across the world. "I can't sit still," he said, and this was quite literally true; his sad eyes were never really with me, even when he was talking with animation. "I figure I have thirteen lives"—he did not bother to explain this—"and have used up about seven. That leaves me six to go." I nodded, expecting him to say that when he reached number twelve he would stop wandering and go home. He didn't, though. "When I get to number thirteen," he said, "I'll die."

The ship sailed at two in the morning, to take advantage of the tides, and at daybreak we were well beyond the mouth of the Tocantins River. To the north rose Marajó Island, which sits in the mouth of the Amazon like a huge cork. Though the

Pará is wide here, the channels are treacherous and narrow; on Mandihoy Bank, which boasts the sole navigation light in all the thousands of miles of river, the hulks of two sunken vessels protrude like black and rotten stumps.

The jungle is remote, rather ominous, on every side. An occasional white egret, like a speck caught on the distant walls of green, the yellow-billed river terns coursing the brown wake for tumbled minnows, and far, floating *urubus*—these are the only life.

The merchant and the missionary left the ship at Belém, and I shall miss them. They have been replaced by an elderly Dutch lady and five Dutch Catholic missionaries, one of whom shares my cabin. Today he is suffering from dysentery and lies miserably in his berth. He is fortunate that illness overtook him here, where he can be tended, for his mission lies six hundred miles upriver from Manaus and the nearest doctor. To expedite their good works, the missionaries have with them a small cabin cruiser, which was hoisted onto the foredeck at Belém: their roadless parishes are huge, the area administered by my cabin-mate alone being larger than all of Holland.

This idea is more startling to me than the familiar statistics on Amazonas—that the basin alone is nearly as large as the continental United States, more than two million square miles, and contains one-fifth of all river waters on the earth, that Marajó Island in its mouth is larger than Switzerland, that the river empties more than twelve times as much water as the Mississippi and carries annually five billion tons of sediment into the sea, where it muddies the water either one hundred or two hundred miles from the coast, depending on the writer. Such figures are impressive, surely, but they seem rather empty when removed from the context of human endeavor; the 238,857 miles to the moon, for example, is a much more awesome distance now that the possibility exists that man, a particular man, will traverse it.

Besides, awe of the Amazon is emotional, not intellectual.

H. M. Tomlinson, whose *The Sea and the Jungle* is one of the few level-headed works in the literature of this region, quotes a description of the implacable "waiting" of the jungle:

> I'm half afraid of it . . . not afraid of anything I can see
> . . . I don't know. There's something damn strange about
> it. Something you never can find out. It's something that's
> been here since the beginning, and it's too big and strong
> for us. It waits its time. I can feel it now. Look at those
> palm trees, outside. Don't they look as if they're waiting?
> What are they waiting for? You get that feeling here in
> the afternoon when you can't get air, and the rain clouds
> are banking up around the woods, and nothing moves.

This concept is accurate and difficult to improve upon. There is a deadness in the air in this terrific heat of the equator, and a sky neither quite shining nor quite raining, but poised between the two, a silver sky of dirty bruises, of suspense. (But later in the day the sky turned a pale blue, and later still an explosion of wind out of the north, the *vente gerol*, burst the humidity apart. Suddenly, more suddenly than in any change of weather I have known, the air was chill. For the first time since the ship left Bermuda I considered putting on a sweater. And night along the Amazon is cool.)

So . . . there is something strange in these jungle airs, no doubt about it, something of foreboding. Man seems ill at ease here. On the bank there is a palm hut, it is true, and an occasional rude clearing, but these are impermanent, as if tacked on the green wall, and the huts in any case will go when the river rises. The rainy season has begun, and already great patches of live savanna grass and whole dead trees drift swiftly eastward. The banks are low on this stretch of the river, and the jungle is never cleared, only bent back. The huts on the higher banks boast a few plantains and occasionally some scraggy, humped gray cattle; these are nomadic settlements of loggers, cutting *macaca uba*, *andiroba*, *sucupira*, and others of the myriad tropic hardwoods. Some of the settlers—the forest halfbreeds, copper-colored, are called *caboclos*—produce manioc and jute, and some tap the wild rubber trees, the *seringueiras*, but most come and go with the river level, subsisting on wild fruits and animals and the river's swarming fish. A frail, small canoe beneath the jungle wall is more forlorn than a solitary sail at sea.

"Its capacities for trade and commerce are inconceivably great," wrote Lieutenant William Herndon in 1851, in the journal of his survey of the Amazon for the United States Navy Department. "Its industrial future is the most dazzling; and to the touch of steam, settlement and cultivation, this rolling stream and its magnificent watershed would start up into a display of industrial results that would indicate the Valley of the Amazon as one of the most enchanting regions on the face of the earth." Herndon's optimism was shared by many who came after, but the Amazon remains as sullen and intractable as it ever was; indeed, it is startling to find how exactly the descriptions of Herndon and such contemporaries as the great naturalist H. W. Bates and the botanist Richard Spruce correspond with the appearance of the river as it is today. The few large towns excepted, the traveler on the Amazon sees almost precisely what these men saw a century ago.

But this is my first day on the river, and the atmosphere is exhilarating, not oppressive. Man has literally scratched the surface of this enormous world, which recedes and approaches endlessly as the ship moves through it—in time of full flood, according to some accounts, the river may become so wide that one is out of sight of land, though this seems doubtful—and the scratches heal quickly in this wild climate without winter. Both the idea and the spectacle are moving—so moving that I could not suppress little squeaks of pure excitement. It is difficult to accept that a wilderness of this dimension still exists, that, despite our airplanes and machines, we cannot really enter it but only skirt its edges. This will change, of course, but it will change slowly; today, should this ship stop at some arbitrary point and send a small boat to the shore, the chances would still be heavily in one's favor that no man, dark or white or copper, had ever stood beneath those trees before.

The trees, at noon, are still remote. There are only the high conglomerate mass of growth, and the debris in the silent river, and the sky. At this time of the day the jungle is glazed over, dead. But in the early afternoon, at the mouth of an inlet several hundred yards away, a great fish, one hundred pounds or more, hurls itself out of the water, flaps like a hooked tarpon in the air, and splashes down again, leaving a soft welt on the thick surface. And later, with the coming of the wind, the sun and rain, both having hung back all day, arrive from separate quarters simultaneously. To avoid the main current, we are nearing a narrow side channel, or *furo*, and moments later, in an incredible light which follows the rain, plunge recklessly into the jungle, our bow wave washing noisily into the stiff arrow reeds on both sides as a small *bigua* cormorant flees back past us toward the open river. For the first time the forest shows its face—great palms and rubber trees, huge domed *ceibas*, soaring high out of the tangle of small hardwoods and lianas. The foliage is luminous and alive, and birds flash everywhere—egrets, bright river swallows, a huge woodpecker, hawks silhouetted in the trees, and, farther on, a scattering of exotic clumsy fowl, a sort of burnished brown chachalaca with white shoulder stripes and the pale tail feathers of a grouse—is this the archaic hoatzin? It squawks and thrashes dismally in the high reeds of the bank. At twilight pairs of parrots hurry down the sky above the tree-tops, their flight trembling and swift. Then sudden darkness, and the jungle is a wall again, a black misshapen silhouette towering above us on both sides, as if the ship were passing down a canyon in the River Styx. It seems to me at this moment, catching my breath, that, even if the jungle should never let me have this fleeting intimacy again, the long journey here will have been worth it.

December 20.

This morning we are approaching the mouth of the Xingú River; somewhere far off there to the southward, toward the headwaters of the Xingú, Colonel P. H. Fawcett, the most famous of South America's lost explorers, disappeared in 1925, still searching for his lost cities of pre-Incas. "The existence of the old cities I do not for a moment doubt . . ." he wrote in that last year. "Unfortunately, I cannot induce scientific men to accept even the supposition that there are traces of an old civilization in Brazil. I have travelled much in places not familiar to other explorers, and the wild Indians have again and again told me of the buildings, the character of the people, and the strange things beyond."

Colonel Fawcett's explorations in the jungles of Bolivia and Brazil extended from 1903 until 1925, and his journals make lurid reading; violent death, whether by murder, disease, drunkenness, Indians, or animals, is a commonplace on almost every page. Much of the carnage he describes came of the evil consequences of the rubber boom, which spread cruelty and greed throughout the jungles for most of a century, before subsiding around 1912; it was found that transplanted rubber trees could be grown more economically on East Indian plantations, and an industry which had built Manaus and Iquitos, and promised swift development of the Amazon, was reduced to a local harvest of wild trees.

Fawcett claims, no doubt correctly, that few of the Indian tribes were warlike until the white man enslaved, exploited, and murdered them for his own ends. For the most part his accounts are sensible and sympathetic, and it is too bad that their credibility is so often undermined by exaggeration and wishful thinking. While scarcely in a position to dispute Fawcett's allegations, not having lived with him in the jungle, I find a number of his observations startling, to put it very mildly. His remarks on the size and habits of the anaconda may be taken as a fair sample; he himself destroyed a specimen of sixty-eight feet, which so upset his Indians that "in the moment of firing I had heard their terrified voices begging me not to shoot lest the monster destroy the boat and kill everyone on board, for not only do these creatures attack boats when injured, but also there is great danger from their mates." Fawcett alleged as well that "their weird cries could be heard at night," which, if true, would make the anaconda unique in the community of serpents; their breath, he wrote, is stupefying to their prey. (Doubtless the breath of a sixty-eight-foot snake can be a pretty stupefying thing, but any victim close enough to smell it would already be, if not on the point of consumption, at least in fairly parlous straits.)

Fawcett has disciples still, and I attracted them like flies all the way upriver. But since I am doing my best to remain hardheaded, I had better not report their stories here.

At Jariuba Point the *Venimos* leaves the Pará and swirls into the main channel of the Amazon. Almost immediately, however, she enters the parallel Arrayolos *furo*, dodging behind the islands to avoid the central current. An hour later we meet our sister ship, the *Viajero*, bound downriver: she takes aboard our Brazilian pilots, and we take her two Peruvians.

A number of new birds this morning—I am keeping separate notes on them, with some vague hope of future identification—and two more large fish seen finning. Probably this is the *pirarucu*, an Amazonian relation of the salmons, which reaches a weight of several hundred pounds. There is also the *piraiba* catfish, said to be capable of swallowing a man whole, though, so far as I know, it has never made the attempt. But the mammals stay out of sight, all but the inia, or Geoffroy's dolphin, which is common along the banks. The high point of my morning—I spend most of my day on top of the bridge, a vantage point known as "monkey island"—was the spectacle of three glorious swallow-tailed kites, that most striking of all land birds, to my mind, now nearing extinction in North America. I remember well the first and only swallow-tailed kite I have seen before today, east of Naples in southwest Florida, and my maniacal cries of excitement—I was very young then and could still cry out—as it turned and swooped back and forth over my head. (Technically, I suppose, this Amazon kite represents a distinct subspecies or race of the swallow-tailed kite, but I am not equipped to make such fine distinctions; birds essentially identical to our black vulture—the ubiquitous *urubu*—osprey, and common and snowy egrets are also abundant on this part of the river and shall be referred to by these names, as the old friends they are.)

To the north, in the afternoon, rise the low hills of the Sierra Jutahy. The jungle changes gradually, with the tall palms slowly disappearing. Here the silk-cotton, or *ceiba*, from the pods of which the fiber known as kapok is derived, is the tallest tree among the few I can identify, its outline blurred by blankets of liana vine. A legion of smaller trees crowds everywhere, and from a distance a species of cecropia appears to bear huge silver flowers. This is the *imbauba*, one of the great number of medicinal trees used by the river people, and its silver flowers are only its great floppy leaves blown over. There are also wild rubber trees and a kind of fig tree, and bignonias which look like the jacaranda. The variety and profusion of species is even more dismaying than among the birds, most of which I can at least identify by family: the hopelessness of attempts at plant identification for anyone but a botanist resides in the fact that the flora of the Amazon basin is the most complex on earth; the majority of all plant species known to man are to be found in this vast forest, and Louis Agassiz once identified one hundred and seventeen distinct woods, including palms, myrtles, laurels, acacias, bignonias, rosewood, cecropias, bombaceas, Brazil-nuts or *castanheiras*, rubber, fig, and purplehearts, in an area a half-mile square.

A few huts, most of them broken and untenanted, their clearings overgrown and their fish traps sagging in the current.

Farther on, some natural savannas, stretching away like park-
lands; apparently they are marshy, for they are uninhabited.
Hawks are everywhere in astonishing variety, and at twilight the
parrots appear again, and a solitary anhinga, marked more vividly
than the species in North America, flaps and glides across the
river. The air is warmer tonight than last, with the huge sweet
smell of the tropics.

December 21.

At daylight Santarém, one of the few towns in the thousand
miles between Belém and Manaus, drifts past against the low
hills to the south. Here is the mouth of the blue Tapajoz, stop-
ping short as it meets the Amazon as if it had struck a wall, and
swallowed without a trace; some distance up the Tapajoz lies
Fordlandia, the site of the Ford Company's great abandoned
rubber plantation and of one of man's more notable failures in
attempts at conquest of this region.

More and more the country has changed to open savanna,
green and sparkling in the light of this first bright day since the
Venimos entered the Amazon—a truly magnificent day. Three
brilliant parrots whirl around the sunlit branches of a tall *ceiba*,
and white egrets are everywhere, and a quadrille of dusky skim-
mers lilts along across the river. These thick meadows are like
outposts of a great grassy plain, the *Campos Geraes*, which lies
off to the northward, cut off from man by some two hundred and
fifty miles of jungle; the plain extends another two hundred
miles to the Tumucumaque highlands on the border of the
Guianas. One day there may be a cattle industry in those grasslands, some fifteen thousand square miles of them, like a huge
unexplored island in this sea of trees.

Between Santarém and Óbidos, a scant sixty-five miles upriver, man's presence is quite noticeable. The banks are higher
here, and the thatch huts of the *caboclos* are larger, semi-
permanent. Nevertheless, in the nearly three hundred years since

Óbidos was founded the face of the river has changed little, and that change is due largely to erosion. At Óbidos, more than six hundred miles from the sea, there is still a one-foot tide. It is a pastel village with Spanish red-tile roofs and looks painted onto its pink sandstone bank; the banks seem inset in turn into the jungle. A church with two towers is built above the town, and the towers sink slowly into the green as the ship moves westward.

December 22.

Last night, toward twilight, I saw the gleaming white head of a kite perched in the dome of a fig tree, and, immediately afterward, two great scarlet macaws, tail feathers streaming, sailed with lazy grace among the cabbage palms along the bank; a third was hauling itself up the trunk of a pale tree with its hooked bill. This morning I saw another in silhouette, and an inia rooting under the bank, and more new birds.

The landscape slowly changes. There are fewer savannas, taller forests, and occasional high red and yellow banks. The ship zigzags back and forth from bank to bank, avoiding the strength of the main current; she stays as close to the bank as possible, and as the river is often fifty feet in depth only a few yards from the shore, this can be very close indeed, so close that branches of the trees at times could be touched with a long fishing pole. With binoculars, and even without, one can study the birds and trees in some detail. (On the downstream run the ship stays in mid-river, and while the trip takes half the time, the river is miles wide in places, and the jungle at best is very remote.) The sole aid to navigation placed on the river since the French geographer La Condamine first mapped it in 1743 is the light on Mandihoy Bank, and the landmarks, such as they are, of the twenty-three hundred miles of river between Belém and Iquitos are stored in the minds of the two river pilots; under their occult guidance the ship streams along full speed ahead all day and night, except in heavy rain or fog. Now and then there comes a resounding boom as a submerged log drives hard against the hull, but otherwise we proceed without accident.

At noon only the vultures and the river terns are still abroad; a turkey vulture, the first I have seen, crosses the glazed river on dihedral wings. At the bank there is a small platform with washed clothes on it, and a *caboclo* woman, in sombrero and pink calico, stands there smiling at us, up to her hips in the brown water.

December 23.

The Río Negro is the Amazon's chief tributary, flowing down out of the wild sierras of Venezuela, and, as its name suggests, it is black; the line of demarcation at its confluence with the Amazon is so well defined that for a few moments the ship is literally in both rivers at once. The stern is still churning in turgid brown even as the bow is slicing through a depthless black; only a few feathers of sediment curl out from the main body of Amazonas to hang suspended in the Negro.

Eight miles above the Negro's mouth is Manaus, the chief city of Amazonas. At Manaus the river's rise and fall can exceed forty feet, and in consequence a part of the city is quite literally afloat; many huts are built on rafts, some of these strung together in long wandering chains, or clumps. There is also a unique floating quay, some distance from the bank; here we tie up. Cargoes are unloaded at the quay—which is littered at the moment with great dark balls of crude rubber—and carried by cable car to the shore, where the permanent wharf, at this time of the year, stands thirty feet above the water line. Though the rainy season is well along upriver, the water has just begun to rise here.

From the river the opera house at the top of the city can be seen; *urubus* wheel and slide above its golden dome. It is said that in the 1890s this opera house, one of the largest in the world, offered the greatest singers of the time, but now it is decrepit, and green reclaimers of the jungle have attacked its cracks and cornices. Like the wide streets and handsome houses, and the large cathedral of arresting robin's-egg blue, the opera house was a product of the rubber boom; it lies at the head of the main avenue like some great monument to better days.

The ship passed the day and evening at Manaus, and in the late morning I paid a call on an affable German, Mr. Schwartz, who deals in wild animals and birds and in decorative local fish, including that tiny pride of American aquariums, the neon tetra. There were two tame river otters underfoot, and somewhere on the premises an escaped anaconda. Mr. Schwartz was rather discouraging about the prospects of seeing much animal life along the Amazon. South American mammals are for the most part small and timid, and man has driven them back from the banks of the main river. The manatee, or sea cow, which is killed for food, is all but extinct except in the wildest areas, the large caimans, or South American crocodiles, are disappearing, and the river otter has become so valuable—it brings as much as eighty dollars a skin—that the Indians pursue it everywhere; Schwartz feels its time on earth is short. In the time of H. W. Bates, who lived on the Amazon from 1848 to 1859, the manatee was a common animal. (Bates's observations, incidentally, contrast strangely with those of Fawcett, Leonard Clark, and other modern adventurers: he never saw an anaconda larger than twenty-one feet, and in all the four years that he lived at Ega, a village of twelve hundred on the Teffé tributary, there was not a single case of snakebite, though snakes were common.) Conservation laws in South America, as in nineteenth-century North America, would be inadequate even if there were some way of enforcing them, and one sees the same forces at work here now which crippled our own wildlife a century ago.

In the afternoon, wishing to set foot in that jungle I had been peering at for a week, I took a taxi out of town, accompanied at the last moment by my fellow passenger, that redoubtable maiden, Miss X. Together we struck off into the wilderness, which turned out to be, if not primeval, at least extremely interesting.

In New England one walks quite gradually into a wood, but not so in the jungle. One steps through the wall of the tropic forest, as Alice stepped through the looking glass; a few steps, and the wall closes behind. The first impression is of the dark, soft atmosphere, an atmosphere which might be described as "hanging," for in the great tangle of leaves and fronds and boles it is difficult to perceive any one plant as a unit; there are only these hanging shapes draped by lianas in the heavy air, as if they had lost contact with the earth. And this feeling is increased by the character of the earth itself, which is quite unlike the thrifty woodland floor at home; here the tree boles erupt out of heaped-up masses of decay, as if the ground might be almost any distance beneath. The trees themselves are so tumultuous and strange that one sees them as a totality, a cumulative effect, scarcely noticing details; there is a strange, evilly spined palm trunk, though, and a crouching plant with gigantic fronds, and a fantastic parasite, like a bundle of long red pipe-cleaners studded with olive nuts, fastened here and there to the high branches, and the looming trunk of a silk-cotton, seen only when one is right on top of it; it soars off through the leathery green canopy overhead.

"We often read, in books of travels," Bates remarks, "of the silence and gloom of the Brazilian forests. They are realities, and the impression deepens on a longer acquaintance. The few sounds of birds are of that pensive or mysterious character which intensifies the feeling of solitude rather than imparts a sense of life and cheerfulness."

And it is true that the jungle seems strangely silent, even when the air is full of sound; the sounds are like sounds from another sphere of consciousness, from a dream, and then suddenly they burst singly on the ear: the tree frogs and cicadas, the shattering squawks of parrots (there were two for a while, discoursing overhead), and the eerie flutings of birds whose appearance could scarcely be guessed at, all of these competing with the little squeaks and cries uttered by my companion, who, receiving no intimation of our insignificance, did not have the proper respect for this sort of cathedral. (I affected a sort of trance, not wholly false, and with a rapt expression disregarded her; and after a time, infected by the atmosphere despite herself, she became silent.) The sounds were remote because there was no sign of their authors, only the still jungle, and occasionally a shadow flicking where the sunlight filtered through above. But a little later, when my eyes had cleared, I saw the humbler creatures I have always known: the subtle gray and brown wood butterflies, the black ants (though these were twice the size of any I had seen at home), and a miniature tree-frog, cedar-colored. And in a clearing the birds showed themselves: *bienteveo* tyrants (this was the bird I saw the first time on top of a warehouse by the docks at Georgetown, British Guiana, a widespread and resourceful flycatcher which, according to W. H. Hudson in his *Birds of La Plata*, will cheerfully consume fish, fledglings, snakes, and mice to eke out its ordinary diet), and flycatchers similar to our western kingbird, and a blue tanager, and a clear-breasted thrush, and one of the blackbird tribe, a flashy black and yellow job, ivory-billed, with an insolent tone of voice. This is the river oriole. Here and there a butterfly of shocking colors, and nondescript lizards in the dry brush.

There came a sudden avalanche of tropical rain, crashing to earth, and immediately, in a small stream, small fish like sunfish leaped and whirled. A water snake, emerald-speckled on a throat distended by what must have been a still-live frog, swam clumsily away, disappearing into a black tunnel where the stream slipped into the jungle wall; at this moment, for the first time, the jungle came into focus for me. I could feel it, hear it, smell it all at once, could believe I was almost there.

December 24.

The forest increases in stature, it seems, as we ascend the river. There are fewer clearings, and the few *caboclos* standing on the bank as we go by, watching dispassionately as the wash from our wake bangs their frail canoes together, look darker to me, more Indian—though even a century ago, in Bates's time, the tribes of the main river banks were already extinct or absorbed by the whites and Negroes. New birds continue to appear, including tropic kingfishers, one of them dark and tiny, with a white nape. In the river the floating debris is increasing, littering great areas of the expanse, but it is the jungle which changes most. A number of trees I have not noticed before, and especially one with a smooth purple-mahogany trunk—I'm told this is the purpleheart. The larger trees have aerial gardens of red-flowered epiphytes, *Bromelia*, and strange silver cylinders—these are hornets' nests—hanging like Christmas ornaments; everywhere, fastened leechlike to the trunks, are the dark masses of white ants' nests. The lowest branches of these trees must be fifty feet from the ground; in the evening light, its pale marble columns mysterious in the greens, the forest is truly beautiful; it is difficult to conceive of a lovelier forest in the world.

Tonight is Christmas Eve.

Christmas Day.

Early on Christmas morning two brilliant macaws streamed out across the river in front of the ship, and in the fiery green of the dawn bank I saw an enormous white flower. I have not seen this flower before.

We are not a religious ship, and, the Dutch missionaries having been left behind in Manaus, there was no formal worship. To soothe our savage breasts the captain played us carols on his phonograph, and a great variety of secular music as well, everything from cha-cha-cha to *The Merry Widow.* The music was absorbed attentively by a gathering of *caboclos* who convened on the bank and in their small canoes at the point near the mouth of the Urucu River where, toward noon, the ship dropped anchor in order that all her company might celebrate Christmas dinner together.

The small salon, decorated by the captain himself, was festive in a heartbreaking sort of way, and there was even a small spruce tree, a renegade from the consignment of Christmas trees left at Saint Vincent. The odor of this humble evergreen, so crisp and strange in the damp, redolent atmosphere of the jungle river, brought me as close as I have come to homesickness—I caught myself easing up to it every little while and furtively inhaling. Past the branches of the spruce, through the bright porthole, could be seen the rapt faces of the halfbreeds on the steaming bank, and the tumbled mass of the jungle rising like a great engulfing wave behind them.

The captain served rum to his passengers and officers in person (this is the custom, and later the officers would serve Christmas dinner to the stewards). He did his courtly best to make a party of it, and to my faint surprise succeeded, pouring our drinks lavishly and with grace. Emboldened by rum, and carried on at table by wine and port, we were able to don our paper hats and snap our snappers with some gusto. The chief engineer claimed the port bottle was his own, and when this claim was contested pointed at the lettering, crying out, "Me bloody name's Fernandez, isn't it?"; behind his head our young Ortega, the swiftest waiter in the world, produced a mask with red nose, mustache, and owlish glasses, and, crossing himself, clapped it suddenly on his own face.

We feasted on ham and turkey of a kind, and there were grapes and nuts in place of the usual dessert "sweet," a tapioca or semolina decked out, according to the joint daily inspiration of the cook and steward, in a variety of brilliant colors and exotic names, and resembling nothing so much, under the effects of the ship's vibration, as a low marine organism, a community of hydroid animals, shuddering with life. This staple item was suppressed upon the Lord's Day, but I have no doubt that naked masses of it, as yet unadorned, are cached somewhere about the ship, quaking away until tomorrow.

The rest of Christmas remains a little hazy in my mind. The noon euphoria was followed, by those officers not on watch, by a humid afternoon of drinking and an access of somber homesickness. Even the chief, who earlier had appropriated the comic mask and kept popping up at portholes all over the ship, now complained bitterly that the company had not sent the ship a Christmas cable. "First ship I was ever on," he grumped, "where they didn't have the courtesy to send the lads a little message." The third mate was snarling and unhappy, and the Second Engineer subsequently succumbed to the eulogies of Scotland, and the good life in the Far East as a tanker "mon," for which he has become notorious on the *Venimos*. (In Haiti one afternoon, forgetting where he was, he abused the longshoremen in Chinese, and a week later, happening upon one of the only two Chinese in Barbados, he celebrated and "went adrift," as these men say—he failed, that is, to appear aboard ship when his watch came around the following day—and this for the first time in twelve years at sea.) Unlike the Brazilian and Peruvian crewmen, who see their families on every run, the majority of the officers have not been at home in months and, in a few cases, years; though the morale of the ship is ordinarily high, there are two officers disliked cordially by the rest, and these resentments flowered on Christmas Day, in company with each man's longings and eccentricities. Nevertheless, these men are generous and intelligent (the most intelligent are Sparks and the third engineer; at least, they thrash me regularly at chess), and on this long voyage—we are now thirty-five days out—I have made good friends among them.

By nightfall morale had restored itself somewhat. There was

a very comic and touching collection of absurd presents which the captain presented to me with a speech at supper, and a fine evening of lusty singing on the afterdeck. "The Londonderry Air" bestirred the lightless jungle, and in the reflective silence afterward the air was tightened by the squeak of bats. Overhead stars livened the whole tropic sky, sparkling outward from the mast silhouettes and crowding down on the black horizons on all sides. Some of these stars, those off to the south, never rise above our night skylines in North America. It came as a start, that realization in the silent evening that these far, endless galaxies I was seeing for the first time in my life.

December 26.

The Paraná de Manycão, a narrow channel cutting across a long bend in the river to the east of the Rio Juruá: a heavy rain this morning, and in the rain I saw three ivory-colored herons with black crests and head plumes and extraordinary bright blue bills. There are still new birds each day as we move westward—the hawks seem to change every few miles—and of the birds seen in the first days on the river only the black vulture, large-billed tern, river swallow, egrets, and green parrots are still in evidence. The mammals remain hidden, all but the bats and porpoises, and so do the crocodilians, but there are periodic swirls of some great fish.

A young native, hunting with canoe and light spear in the arrow reeds. The ship starts up the egret he is stalking, and he stares at us impassively over his shoulder as he drifts astern. There are a few more of the large white Christmas flowers, and red flowers of the wild banana trees. And at last, a monkey, a large black one, hurling himself out of a high tree onto the lower canopy, where he scrambles a moment before disappearing among the leaves. With those shaken branches, the whole forest quite suddenly comes alive.

December 27.

Sometime tomorrow we shall reach Peru. There are more flowers here—yellow ones, and small red and pink-purple, growing on the vines—and a new yellow-flowered tree, quite large in size. A palm in this country, called the *ubussu*, has enormous fronds, like an outsize fern, which dance violently in the slightest air. Parasites and air plants are everywhere, some flowering and lovely, others grotesque; one tree has spheres, like linked coconuts, hanging down its trunk. I think this is the cannon-ball tree, *Couroupita*. Another tree, unnoticed until today, has bark gray with a greenish tint and very smooth, like the skin of some ancient dinosaur.

Strange whirlpools and eddies increase along the banks; the river has risen markedly. The banks are clogged with snags and floating islands, and spinning logs which, moved slowly upstream in the eddies, look deceptively like animals. Some of the trees are caught on the bottom and yaw viciously in the current, and others sink mysteriously, to rise some distance away; the dull boom which shakes the ship when one of these trees is struck at the wrong angle is now periodic. A heavy bird with the head of a fowl and the flight of a vulture is common on the banks and floating debris—this is the *camungo*, or screamer, a great black and gray relation of the geese, with long spikes or horns on the shoulders of its wings.

The animals come forward as we move upriver. This morning a group of four or five red howler monkeys, rusty in the sunrise light, observed us from the top of a tall tree, and this afternoon I saw a sloth. This unprepossessing mammal, long-armed, with an earless face like a husked coconut, was apparently roused out of its torpor by the ship; it was climbing upward and inward toward the trunk of its bare tree at top speed, which is to say, about as fast as a very old fireman on a ladder. Its dingy coat was green-tinted with algae and lichens, which serve it as a kind of camouflage; by the time it reached a crotch behind the trunk and hunched down, resembling some parasitic growth, the ship was already past; I observed its last precautions through binoculars.

December 28.

For the second straight day the river was shrouded in heavy fog in the night and early morning, retarding us. Gray weather, and the morale of the ship is now at a low ebb. All of us are drinking more, and the chief confesses—not entirely without his usual considerable charm—that he is sorry for himself. Probably it would not be far-fetched to say that the climate, abetting fatigue and drink, has brought home his age in a very painful way; he is to retire after this trip, and while he is longing to go home to his garden near Bristol, he is a man who loves life, or loved it once, and he sees in retirement some sort of admission of defeat.

The third mate is also sorry for himself and angry at the world. In the beginning of the trip he was looking forward to Peru—I remember his enthusiasm on one blue day at sea, south of Bermuda—but now he cries out his hatred of the river and of "the stinking nay-tives," the trees, and the humidity—it doesn't matter what. He is a good-looking boy in his early twenties, with a wife in England and a child he has never seen, but there is more violence than love in him, and an unquenchable frustration that his natural assets have brought him nothing but responsibility. He speaks longingly of a trip in a sloop around the world, away from everything.

A solitary red howler in the morning, perched disconsolately on a long limb, and at evening great flights of green and white parakeets, birds by the thousands, their electric screeching clearly audible above the engine even at a distance. They bank and whirl among the trees in bands of four or five hundred, perpetually excited. There are also large black and yellow river orioles, and here and there the trees bear dozens of their hanging fiber nests, some of these three feet in depth.

December 29.

Last night the *Venimos* arrived at the Brazilian frontier post of Benjamin Constant (called formerly, I have read, Remate de Males, or "Culmination of Evils"), on the Javarí River; the first sight of Peru was a light across the void of jungle darkness. We then moved on to the military post of Tabatinga, and finally to the border village of Ramón Castillo in Peru; at one point, under flashes of slow lightning which illumined the horizons, the faceless corners of Brazil, Peru, and Colombia could be made out simultaneously (I got up out of my berth to observe this minor marvel, but I can't really say I got much out of it).

This morning Peru lies to port and Colombia to starboard. The Colombian foothold on the Amazon (between Manaus and Tabatinga the river is called the Solimões, and in Peru the Marañón, but it is still Amazonas, "El Río Mar") is small, and the jungle here seems low and scrubby. Colombia is left behind in the middle of the morning, its one distinctive feature a delicate pearl-gray hawk with a black and white barred tail, which circled out across the bow before sliding back over the trees. I have not seen this species before, and because I think of it at this moment as Colombian, I hope unreasonably that I shall not see it again.

December 30.

The weather remains overcast and somber and very cool for the equator—72 degrees plus at times. Without sun the jungle assumes a monotone and oppressive aspect; even the bird activity seems diminished. Tonight the ship arrives at Iquitos, forty days out of New York, and though she has been comfortable and pleasant, I can't say I'll be sorry to leave her. But I shall miss my friends; the chief came this morning and gave me his address, asking me to visit him, and I certainly hope I shall.

December 30–January 2.

The town of Iquitos lies some twenty-three hundred miles upriver, and less than three hundred feet above sea level. To a lesser extent than Manaus it has the boom-and-bust aspect derived from better times; its few large houses seem out of place and incongruous on the dirt side streets. Nevertheless, the town, overlooking a wide curve in the river, remains Peru's chief port on the Amazon; as in Manaus, a part of its community, called Belén, is afloat.

While in Iquitos I celebrated nightly with the ship's officers our arrival in Peru. One of these four nights was New Year's Eve, and this was spent largely at the house of four very young Peruvian girls, friends of my own friends on the ship. (Some seamen here also have informal Indian "wives," and one was presented upon his arrival with a baby girl, alleged to be the fruit of his last voyage; he played the proud father with good grace until someone suggested that he use his arithmetic.) These ecstatic sisters, with their mother and aunts, baby brothers and sisters, and a puppy which, to the naked eye, was perfectly round in shape, welcomed four or five of us with beer and wine, firecrackers, a chicken-and-rice dish, dancing, and a great amount of innocent hospitality, and I shall remember that family warmly for a long time.

Iquitos, like the other river towns, has its share of wanderers, including an ambiguous German guide whose history—some of it conflicting, but all of it propagated by himself—includes a period spent in North Africa as driver to General Rommel. On the subject of wildlife and Indians this man seemed fairly dependable; he affirmed the virtual disappearance of the manatee and river otter and the fact that the caimans are shot on sight for their hides. The shops in Iquitos are jammed with stuffed crocodilians, which, understandably, do not sell well as items of interior decoration; nevertheless, they continue to be slaughtered. One sees another aspect of the North American pattern, with the Indians, for a tiny gain, hastening the decline of the natural resources they depend on. (Some of the waste, it must be said, is of their own devising: they destroy many more fish than they can use by grinding the barbasco plant in the bottom of a dugout, which is then overturned in a lake or stream. The poisonous barbasco—the source of rotenone, used in insecticides, and first described by La Condamine—litters the surface with dead and dying creatures. This practice is against the law, but again, the law is all but unenforceable.)

Herr D., among others, deprecates the legends of Indian ferocity. In his opinion the celebrated killings in recent years by the Jivaro tribes of the upper Marañón and the Aucas of the Ecuador border, north of here on the Napo River, were provoked by the rape of an Indian woman in one case, and by total and foolish neglect of Indian customs in the other. The Jivaros have been "contacted" by the missionaries, and pictures and artifacts of this handsome and colorful people, including their toucan-feather headdress, eight-foot blowpipes, and great bows and arrows, are readily obtained. Nevertheless, a German explorer was killed by a sub-tribe of the Jivaros, the Muratos, only a few months ago, a fact extremely vexing to Herr D., who takes hunting safaris into that region. Perhaps he fears that his rather lurid advertising—"Fish with the Chabras Headhunters"—may backfire. Herr D. is sure his fellow German committed some blunder or atrocity, though the facts are still mysterious; he himself claims to have spent six weeks with the Aucas prior to their massacre, a few years ago, of five American missionaries. They are, he says, a very gentle people when they do not feel their rights are being infringed. The one dangerous tribe left in this region are the Mayorumas, or "Mayos," a short distance southeast of

Iquitos on the Brazilian border. (Lieutenant Herndon mentions the danger from the little-known Mayorumas in the journal of his explorations for the United States Navy Department in 1851—"Our men are much afraid of this people"—and an account of 1904, quoted in the excellent *Handbook of South American Indians* of the Smithsonian Institution, demonstrates that their hatred—or, more probably, fear—of all outsiders is not limited to the white man.

> The Mayoruna used to trade with their enemies. They went to the river and blew bamboo trumpets to signal the traders on the opposite side. The latter crossed in canoes and, without landing, held articles for exchange on the points of their spears. The Mayoruna gave parrots, hammocks woven of wild cotton, feather head-dresses, and various small objects, and received knives and other iron tools. The traders then separated, shooting arrows at each other.

In recent years the Mayos have been infiltrated by outlaws—Peruvian, according to Brazil, and Brazilian, according to Peru. Reports received from other tribes by a missionary I spoke to before leaving South America indicate that soldiers of undetermined nationality have recently invaded and wiped out the largest settlement of these Indians, though killing Indians is officially illegal in both countries.)

On New Year's Day a Captain C., representing a oil exploration company in the area, was kind enough to take myself and some young Germans (Germans are mentioned frequently in this account because they are met with frequently in South America) up the Nanay and Murumu Rivers. These are black, clear streams, and although the wildlife seen was inconsiderable—some large blue-tinged anis, river orioles, egrets, a swallow-tailed kite, a new, black swallow, and a strange community of small bats fastened to a swaying stick out in the open water of the Murumu—I was glad of the chance to see some of the flowers and butterflies close at hand, and especially the great sky-blue morpho; there were numbers of these, some pure blue and some with a black border on the wings, bouncing along in their curious toylike flight.

On our return we paused at the hut of a *caboclo*; the children there took the odd white *guaba* and distasteful *calomito* fruits from the trees for our inspection, as well as the red seed of what looks like a sort of chestnut but is not, used by the Indians as a stain. Captain C., incidentally, swears by the efficacy of Indian medicines, which he claims have cured him of drastic fevers, and of course a number of their medicinal plants are now in general use; *oche*, one of the poisons used by the Jivaros on their arrows, is an ingredient in tranquilizer pills used in the United States.

The following day I paid a visit to the the Iquitos aquarium and natural history museum, where I had a good look at the nervous red-throated piranha, the great *pirarucu*—or *paiche*, as it is called in Peru; most Amazon creatures have both Portuguese and Spanish names, which can be confusing—the giant river turtles, and the dreadful matamata turtle, with its ragged, camouflaged head; the museum upstairs was also useful for verification and identification.

January 3.

From Iquitos, I was anxious to leave by riverboat for Pucallpa, which lies on the Ucayali tributary, six hundred miles farther upstream. But the next boat did not leave for nearly a week, and I decided at last to fly out with the Peruvian military air transport service.

Today is bright, and little puffs of mist hang over the jungle, which is so dense that the ground is closed out entirely. The upper Marañón curves off toward the west, toward the mountains, into the country of the Jivaros—"The region traversed by the Upper Maranhão," reads the present-day South American pilot, on board the *Venimos*, "from a point in about latitude

5 degrees, 30 minutes south, longitude 78 degrees, 30 minutes west, is inhabited by warlike and hostile tribes of Indians known as Jibaros, Huambisas, Aguarunas, and Centipos." We cross a country of bright, algaed sloughs of a sulphurous green, and strange lakes with sharp corners, or shaped like boomerangs— there are an unaccountable number of these—some muddy and some, nearby, jet black; and on up the Ucayali, which, with the Marañón, is a main tributary of the upper Amazon. The river is muddy, creeping up over its banks, and in the bends lie streamlined, sculptured islands. Below, the settlement of Requena, with its rusty roofs of corrugated iron; inland from Requena lie the territories of the dangerous Mayos. The jungle is cut by dark, serpentine creeks with no sign of life along their banks, and now we are over a vast swamp, black water and low clouds: at this height the country can scarcely be told from the coastal swamps of our eastern seaboard, or of Newfoundland, or even of the Yukon delta. But it changes again, a forest of palms, and there is a mirage effect, as if the palms stood suspended above the river water which has flooded them. A sudden storm, and a short time later, with superb Spanish abandon, the plane careens downward through dense clouds, breaking through just above the tree tops, and settles heavily on the mud runway of Pucallpa.

January 3–January 7.

The town of Pucallpa is the terminus of a road across the Andes from the coastal ports and Lima to the Ucayali and the Amazon. In former times Peru had the alternative of transporting its jungle products up over the high mountains by Indian or muleback, or shipping them nearly three thousand miles down-river, around northern South America and through the Panama Canal, and south again to Callao; except for the small amounts that can be taken out by plane, it still has this alternative in the rainy season, for the last part of the road, from Tingo María to

Pucallpa, has never been surfaced and becomes all but impass-able when wet. The money set aside for surfacing the road has long since vanished, in the graceful and mysterious manner of these countries, but eventually the *carretera* may be completed, and when this happens Pucallpa will become an important city and may well replace Iquitos as the capital of the jungle. At the moment, however, it is a frontier town, ramshackle and muddy, without a paved street to its name; the great majority of the dwellings here are thatched.

Nevertheless, it is more interesting than Iquitos or Manaus, which might be small towns anywhere. The jungle is very close here, and Indians come into the streets—flat-headed, barefoot Shipibo women, for the most part, with nose ornaments hanging to their upper lips. They wear embroidered skirts and shawls, and thongs tied around their ankles, and their hair, cut in a straight line across their foreheads, extends straight down their backs. The nearest village of Shipibos is about fifteen miles away, at the far end of a large lake, Yarina Cocha. At the near end of this lake is the Peruvian base of the so-called *lingüísticos*, a group of religious men and women, mostly American, who specialize in the translation of the Bible into the Indian tongues. There are thirty-one distinct languages in the Peruvian *selva* alone, and the *lingüísticos* have people working with twenty-nine of these groups—all but the Mayos, who are not hospitable, and one other tribe which is known to exist but which, to date, cannot be found.

I obtained this information, and a good deal more, from Mr. Jack Henderson, the base director, after an erratic journey to Yarina Cocha by bus and on foot. The work of the Summer Institute of Linguistics, to give the organization its official name, has received a good deal of well-deserved publicity—a converted chief of the Chapras tribe, Tariri, has even appeared on tele-vision in Hollywood—and there seems no reason to celebrate it here, but Mr. Henderson was also very helpful in regard to local information and confirmed two stories I had heard downriver. First of all, missionary work throughout the *selva* has recently been hampered by the natives' conviction, spread by their medicine men, that Indian flesh and its oil are used as fuel for the white man's airplanes. And second, one of the *lingüísticos*, a girl, was actually attacked by an anaconda. For once Colonel Fawcett had been borne out, and so had my friend Picquet in Belém. Apparently, the girl involved was sitting in a canoe at the river bank in front of a Chapras village, awaiting her partner, a trained nurse, when the river boa rose behind her and seized her at the elbow. She was able to fight free of it and reach the bank, but not before being bitten severely on the arm and side; the incident was witnessed and confirmed, apparently, by the girl's partner and the Indians themselves, and she still has the scars to prove it.

Mr. Henderson recommended to me an independent missionary in the nearby village for further information as to wildlife, and, after a fine lunch served by his wife, I walked back down the jungle road. Songbirds and doves were everywhere, including a black finch with a luminous breast of dark, deep red; there were also two kites, which are common around Pucallpa.

The missionary, Mr. Joseph Hocking, came to his calling indirectly, having formerly been an expert on snake venoms and anti-venins for the pharmaceutical firm of Sharp & Dohme; he is an enthusiastic amateur naturalist and still corresponds with museums and zoologists in the United States. Mr. Hocking is a bald, cheerful man with an attractive family, and his specialty is aiding the local people toward improved agricultural practices. He operates an experimental fruit farm—he fed me a variety of fine mangoes—and raises the only prosperous chickens I have seen to date in South America, feeding them a nutrient meal of his own invention consisting of ground-up caimans. Formerly, he said, large caimans were so common in Yarina Cocha that at times the airplanes of the *lingüísticos* had difficulty finding a clear path in which to land. The big animals are rare now—in part, he admits, because of the local industry he himself set up by advocating their use as chicken feed. According to Hocking, the caimans will attack, though usually when cornered, by accident or intent, in a narrow place or slough. Snakes and snakebite, in his experience, are much exaggerated dangers, though the bite of the bushmaster, called by Fawcett "that double-fanged abomination," is almost invariably fatal in a matter of minutes. (The bushmaster is commonly twelve feet in length, enormous for a pit viper, and the quantity of its peculiar venom so great that even if a quantity of serum was at hand, a sufficient amount could not be transmitted to the victim in time to save his life.) But the bushmaster is nocturnal in its habits, as is the more common fer-de-lance; both of these species, with the large variety of other venomous snakes, usually succeed in keeping out of man's way. Hocking supports the usual theory about that small but notorious destroyer the piranha, that it will not attack unless blood is in the water; the piranha is common in Yarina Cocha, but children swim there freely nonetheless. Mr. Hocking's children keep a pet tapir, a *matamata* turtle, and a small boa constrictor on their premises, which are lively and cheerful. I hope it won't embarrass Mr. Hocking if I report here that he is extremely well liked and respected throughout this region.

Mr. Hocking's remarks on the crocodile, piranha, and poisonous snakes tend to bear out the results of my own unscientific survey of the dangerous fauna of the Amazon. A number of intelligent people, including a few who can be considered trustworthy, were earnestly consulted. Here are the dubious conclusions: in answer to the question, What do you think is the most dangerous creature in the Amazon? (or, *Qué a su opinión, es el animal el más peligroso de Amazonas?*), the name which came up most often was that of the *sucurucu* (Brazil), or *shushupe* (Peru)—the bushmaster. Next came the *gergón* (Peru), or *jararaca* (Brazil)—the fer-de-lance. And this was true despite the fact that, according to many, it is possible to walk through the *selva* for days at a time without seeing a snake of any description. This leads one to suspect that the two largest of the venomous snakes are less prevalent than awe-inspiring. (Hocking, in fact, tells a terrible story which he believes to be true: not long ago, in Brazil, two men played a joke on a sleeping friend by slapping him on the arm with two thorns on a stick after placing a live bushmaster on the floor. Seeing the bushmaster and the two spots of blood upon awaking, the man was convinced his doom was sealed and dismissed his friends' frantic reassurances as attempts to comfort him; within fifteen minutes he had died of shock.)

No other creature received more than a single vote. Few jungle veterans have ever seen an anaconda large enough to do them damage (to Fawcett, perhaps, this would indicate that few have ever done so and lived to tell the tale); the giant specimens —thirty feet is very big indeed—usually occur in ponds or swamps, away from the traveled rivers. (Nevertheless, an imposing source of information, the well-known jungle hand and hôtelier of Pucallpa, Señor Fausto Lopez, has described to me this very day an anaconda which he saw killed by Indians during the course of a journey by raft, or balsa, down the Huallaga River from Tingo María to Iquitos; this animal, which the Indians assured him was old and harmless, measured thirty meters, or more than ninety feet, in length.) The jaguar has some kills to its credit, but these are extremely sporadic, at least in the Amazon: the evidence seems to suggest that *el tigre*, like the other great cats of the world, is chiefly dangerous when wounded, or when so old and decrepit that human beings are the best it can manage in the way of food. The electric eel, tarantula, scorpion, vampire bat, and other creatures can all be deadly under special circumstances; a missionary from near Atalaya has never known a fatal case of snakebite but has lost a young Indian to a scorpion. In general, however, these small things are considered pests: the vampire, with its swift digestion, adds insult to minor injury by befouling the sleeping quarters of its victim. In the end the creatures most disliked are the biting insects and the *candiru*.

These are not fatal, and the conclusion one must come to—not without a certain loss of romantic illusions—is that a human death caused by any one of the dread denizens of the jungle is so rare that Theodore Roosevelt once called potential danger from these animals "trivial." The rare animal fatality, however, coupled with those caused by disease, drowning, starvation, and, very occasionally, wild Indians, reminds one of the forces still operative in this huge river world.

There is a man in town named Vargaray, from upriver at Atalaya, known locally as an *hombre muy serio*—not given, that is, to flights of fancy—who has seen a fossil mandible lying in the jungle near the Inuya River so huge and heavy that "five or six men" could not lift it. I expressed my doubt politely, I thought, by inquiring why the missionaries in the area had apparently never seen or heard of this phenomenon, and Vargaray retorted, not without mild contempt, that the *misionarios* knew nothing of the *selva* except the Indians of the few small villages on the bank where they had elected to spread the Word. A friend of mine, Señor Cruz, subsequently vouched for Vargaray, as did Señor Raul de los Ríos, whom Mr. Hocking describes as a fine naturalist and taxidermist, and who is plainly an educated man. And it is true that fossil mammoths have been discovered in South America, though none so huge as to satisfy Vargaray's description. His story, like most stories of the Amazon, leaves one with a nagging doubt, a fleeting impulse to scrape up an expedition and go plunging off into those imperturbable green walls.

Here at Pucallpa the jungle is visible from my window in the Gran Hotel Mercedes; it lies but a short distance away, on the far side of the Ucayali. Tomlinson's Englishman of Belém never seemed more right: it seems to wait. But in Pucallpa, where tourists are a novelty, a man who says he wishes to go to the jungle simply to look at it is not taken seriously. A Peruvian who might rent his boat is never there, and the assurances of my new friends—one makes friends quickly in Spanish countries, and loses them just as fast—that something can be arranged never seem to come to flower. In consequence, I shall leave the Amazon tomorrow with the uneasy feeling that the jungle has eluded me.

And yet a curious apathy has overtaken me. I can't say that I'm not frustrated, but I can see how tempting could become the Latin concept of *mañana*, that eternal procrastination so foreign to us brisk northerners. It is particularly insidious in an outpost like Pucallpa, cut off from the world by the jungle and the river, the road out impassable much of the year. For example, I am ignorant of what has happened in the world in the past month and do not care—*mañana* I shall find out. I sit with the rest and drink and wait, and watch the hogs and vultures in the muddy street. Sometimes, in a desperate attempt to pierce the jungle, I journey out of town on the tiny bus, or on a truck, poor great gringo that I am, swaying above the press of small humanity like a praying mantis in a beehive. Miles later I get off and unlimber all my optical accouterments, but I am really more an object of curiosity than an observer, for the jungle I glimpsed along the river is never really there, not that jungle of giant trees and mystery which stays always in the distance. The most interesting object I have seen here, in fact, was a large green iguana, which I found downtown, consorting with some hogs. The humidity defeats me after a while, and I hobble back to town in my explorer's boots for the siesta. My skin, dark brown three weeks ago, appears to have turned yellow. At night large frogs appear in the deep rain ruts of the street and fill the darkness with a sound like Chinese blocks, and a bat whirls up and down the upstairs corridor of the Mercedes. Early in the morning men dead drunk on the cane alcohol, *kachasa*, reel past, talking to the pigs, and another man, not drunk at all, plays a guitar as he goes along and sings in a clear voice a repetitive, sad *huainu* of Peru.

By the last day I have given up entirely. In the *cantina* a small boy is polishing my explorer's boots, and out in the street a stricken pig, diseased or mad, lurches into the ditch and topples over. A few children gather to contemplate its final moments, but the rest of us, sitting there, haven't time. An Indian in an extraordinary costume of feathers and red silk, wearing high sneakers, hurries through the *cantina* on an unknown errand, arousing a brief murmur, like a swirl of flies.

Having aroused a brief murmur myself, I am seen off at the airport by my admirers. The plane follows the narrowing Río Pachitea into the foothills, sliding briefly into the village of Tournavista, then climbing to the mountains. Below the wing a vulture slips past, buff-colored with black primaries, the king vulture. This is the last creature of the *selva*, for now the heavy rain clouds sink, and the forest wavers in the swirling mist and disappears. An evil limbo, and the plane surges up into the sun. Across the rolling waves of clouds off to the westward stands the great snowy cordillera of the Andes. Frost forms on the window glass, and behind it a world blue and clear and cold, and a sun so bright, and so violently unlike the shrouded sun of Amazonas, that it is like coming up out of the darkness.

3. SIERRA

CROSSING THE PERUVIAN ANDES, from the jungle to the sea, a plane must fly at an elevation of well over twenty thousand feet, and one thus obtains a striking first impression of the sierra. The rivers sink, the cloud forest gives way to chaparral, and the chasms and dark gorges of the upper slopes loom in wind-driven mists. Then sunlight flashes coldly on the silver wings, and a bed of bright white tufts quite unlike the gray shrouds of the eastern slope stretches away westward toward the snow peaks.

The Andes form the Pacific face of South America, from Colombia south into Tierra del Fuego, and consist of a series of parallel ranges, or cordilleras; between these ranges lie wide, high plateaus, the *altiplano*. In central Peru the *altiplano* is a rolling barren of thin greens and somber browns, traversed irregularly by ridges and sharp ravines, and pocked by odd black ponds. Under the snow peaks a series of blue glacial lakes occurs, lakes in the sky. One gets an impression of vast emptiness and air, but then a settlement breaks a corner of the wasteland, like an outcropping of dull red rocks. Here and there a hut, a stray bead on the thin string of a road leading east and west.

The plane passes between peaks of the western cordillera

and immediately noses downward, so sharply that the heart leaps to the throat. The descent to the coast is very steep, and on a clear day one is able to see from the crests the misty blue of the Pacific and even, incredibly, a broad scalloping of white which proves to be the ocean surf. Beneath the plane, the mountain flanks differ markedly from the green maelstrom of the eastern slopes; they are bare and brown, a consequence not only of the sierra's eastward drainage but of a rainless climate induced by the Humboldt Current, passing northward along the coast. The Pacific here is cold and deep—the southern tip of the so-called Milne Edwards Trench, not far to sea from Lima, reaches a depth of well over three miles—and the Island of San Lorenzo, now visible to the northward, may be thought of as a foothill of this great mountain chain which rises so abruptly from the sea.

The desert aspect of the Andes is the one which confronts travelers arriving by the usual routes, by sea or by air from the north; the western foothills which compose the coast are part of the great Atacama Desert which extends some fourteen hundred miles, from Ecuador far into Chile. Driving south on the shore road from Lima, one sees it at close hand—a lunar world, a dead, windless world of giant dunes and cones, half sand, half dust. The vague mist which hovers on the coast—in the winter months, from April to September, it forms an overcast, an unbroken pall—contributes to the unreality. Out of this mist, beyond the surf, rise the ghostly shapes of the sea-bird islands, dead white with guano.

The road passes the pre-Inca ruin of Pachácamac, half covered by the creeping tongues of dust; beyond, the precious green fringes of a rare westward-flowing stream. The Pachácamac people must have used this stream, and the Quechuas use it still; these mountain Indians, wandered down from the sierra, inhabit huts built of the ruins.

North of the fishing village of Pucusan a road leads off to

a settlement of summer houses overlooking a neat cove between two headlands. The place is called La Honda, and while its terrain of dust and shale, broken only by gray cactus, is at first oppressive, the sense of mystery of the place, the ominous juxtaposition of sea and desert and pale mountains rising one upon another toward a cordillera invisible in the haze soon seem very beautiful. A pair of vultures slide back and forth across the cliff faces, riding the gentle air currents in the fierce sun, and some large gray porpoises rise silently and sink again in the outer bay. One day an osprey fished beyond the rocks, and on another day I saw a solitary oystercatcher. But the great sight on this coast is the multitude of sea birds, which feed on the swarming sea life of the Humboldt Current—the small, whining gray gull or *torero*, the kelp gull, Belcher's gull, and Franklin's gull (a North American species, and the only gull to migrate to the southern continent), the Humboldt pelican, the small red-legged cormorant, but especially the famous guanay cormorant, cleaning up after which, on the guano islands, is a most profitable industry in fertilizer, and the *piquero* booby, still more numerous: in the numbers of these latter species, whirling in like locusts on a shoal of anchovies beyond the cove, may be seen one of the last spectacles of wild natural profusion left on earth. (In recent years a slight increase in the temperature of the Humboldt Current has threatened the ecology of its plankton communities and, by extension, the huge populations of fish and birds, and the guano industry.)

I made several trips to La Honda, in January and again in March, as the guest of Alfredo Porras, and though I kept an eye out for the Humboldt penguin, the delicate Inca tern, and the Andean condor, that largest of flying birds, these three species eluded me. But I went often in the late afternoon to the headlands down the shore, where pelicans glided past beneath the cliffs or sailed on the still sea like plastic toys, and the *piqueros* and red-footed cormorants clustered on an offshore skerry; the latter bird, unlike other members of its dour family, emits a cheerful chirp, quite audible across the wash of ocean on the sea rocks. Beyond, guanays and *piqueros* by the thousands moved up and down across the gold reflections of the setting sun. The great piles of crumbled shale which form the cliffs are full of fossil shells (Darwin found sea shells carried up by the emergent Andes high in the peaks of the Chile-Argentine frontier), and an Inca or pre-Inca wall, now all but subterranean, trails along the cliff edge. Once, returning homeward with a friend, we descended the steep back slope of one of these mighty dunes in the twilight shadows. A week later our tracks were still visible from a mile away, and in that strange rainless and windless land where everything seems at an end, they may be there still.

In the middle of January I left Lima, bound for Cuzco in the mountains. Before turning inland, the plane travels out over the sea to lessen the steep angle of the climb. It struck the coast again high over La Honda and climbed the brown mountains to the snow-splotched peaks. Below lay a wild region where thin streams trailed off disconsolately from the snow pools, sliding down barren slopes into the gorges. A small Indian village perched among *andenes*, the ancient agricultural terraces of the Incas, still in use, which are civilization's most notable imprint on this landscape. There was no road to be seen, and one supposes that these Quechuas live very much today as they did five hundred years ago, under the Incas, tilling the small bitter *chuño* potato which is the chief item of their diet.

The valley of Cuzco is an oasis in the *altiplano*, wide and fertile; one sees immediately why it became the center of Inca civilization. The city itself, more than eleven thousand feet above sea level, is beautiful—it has a clean terra-cotta quality reminiscent of Italian hill towns—but its essence lies less in its architecture than in its setting in the valley, in the cold mountain sun reflected from its Inca walls and Spanish steeples, in the mute Indians and haughty llamas, in the relentless bells. The walls and foundations excepted, the architecture is colonial Spanish, handsome enough from the outside, but with that Spanish

interior clutter which, in the churches, drags any sense of exaltation and transcendence back to earth. Here, as in Spain, one is
startled by the vulgarity of the trappings, and the violence. An
especially gruesome Christ, in the cathedral, is covered from head
to toe with sores and lacerations and a veneer of filth, the whole
decked out in a bright cheap purple skirt.

How affecting it is to see the Indian, unchanged by the intervening centuries, paying to Mass the same mindless coca-
numbed obeisance that his forebears awarded the Temple of the
Sun. There he kneels, ragged and hunched against the cold, before the same gold and silver, now long since refashioned into
the panoply of the Church. (The Christians who had the Inca
Huayna Capac drawn and quartered in the square outside the
cathedral tore down the Inca temples, using the great heathen
stones in the construction of Cuzco's myriad churches. Even
today the Church of Santo Domingo is being rebuilt with the
stones of the Temple of the Sun, Moon, and Stars, some foundations of which, serene and simple, may still be seen in the weeds
of the old churchyard. Of all the churches that I visited, I admired only the small La Merced, with its stonework of pink and
gray, its gentle ornament and fine gold filigree.) The pale priests
wave pale hands in the showcase light around the altars, and
the small Indians, of the color and texture of the earth itself,
crouch in the darkness, their round heads silhouetted by the
trays of flickering candles. Outlandish bells resound. Around
them, mysteries—the dim chapels behind bars, the old soiled
paintings of forgotten saints, the heaped-up altarpiece of silver.
Then the orisons of the choir, and the bells toll out across the
city. Despite the gulf between poverty and pomp, one is stirred,
as the Indians must be. But a child, frightened rather than
moved, begins to wail, its voice rising painfully with the ho-
sannas: its pure animal reaction, juxtaposed with its parents'
hopes and edifices, renders the latter, in the Camus sense, absurd.

But this is a journal of the mountains, and these random

notes are out of place here; I have neither the resources nor the sympathy to comment fairly on the Spanish architecture of Cuzco. There are many fine books on the Inca civilization and Spanish seizure, among which Prescott's classic *Conquest of Peru* probably remains the best.

A number of ruins lie quite near the city—the Inca baths of Tampu Machay, the small fort of Puca Pucara, the Kkenco ruin, with its amphitheater and central monolith (alleged by the guide, no doubt falsely, to have been the scene of human sacrifices), and the massive amphitheater and terraces which are all the Spanish left of the vast edifice known as Sacsahuaman.

Sacsahuaman is mighty, even now. "Many of these stones," as Prescott wrote of the Temple of the Sun, "were of vast size, some of them being full thirty-eight feet long, by eighteen broad, and six feet thick. We are filled with astonishment, when we consider, that these enormous masses . . . were brought from quarries from four to fifteen leagues distant, without the aid of beasts of burden." Our astonishment is increased by the knowledge that the Inca, who used clocks, metal alloys, agricultural terracing, aqueducts, guano fertilizer, and many techniques of the welfare state, had failed to discover the wheel, and by the phenomenon, evident at a glance, that the enormous stones are fitted like watch parts: one cannot, as all writers agree, pass a knife blade between them. In places they even curve into one another, as if squashed together while still malleable, like clay. (The late explorer Colonel Fawcett has suggested that the Inca possessed an herb which softened stone, and this theory, which is not confined to Fawcett, makes as much sense as many of the rest.) On the uppermost terrace of Sacsahuaman stand two great tables, used apparently for animal sacrifices, a huge water clock, and some stone benches. From here one may gaze down past a shimmering grove of Australian eucalyptus—this resourceful tree is now widespread in South America—to the steeple-spined roofs of Cuzco. Farther down the ridge an enormous white Christ broods over the town, in garish competition with the ruin; it is marvelously out of place against the spare distances of the Andes. Elsewhere, the eucalyptus groves excepted, the prospect is as it has always been, a wind-swept alpine tundra of bright wild flowers, finches, and miner birds, mounting to the dark horizons of the cordilleras.

The road from Cuzco to the village of Pisac climbs onto the plateau, passing Sacsahuaman and Puca Pucara before angling off to the eastward. This is a region of streams and soaring hillsides, thatched Quechua huts and winding valleys carpeted with blue and white potato flowers; the Indians themselves were bound for Pisac, for Sunday is their market day. They were all along the roads, moving rapidly in that trundling shuffle of theirs, bent forward, as if forever doomed to walk uphill. They peered without expression at the car—I was sharing a hired car with a missionary on leave from the jungle—for the Peruvian Quechua neither smiles nor scowls, and this deadness of face seems incongruous by contrast with the gaiety of his dress; both men and women wear striped ponchos or shawls, and their wares are tied in many-colored *qquepinas*, a sort of sling-sack carried on the shoulders and tied across the chest. The women are barefoot and black-skirted for the most part, with everything from white straw fedoras to tasseled black woollen disks in the way of headgear, while the men wear sandals, black Spanish knickers (their costumes at times seem almost a parody of colonial Spanish dress, which to a certain extent they are), and vivid wool caps with tassels and earmuffs. These knitted caps, earmuffs and all, are worn even on the hottest of middays; the bareheaded Quechua is almost as uncommon as the one who smiles.

The children too are small bundles of dirty colors, like rag dolls in elfin hats, trotting barefoot in the cold mountain mud. Unlike their elders, they still smile a little, and with their clean, neat features can be very pretty indeed. But at puberty they are no longer children. Their faces broaden, and they assume the squat stolidity of manner which marks the tribe. (Technically the term "Quechua" or "Quichua" does not denote a tribe but rather, a great linguistic group embracing some twenty million mountain Indians of Andean countries, from Colombia to northern Argentina, as well as a jungle tribe of northern Peru; it is the second language of the latter country. Agricultural peoples, they have always been far more numerous than the jungle tribes, and in Bolivia comprise well over half of the population. The mountain Indians are divided into very few tribes; almost all speak Quechua and, where they maintain their traditional dress, are known collectively as Cholos. Like the jungle Indians, they pay small attention to nationality, and are restricted less by the frontiers than by their own sedentary natures.)

The bridge at Pisac, crossing the Vilcanota, was choked with Indians hurrying to the market in the plaza. Under two great *pisonay* trees women sat sturdily upon the ground, feeding babies at long brown breasts while they sold fruits, vegetables, medicinal herbs, alpaca hats, slippers, rugs, and scarfs, fake Inca trinkets for the tourists, and the crisp green coca, a narcotic leaf from which cocaine is derived, and which serves to inure these people not only against hunger and cold but against their grim existence. Meanwhile the men, lined up against an adobe wall, drowned ancient sorrows in the thick, pasty maize beer known as *chicha*. They seemed to find small happiness in their drinking and were, if anything, sadder and more hopeless than before.

We left the Pisac market in mid-morning and traveled down the Urubamba valley, under long avenues of eucalyptus. Yucca cactus and the great century plant were common, but the dominant growth in this loveliest of all valleys I have ever seen is the Spanish broom, called *retama* here, and said by our driver to be good for the human heart: the broom choked all the road shoulders and river bars with yellow blossoms. A few doves and songbirds, and over the river a solitary *serranita*, or Andean gull. In many of the small villages Inca stonework was still apparent, trapezoidal doorways and all, and some of these ancient walls served to support small thatch huts of adobe. Some of the huts in every settlement had a kind of flowered mast above the door, which indicated that *chicha* had been made there and was obtainable.

The driver recommended that we dine in a small hostel in the town of Urubamba, where he joshed and poked the fair proprietress while we washed down with beer an unidentifiable flesh served with hot peppers. The missionary did not touch the beer and toyed unhappily with the food, being distressed not only by the insanitation of the place but by what he took to be the low moral tone of its inhabitants.

At Ollantaitambo, adjoining the modern village, lies one of the most notable ruins of the region: one passes through an Inca gateway in an outer wall and climbs to the top of the ruin on a wide stone stair. There are roofless structures of all kinds, built of a kind of yellow shale, and a ceremonial area littered with cut monoliths of reddish granite: Hiram Bingham, who located the Machu Picchu ruins in 1911, estimated the weight of these Ollantaitambo stones at fifteen to twenty tons, and yet they are dwarfed by numerous examples at Sacsahuaman. On the steep hillsides opposite perch more *ruinas*—schools, prisons, storehouses, it is said—and below, in the court of a modern habitation, there is a lovely fountain, fed by a mountain spring. This is described locally as a sacred bath of Inca sun virgins, and one may as well believe this.

On the return to Cuzco we crossed a bridge at Urubamba and climbed up onto the plateaus, in the direction of Anta. In the late afternoon the *puna*, as the highest wastes are known, was sharp-shadowed and bleak. A church on the Anta road is beautiful in its desolate isolation; it is used for but one service a year, in the winter month of August. Farther on a shallow lake, stalked by restless rays of an obscured sun, reflected the clouds and buttes in faint pastels; along its reedy edges coots, grebes, ducks, spotted sandpipers, and lapwings cried and fed.

In the villages, by evening, the Indians were totally drunk, and there were many fallen; even the fallen were unsmiling. In this state the Quechua looks more slack-jawed and brutish than the most primitive man imaginable. (A team of American psychiatrists—why is it, of recent years, that Americans are always said to operate in "teams," as if an individual American, without his insipid "togetherness," would be helpless?—contrived last year to administer the Rorschach test to Quechuas and "proved," to the satisfaction of my informant, that these people are rife with hatreds and resentments—of the *peruanos*, presumably. But they are so subdued by their own poverty, and by their failure to realize how very numerous they are, that a Quechua revolution, while one day inevitable, remains remote. In dealing with them it is hard to make out whether they are as stupid as they seem or just perverse; the Quechua laborer for one of my friends in Lima was told over and over again not to water the flowers in the heat of the day, when the soil would harden like adobe, but he went right on doing it, patiently destroying the garden. One day his employer, observing this, rushed out in despair and shook the man. "How many times," he shouted, "have I told you not to do that!" The Quechua gaped at him a moment. "Eight or nine times," he murmured sadly.)

Beyond Anta, in a eucalyptus grove, some people were dancing to a sad, slow *huaino* of Peru; when we paused to watch, they brought us beer, which the driver and myself and a friend of the driver we had picked up during the day drank heartily.

Through various causes, not the least of these some remarkably bad planning, I crossed the Andes nine times in five months, at various points from northern Peru to Tierra del Fuego; also I traveled them overland, in three installments, from Cochabamba in central Bolivia to a point well past Quillabamba in south-central Peru. The last part of this journey, from Cuzco north to Machu Picchu and Quillabamba, occurred in early April; from the mountains I went on down the Urubamba

River into the jungle on an errand described in another chapter.

From Cuzco the small Diesel car to Machu Picchu climbs in a series of switchbacks to the high plateaus which surround the city, passing upward through groves of eucalyptus trees to the open slopes; it was April ninth, a clean, clear mountain day, and banks of blue lupine, yellow daisies, and other flowers reminiscent of our own alpine tundras in North America crowded almost to the windows. Near Anta the track crosses the old stone Inca highway—at twelve thousand feet, this is the highest elevation of the railway—and starts on its long descent, winding down across the bare *puna* and into the deep Pachar Canyon, which opens eventually on the Urubamba Valley. In the canyon the flowers change. There are several vivid red varieties, and one of these is the so-called Inca flower or *cantuta*. Toward the foot of the canyon the seas of yellow broom make their appearance; in the valley itself, as the banks steepen into canyons and the river plunges down around boulders, the broom is replaced by the strange mosses, cacti, and gray air plants. The river gains rapidly in speed, from the slow rush at Ollantaitambo, where a base of mighty Inca stones supports the modern bridge, to the swift plunge of white water into the deepening gorges which extend to Machu Picchu. The stream boulders are multicolored: white marble and gray limestone, with red porphyries and blackish slates. North of Ollantaitambo a bright snow peak peered over the dark shoulders of the mountains ahead; it was still in view when the outriders of the tropic zone, acacias and strangler figs, appeared, and a small flock of green parakeets whisked screeching up the valley, like heralds of the *montaña*—the "high jungle" in the eastern foothills of the Andes. Long shreds of cloud settled into the ravines, and the overhanging walls climbed higher, until the train hurried along in shadow, like an ant in a deep crack.

At an arbitrary point, it seemed, there was a siding and a hut, and the *ferrocarril* stopped. High above, visible in the outline of the rim only because one knew it was there, was Machu Picchu; through the dark mountain passes which surrounded it the fog poured like smoke.

To reach the ruins one crosses a footbridge over the torrent and ascends the mountainside in a small bus. The climb from the river is said to be three thousand feet, and this is not difficult to believe; the bus took more than twenty minutes to go a lateral distance from the river of a few hundred yards. At the summit a modern lodge has been erected, rather too close to the ruins for my taste; the latter stretched away along the spine of the ridge and extended upward to a sort of outpost on the very peak of Huayna Picchu. This great dark cone stands guard over the roofless city, where grasses blow and brilliant flowers bloom in the dead houses. Far below, the Urubamba winds around the base of Huayna Picchu like a brown string; other peaks, dark and green, crowd forward from the north, east, and south, the ravines between them filled with flowing mist. This is an impossible terrain, impossibly steep and inhospitable and, in the end, oppressive. (*In situ*, the dispute as to whether the Machu Picchans were Inca or pre-Inca seems very much beside the point. When Hiram Bingham located the rumored city, an Indian family still farmed the overgrown terraces, which suggests the interesting possibility that Machu Picchu, lost in its clouds, has always been inhabited and, to judge from the numbers of Germans and Americans who range it now with their clean limbs and glittering equipment, always will be.) And it is Huayna Picchu and the dark masses, the restless clouds prowling the peaks and the dreadful plunge to the swift river—the mystery, indeed, as to why and when a people would come here to live and why so suddenly, as it is thought, desert the place—which make this ruin so remarkable: if one can separate it from its surroundings and its mystery, Machu Picchu itself, despite its extent and its excellent state of repair, is less noble and less moving than Sacsahuaman, where stupendous monoliths lie juxtaposed to a living city. A visitor there five centuries ago, like the visitor today, would have known the click on stone of llama hoofs descending past it down to Cuzco, the far, solitary red of a cap or poncho, still as an alpine flower against the bleak tone poem of the *puna*, the lonely fluting of an Indian herdsman, playing the thin high *huaino* of the sierra with all the power of his muted soul.

The train south to Lake Titicaca and Bolivia leaves Cuzco at 7:30 in the morning, climbing gradually onto the *puna*. This land much resembles parts of Wyoming and Montana and, higher still, the foothills of Mount McKinley—the same blue lupine and bunch grass, dwarf willow and alder, of our own alpine tundra. But there are many unfamiliar flowers, including a lovely species of silver blue, in clumps, and yucca cactus, and the sage-like *tola*, and representatives of bird families not usually found at these altitudes in North America—coot, and a variety of hawks, and white egrets, and the *serranita* gull, and, most astonishing of all, their color reflected in a long, shallow lake beneath snow peaks, a flock of forty or more flamingoes. The pink of these strange birds as they rise against the distant snowfields is an ornithological incongruity beyond description.

Much of the day it rained, and in the cold mountain fields the Indians sat on rocks, stolid as owls. The spot of red which signaled a distant herdsman was present in every distance, like an emblem of Inca days. Here and there, skulking in a ravine or padding along under a hillside, a solitary black sheep dog, semi-feral; these animals were often miles from the nearest hut or herd of llama. A lone horseman—horses are uncommon at this altitude—a far glacier, a large wheeling bird . . .

And in the station at Juliaca I could not open my window in time to give money to a blind old beggar. The pretty Indian child leading her, shuffling along underneath the window as the train drew out of the station, smiled a forlorn smile of understanding. The little girl stopped at last and waved, and the wave stayed with me all the rest of that long day.

The train arrived at Puno after dark; the passengers for Bolivia went through customs before boarding the lake steamer *Inca*. In order to make the most of its tiny staterooms, the *Inca* travels only at night, which is very unfortunate indeed. One would like to contemplate Titicaca, which, at 12,000 feet, is the highest large body of water in the world—it is 138 miles long, in fact, by 69 miles wide, and at sunrise the *Inca* was still trudging down its length, passing close by the sacred Islands of the Sun and Moon. It was a cold, clear morning in a world of white mountains and blue water. Along the eastern shore drifted the curious reed balsas, or raft-boats, of the Indians.

We debarked at Guaqui, in Bolivia, while the day was early, and I was offered a ride in their hired limousine by an affable South African and his wife. On the way to La Paz we stopped for a time at the pre-Inca ruins at Tiahuanaco. The modern village of this name is only a few miles from Guaqui, and its foundations are largely of stone taken from the ruins; the church itself was constructed in this manner and has two of the great stone idols for which these ruins are best known, standing like sentinels at the gateway of the House of God.

The ruins are spread over a wide area of the *puna*, beyond the village. Excavation has been limited, and probably much remains to be discovered. Walls, storerooms, aqueducts, and an imposing "Gate of the Sun" have been unearthed, in addition to a number of the figures sometimes referred to, due to their woeful expression and for want of more exact archaeological information, as "crying gods." Most of these have been removed to La Paz, but one still stands on the ruin itself, and another lies face down at the bottom of a pit, half excavated. To my uneducated eye they are not dissimilar to the monoliths in photographs of Easter Island, which may or may not tend to bear out the common theory that the creators and rulers of these civilizations were not Indians at all but peoples from the Pacific who made the *Kon-Tiki* voyage in reverse. One area of the ruins, protected now by an adobe wall, is thought to have been a seat

of justice; fine designs are engraved in its fallen stones, some
of which are enormous. Crude ceramics and artifacts, including
tools of copper and copper-bronze, have also been located.

The road from Tiahuanaco to La Paz leads across an *altiplano* far more desolate in aspect than its counterpart in southern Peru; it is higher and is brown rather than green. The adobe
huts of the Quechuas (actually, the Indians of this region are
called Aymaras, though the two groups are closely related; farther
south and east, in the region of Cochabamba, they are called
Quechuas once again) seem poorer than those in Peru, and there
is an increased number of the strange wandering black dogs.
The Indians themselves, on the other hand, look cleaner and
more active and have been known to smile, possibly in consequence of a heightened morale induced by Bolivia's agricultural
reforms; they are not so colorful as their cousins in Peru, though
the most apparent difference in their dress is the brown derby
hat worn by the women. At one point the car passed a funeral
procession, and the file of Indians was reflected in long rain
puddles as they shambled over the plain toward the road: the
corpse was draped in a shiny black material and was carried on a
sort of thin stretcher which sagged sadly between the four pall-
bearers.

La Paz is situated in a canyon, and one comes upon it very
suddenly: the plateau terminates abruptly, and there is the city,
flowing down the steep slope below. From its highest point to its
outskirts, on the floor of the canyon, there is a fall of nearly
two thousand feet. It is a pretty, light, airy city, and its setting
is enhanced by the towering snowfields of Mount Illimani, rising beyond out of the clouds which shroud its base.

From La Paz I traveled to Argentina, Chile, and Tierra del
Fuego, and subsequently to Uruguay and Brazil. In March I
returned there from the opposite direction, arriving in the Bolivian frontier town of Santa Cruz de la Sierra by way of
Corumbá, in Mato Grosso. The Andean foothills mount directly

behind Santa Cruz, which is perched at the edge of the low jungle, and the plane west to Cochabamba rises swiftly among the red cliffs and wooded gorges of the mountain-jungle valleys, known as *yungas*. Not far to the north of here lie the terrains of the savage Yuquis, who killed two hunters a few months ago and threatened the missionaries who were trying to befriend them; according to the Protestant missionary publication, *Black and Gold*, the Bolivian colonists' commission for developing the hinterlands may try now to eradicate the tribe. (This solution would be inadmissable, officially at least, in Peru and in Brazil, but Bolivia, which is primitive and poverty-stricken and cannot afford to have an entire region go undeveloped for the sake of a few savages, makes less bones about its methods.)

The cloud forest of the steepening slopes, and a number of fine waterfalls and cascades which drain the bare upland valleys. Occasional eucalyptus in the hollows, and muddy lakes which, because of the torrential rains of February, have overflowed their edges—one can make out the flooded hedgerows which mark the fields. The railroad from Cochabamba to La Paz has apparently been washed out by landslides, and so I shall travel on from here by bus.

Cochabamba is a pleasant town in a pleasant climate, hot and dry, and planted generously with palms and flowering trees. Mountains rise at each end of its sunny pastel streets, and there are two shady plazas, full of flowers and wild doves like mourning doves; at twilight, on the day of my arrival, the streets glowed with the warm suffusion of the sun.

I was sorry to leave this town the following morning, and I very nearly didn't, for the ancient *góndola* was full to bursting when I arrived at the bus office around sunup. The passengers clamoring for space included a small boy carrying live turtles and a large old woman occupying two seats, neither of them hers, on the grounds that she was not only fat but sick. The *góndola* was scheduled to leave at seven a.m., but as South American transport companies, whenever possible, sell more seats than actually exist, it was seven forty-five before the shouting died down and all thirty-eight passengers had been wedged into a space optimistically alleged to contain twenty-four. The boy with the turtles had been shouldered off the bus entirely, and the extra fourteen included eight legitimate passengers without seats, two excess conductors who contributed little besides body heat, and a family of Indians related to one of these, who were gathered aboard around the corner from and out of sight of the manager of the bus line; the latter was so indignant about the abuse he had received for having oversold his ancient contraption that he had threatened openly to cancel the whole service. The Indian woman, in her derby and shawl, sat on the floor of the bus, nursing her baby, and the Indian men stood in the doorway for thirteen hours, uncomplaining. I followed the lead of the Bolivians and churlishly held my seat: Indians are expected to endure in these parts, and I am now in a position to testify that they can sleep standing up, like horses. The woman, whose head rested on my forearm most of the trip, kept dozing off and letting the baby roll away into the aisle; the baby was of a stoic or resilient turn of mind, however, and held its tongue throughout the day.

I was in the front seat on the right, the only seat aboard which would physically contain my legs, since here they could protrude into the entry. As it was, the legs dropped away into a maelstrom of swaying bodies; I scarcely saw them all that day, and was able to see the road ahead only in glimpses. Altogether, there were six men between the front seats and the windshield: the driver, a friend of the driver who perched between him and his side window, and four others, friends of one another, between the driver and the door. The conviviality of this arrangement did not quite redeem the perils, once we got up on the high curves. The mountain roads of these countries are famous (so famous, in fact, that I hesitate, if only momentarily, to add my own account of them to the vast literature on the subject) for the breathtaking views which lie just beneath the unfenced, unbanked shoulders; both roads and vehicles are always in poor repair, and to the helms of the vehicles cling driven men, innocent of fear and common sense. This particular road, mounting and descending the steep valleys west of Cochabamba, is often no more than a ledge. The ledge has crumbled away in places, and as the drop, at times nearly vertical, can exceed a mile, one is made extremely unhappy to observe how frequently the driver's vision is obscured by arms reaching for bottles or throwing fruit rinds out of windows or clutching at paper bags to be sick in: there was a drum of gasoline in the aisle from which fuel was siphoned periodically to a tank located beneath my seat, and possibly its leaking fumes accounted for the great amount of illness.

The driver, in any case, was neither disabled nor dismayed by these conditions and plunged forward with a will. He yanked the swaying, topheavy bus around long series of blind hairpin turns, hugging the outside edge in order to maintain speed, and blaring down on the next turn as if bent on the total demolition of any opponent who might appear from the opposite direction; the opponent, in the unlikely event that he had sufficient time, would have had to seek out a place where he might pull over, as our own man was much too proud to do so. During this part of the journey, at least, I was quite unaware of my physical discomfort.

At last we gained the altiplano, and the rest of the trip, while interesting, was uneventful. The Bolivian plateau is very high, and even in sunlight its color is a deep unbroken brown. The Indian villages scattered along the road are built of this same earth; the huts seem to grow out of the ground, low and humble as the outcroppings of moles. They are thatched with mud and straw, with tiny holes for windows. These Indians still use their ancient digging sticks and hoes, still grow their traditional tubers and rough vegetables, to the list of which they have added wheat and barley. The men with their long staves, the bundled children, the burdened women—in central Bolivia the Quechua women wear white top hats of straw, but as one approaches La Paz these hats give way to the brown derby of the Aymaras—trundle along the roads or stand staring in the fields. The llamas, too, seem built into the land. A child's head in its brownie hat, still as a stone, observes the passing of the *góndola* from behind a hillock or mountain boulder; the child may be miles from the nearest hut, as if it had grown there on the *puna* like a toadstool. But other children have learned the rewards of beggary: they bound like vicuñas to the roadside as the bus nears and hurl themselves upon the ground in postures of terrible deformity, legs twisted, mouths ajar. They wave their idiots' hats for alms and rend the mountain air with forlorn cries.

Sooner or later the traveler in South America may happen upon a revolution, and especially should he choose to spend much time in Bolivia, where the government is chronically so fractured and unstable that it can scarcely be called a government at all. An unpromising situation was made worse by the revolution and agricultural reforms of a few years ago, which, while commendable in principle, included the nationalization of the valuable tin and silver mines, and gutted the poor national economy by placing the country's exploitation in the hands of amateurs. These amateurs disapprove of one another, not infrequently with good reason, and while I was in Bolivia the town of Santa Cruz de la Sierra and surrounding territories were physically controlled by the opposition party, in a state of open rebellion which, in any other land, would have to be described as civil war.

In La Paz on Saturday morning of March 19, about five a.m., I was awakened by a cascade of gunfire—rifle shots, then machine guns, and finally the dull boom of mortars. I was staying with friends, Dorry and Ted Blacque, whose handsome house overlooks the steep gorge of the Choqueyapu River and is situated on a line between Army Headquarters and the Defense

Ministry; the house is still bullet-pocked from the last revolution, in 1952. I got up and went downstairs, where the maid was very nervous and upset. "*Matan la gente, matan la gente,*" she said to me, wringing her hands. "They are killing people."

The firing continued, way off down the canyon, and two hours later the Bolivian Air Force, represented by two ancient United States Navy SN1 trainers, came droning past at a low altitude. A heavy boom, and the planes swept back down the gorge: apparently they had dropped some sort of explosive, presumably from the after cockpit. Apparently, too, someone had shot at them, for they did not repeat the maneuver; for the rest of the day they circled the city at prudent heights, just barely visible, while the radio ranted excitedly about aerial reconnaissance.

The radio had by now informed us that the glorious people's revolution was being threatened by a dastardly counter-revolution led by the *carabineri*, or military police; clearly these wretches were in cahoots with the plotters in Santa Cruz. The counter-revolutionaries were trying to gain control of the plateau rim surrounding the capital. Already one side or the other had hurled a mortar into the home of the innocent family Cuba, wiping it out, and the toll of dead and wounded was mounting rapidly. The chief of the *carabineri* had been sentenced to death, ten thousand armed *campesinos* constituting the civil guard had been called in from the countryside to assist the patriotic soldiers of the Army, and a national emergency had been declared.

There was a steady whackety-whack and dum-dum-dum of fire—81-millimeter mortars and .50-caliber machine guns erupting among the rifle shots. By mid-morning the fighting was confined to the heights across the gorge. I had ventured out with binoculars and camera and was able to see, from a very safe distance, the explosions of mortar shells and the lines of scurrying men. It was impossible to determine which group was fighting which, or whether the thing had not become a free-for-all. The wide sunny streets of the city were empty of everything but suspense, though a few uneasy people stood in doorways. Here and there on corners stood groups of soldiers or some defected *carabineri*—these were rather self-conscious and tried to look as peace-loving as possible—or some irregulars of the civil guard, with armbands and ancient rifles. I talked with a group of the latter, who were excited and a little drunk, and who told me that the fighting was very close. This was untrue, however.

Farther up the hill a crowd had gathered outside a small hospital, where a casualty list had been posted; in this part of the city, so far, there were one dead and twenty-three wounded, a happy evidence of wretched marksmanship, since the blasting had been considerable. The atmosphere at the hospital was serious, but elsewhere the people, emerging in increasing numbers, only shook their heads, and many grinned; the civil guard, especially, was enjoying itself, for, as the radio reported later, "the noble women of our city rushed to provide their men with food and wine and cigarettes." To judge from appearances, the greatest of these was wine. A squad of soldiers which came hurrying by, carrying mortars and radio-telephones, was very anxious that I take its picture and obligingly struck martial poses when I did so. But one elderly Bolivian who borrowed my binoculars was ashamed. "*Muy feo*," he kept repeating, "*muy feo*—very ugly." Then he mourned, "Now a country like Argentina, countries like that, it is only once every twenty years or so, but here—why, it is practically every other year."

On the way back to the house I ran into a truckload of *campesinos*, Indians mostly, which an array of noble women had plied with *chicha*. A great deal of the damage on these occasions is done by drunken peasant boys who do not know how to use their rifles, and the city is invariably faced, after each revolution, with the problem of getting all these armed men out of town.

By noon the firing had substantially subsided; from the edge of the gorge I could see a file of men, *carabineri*, marching down the ridge opposite, waving a white flag. But the noon lull must have signified only lunch and the siesta, for around two the firing started up again. Directly across from the house where I was staying, a squad of soldiers scurried up the stairs of a skeletal new building without walls, and threw themselves on their stomachs at the corners of the roof. Their attackers did not materialize, however, and a little later they trooped down.

After this the firing dwindled to a halt, though there came an occasional round throughout the evening. Another short burst occurred the following morning, and I supposed that this was an execution. By five that afternoon the radio had announced that the people's government controlled *"perfectamente la situación"* but was still uncertain whether or not a state of siege would be maintained throughout the city. We drove out later, in hopes that a Russo-Hungarian ballet scheduled for that evening would still go on, but the theater was dark and cold, and the bare, bright streets a little ominous; only a few *campesinos*, very drunk, loitered forlornly on the corners, looking belligerent and confused. Like the rest of us, they seemed uncertain what the whole thing had been about. There was even some talk that the counter-revolution had been staged by the government to consolidate its factions at the small price of a few Indian dead.

The next day the city was calm again, and I flew out across the western cordilleras to the coast and north to Lima.

In southwestern Bolivia and the northern extremities of Argentina and Chile the Andes reach their widest point, and the character of the *altiplano* is quite different from that to be seen farther north. This land is not only bleak but quite surreal, a dusty brown waste littered with curious heaps and windrows of rocks, raked up neatly by some giant hand. Dark, erratic weather increased its doom-ridden aspect, with small swift rains and looming cumulus and beyond, as the plane moved southeastward toward Buenos Aires, blue-black caverns of thunder between thick cirrus and the stony land. The light effects played ominously on these windy wastes of high sierra, made all the more desolate by what looked like dry riverbeds of another age and by a mute human habitation, scarcely discernible, and separated from visible roads or water by league upon league of savage ridges, cliffs, and canyons. To the rare traveler on the ground, this must be among the most awesome landscapes in the world.

The plane, sorely buffeted, struggled up over the last cordillera. It descended rapidly to the eastern slopes, where snaky brown streams glinted through a still, unearthly mist at the edge of a climbing forest. The streams joined the complex patterns of the larger rivers in the foothills, and then, where the Bermejo River coils outward into the flat jungle of northwest Argentina, the hills disappeared entirely. This region of low forest and arid scrub, all but uninhabited, is called the Gran Chaco; it extends far to the northward, across most of Paraguay and a large part of eastern Bolivia. The plane crosses several hundred miles of it before the scrub gives way to a vast treeless plain—the Pampa. On this part of the Pampa there are few houses, but the network of civilization may be seen in long dirt roads.

The plane is high, and at seven in the evening the sun is still bright on the cloud crests of the horizon. For the people below, sundown is past, and the land lies shrouded in shadow. Just north of Santa Fe the maze of islands, marshes, creeks, and sloughs which fill the shallows of the River Paraná slide beneath the plane. Like so many of the variegated wildernesses of South America, this alluvial wasteland is enormous: the main stream of the river is all but lost somewhere in the middle of it. At the mouth of the river lies the great estuary known inappropriately as the River Plate.

South of the Gran Chaco, through Patagonia and Tierra del Fuego, the eastern slope of the Andes is barren, while its western slope, in the long southern reaches of Chile, is relatively wet and fertile; this, of course, is the exact reverse of the situation farther north.

Moving westward from Buenos Aires to Santiago, the rich

farming plains of Buenos Aires province, with their islands of trees, give way to a dry pampa, and the Pampa in its turn to arid lands which merge at last with low, wrinkled foothills, the Sierra Córdoba. The foothills here are token, a narrow fringe of red-sand and gravel buttes, of meager plateaus. Then the dark mountains rise, snow-covered. The snow on these peaks, which appears more copious than in Peru, seems out of place until one recalls that to the southward, on this continent, lie the cold countries. Also, the sierra finds its summit here: the Andes claim none of the world's five highest peaks, but they can boast the majority of the world's first twenty. To the north the white crowns seemed to drift among the clouds, airborne and fleeting: one is Tupungato, 21,484 feet high, and, farther off, a colossus which must be the Andes' highest, Aconcagua. At nearly 23,000 feet, Aconcagua is only 4000 less than Everest, and the spectacle drives all quotidian odds and ends straight from the brain. Then the mountains plunge toward the Pacific, and the plane slips down the western slope into the dry, pretty valley of Santiago.

Seven hundred miles south of Santiago lies the town of Puerto Montt, on the Gulf of Corcovado; from this point onward there are neither roads nor rail, for the great archipelago which constitutes all of southern Chile except the steep mountain slopes begins at Chiloé Island on the Gulf and sails down to the Hermite Islands and Cape Horn.

In Chile, in clear weather, the Andes are constantly in sight and march along with anyone who cares to take the *rápido* from Santiago to land's end. The train leaves the capital at seven in the morning and is scheduled to arrive at midnight—on January 30, 1960, it was only two hours late, a feat unusual in South America—but the journey is well worth the slight fatigue.

Below Santiago the desert gives way almost immediately to the rich land of the central valley, green bottom land and vegetable farms, succeeded by pasture land and pine barrens—though in fact there is no clean line of demarcation between these areas, which are interspersed. Small clear streams with gravel sandbars slip across the valley from the mountains, cut deep as trenches into the land. In the face of Chile's poverty, these good lands seem sparsely inhabited, scarcely exploited, though they are far from boundless.

To the eastward, as the day goes on, the cordillera diminishes in stature; it will sink into the sea at last at Staten Land, off the eastern end of Tierra del Fuego. Nevertheless, the snow increases, and as the highest mountains of this region are apt to be volcanoes, one sees a long, low range posted periodically with white-capped cones, including Villarica, Lanín, and finally Osorno, on the far side of Lake Llanquihue from Puerto Varas; I spent a few days in this town, which lies just north of Puerto Montt. It was long past dark when I arrived there, and I did not see Osorno until the following morning.

The Chilean mountain-lake country, in aspect anything but violent, was torn apart a few months after my departure by one of history's most dreadful earthquakes. It is said to resemble Switzerland, and to a certain extent it does. It is rolling dairy land set among blue lakes and snowy peaks; the pastures are firmly fenced, the cattle tame and fat, and the Germans plentiful. But the mountains are more distant and less lofty than in Switzerland, and the atmosphere therefore more open, less pinched-in. And then there is the sense of the vast ocean a few scant miles to the westward. It is hot and clear in the summer days, and cold at night.

I passed most of my time in the woods and pastures above the town. In one plowed field a conclave of odd birds had gathered—forty or more brown raffish hawks of the vulturish caracara family, here called *chimangos,* and the turkey vulture or *gallinazo,* and numerous loud lapwings, strikingly marked, and the black-faced ibis, short-legged and fawn-colored on the neck, with its hollow, gloomy call. The common songbirds were the Chilean song sparrow, rusty-collared, and the tit-like tyrant, a dingy little bird with a bedraggled head plume which acts more like a warbler than like the flycatcher it is. There was also a sort of dusky robin with a voice quite like that of its relative in North America.

The trees, like the birds, were unfamiliar, and a number of the field flowers were quite strange, as were some lovely varieties in the woods; at the edge of the woods I saw a small thick brown snake but did not detain it. Beyond the woods lay more pastures, broken by the cheerful black-and-white of cows, and then the cold blue lake and the volcano; this much was Chile. But when I lay down in the warm pasture grass I felt a surge of homesickness: the grains and wild grasses, the purple clover and yellow dandelions, the thistles, yellow-jacket bees, the saw of grasshoppers, the green aphids, the robin song and tink of sparrows, a distant bird which sounded like a yellowthroat, and a sparrow hawk hovering above a grass clump on the far side of a sunny, wet, redolent meadow—I had to look across the lake to the volcano, with its Chinese hat of snow, to remind myself that I was four months and five thousand miles or more from some high New England pasture in the early days of May.

4 ♦ TIERRA
DEL FUEGO

THE SOUTHERLY LIMITS of ordinary travel in South America are the towns of Bariloche, in the Argentine foothills of Andean Patagonia, and its Chilean counterpart, Puerto Montt, which lies at the head of the Corcovado Gulf and the Chilean Archipelago; these not-far-distant towns are linked in a rather spectacular tourist route through the lovely mountain lakes of both countries, with good connections to Santiago and Buenos Aires. Land's end, on the other hand, is more than one thousand miles to the south, in the Hermite Islands—the wild sea rock called Cape Horn. To proceed farther than Puerto Montt, one should probably have a better reason than my own, which is nothing more than a desire of long standing to lay eyes on Patagonia, the Strait of Magellan, and Tierra del Fuego.

Heading southward down the Gulf of Corcovado, the plane from Puerto Montt to Punta Arenas, on the Straits, crosses the first island of the archipelago. With its deep coves, pretty farms, and broad gray beaches, this island is quite unlike those at the southern end of this greatest of the world's archipelagos. There are other, smaller islands, and, off to the westward, the Chiloé Channel and the Pacific. Though the day is clear, Chiloé Island, the largest of the group, rises and fades in its attendant clouds. To the east the Andes, slowly diminishing in stature as they move southward, are bright with snow; in the early light the lower slopes and the islands alongshore are a somber black beneath white wisps of cloud, while the islands to the west are brown and green. There are literally hundreds of islands to be seen, all but the smallest maintaining a few farms, but the sea around them is flat and empty, with only a few small sails of fishermen banded together on a distant shoreline.

Farther south the island forests are unbroken; there is scarcely a sign of human habitation. The islands vary from a few hundred yards to fifteen miles in length, and one of them is nothing more than a great flat-topped monolith of rock, jutting up out of the sea like the base of a fallen monument, with only the barest fringe of boulder shore below.

Now the plane heads inland, skirting the twisted peak of Corcovado, with its vertical columnar crest—"the lofty-peaked Corcovado," Darwin called it, "well deserving the name of *'el famoso Corcovado.'*" Below, blue glaciers turn like diamonds in the sun, feeding cold emerald lakes shut away from the world by cliffs. A dense forest crawls up steep ravines and sunny flanks to tree line, and lonely rivers wind their way among cold bars of gravel, but the prevailing elements are sky and snow and granite. High among the peaks bright ponds of glacier water are inset; from these white streaks of foam rush off down the shadowy ravines, headwaters of a stream, perhaps a river, with no name. Farther south lakes of ice blue are pinned in by boreal forest, and an occasional lake, quite out of place here, the color of pea soup.

The Pacific is no longer visible. We cross an *altiplano* of barren alpine tundra, broken here and there by a few shrub-bordered streams, a thin patch of forest, and curious terraces and hillocks. The wind howls over this brown world, and by the time the buttes rise up around a mountain village the two-engine plane is bounding like a kite, with dreadful uproar and vibration. We are now trapped in a sort of gorge, with a mountain river on the south side, and after a brief and extremely unpleasant interlude of jolts and plunges, touch down on a narrow terrace between butte and gorge—Caihaique.

Mountain flying is, for me, the worst aspect of an uneasy means of travel, though on rare mountain days without wind and downdrafts it can be both exhilarating and intensely beautiful. Today there is a distinct *malaise* among the passengers; we push out through the cabin door like frightened sheep, and it is nearly an hour before we can be herded in again. Had the plane not been the only means of departure from Caihaique, I suspect it would have left a number of its passengers right there.

I have come to regard myself, without any real justification, as a connoisseur of bad moments in the air, and it is my heartfelt opinion that the take-off was worse than the landing. Not only did we barely clear the end of the rude runway but, confronted with the oncoming Andes, the pilot was forced to bank so sharply in the wind that the right wing, for one terrible moment, seemed caught irretrievably at a near-vertical angle: one gust, it seemed, and the plane would be flipped on its back like a turtle. The pilot may have been shaken too, because for the next hour or more the piloting of our fragile craft seemed to me to lack authority. We rose and fell, turned in half-circles, speeded up in sudden bursts to clear unseen obstacles ahead, and in general careened around among the mountains in a decidedly haphazard manner.

Through this taxing period our peril, if any, was increased, to my mind, by the presence in the pilot's cabin of a big, saucy German girl. On the ground at Caihaique she had won the hearts of the *chileno* airmen, who were half her size, and was invited to pass the remainder of her journey in the cockpit. I don't say she was at the controls, but it may have been some gallant attempt to win her admiration which shook my easily shaken confidence in the Latin fliers.

The indecision was most pronounced over Lake Buenos Aires, a magnificent blue water saddling the Andes of both Chile and Argentina, stretching east and west for more than one hundred miles. In the swift clouds one saw two almost identical fields of blue, one of these being the sky and the other— not always the lower one, either—the lake. It was difficult to concentrate on it, though, for here the wind had reached its zenith, and the plane was doing some spectacular gyrations. Then suddenly it swung, or was blown off, to the eastward, descending rapidly at a steep incline, and the steward came down the aisle saying "No *fumar, no fumar*—no es-moking!" This struck me as an unnatural request, there not being a landing field for a hundred miles, much less a good reason to land. I didn't have the pluck to request an explanation, though. And after a time the wind, plane, and pilot calmed a little, and we headed south again across the barrens of Argentine Patagonia. We had not regained altitude, and while at times we were skimming the plateaus at no more than a few hundred feet, this unusual tactic enabled me to get a better look at a wild country I had come far to see.

Patagonia—loosely, "land of giant feet"—was named by the small Spaniards in honor of the large footprints of the Indians; the Tehuelches, especially, were very tall, many of the men being six feet four inches and more. While the name Patagonia is sometimes used to describe all of South America south of the thirty-ninth parallel, including the Andes and the Chilean Archipelago, it signifies more exactly the great treeless barrens on the Atlantic slope of the mountains, from the Argentine Pampa south to the hook of the Andes, including those parts of Chile on the eastern shores of the Strait of Magellan and most of Tierra del Fuego.

North of the Strait, Patagonia is extremely desolate, far more so than one expects. Between Lake Buenos Aires and Cardiel the bare plateaus of the western foothills support only a thin grass and the poorest sort of ground scrub, though gradually, as we move southward, some tundra ponds and sterile-looking creeks appear, supporting a wan green along their edges. On this wind-swept day of swarthy clouds and sun, the view across this wasteland to the receding mountains is oppressive. Far off beneath the snows, another huge lake, Argentino, spreads away. The land rises and falls more gently now, so monotone and lifeless that one has the impression—not inaccurate, from a geological point of view—of the floor beneath the sea.

The Santa Cruz River, green-silver and snaky, starts east across the desert toward the Atlantic; then a high, grassy plateau, an island in the waste, and here there are several bands of dark horses, never more than eight together; one band runs wildly, black manes flowing, at the low passage of the plane. There have been wild horses in Argentina since the early sixteenth century, when, as in North America, a few escaped the Spanish, but they are shot down commonly by the ranchers and are growing rare now except in these deserted regions. There are also small bands of a lesser, light-colored animal: these must be that small wild camel, the guanaco, though I cannot be certain, even with binoculars. However, they are far from any road or sign of man, and neither their color—a pale brown—nor their small numbers suggest sheep.

The land descends and softens. Here is Lago Blanco, accurately named; we have crossed the frontier again, into Chilean Patagonia. To the west spreads slowly what looks like another of the great blue lakes which stretch across the Andes, but its blue is deeper, colder. This is Otway Inlet, a long arm of the sea, which comes in from the Pacific reaches of the Strait of Magellan. The eastern straits are visible far ahead, and in a little while the plane curves out over the water; Punta Arenas, the most southerly city in the world, gleams in a weak sun down the coast. Across the water, some twenty miles or more, is the purple shadow of Tierra del Fuego.

February 2–4.

The area comprising south Patagonia, the Strait, the islands and channels, and Tierra del Fuego is sometimes called Magallanes, and it has been vividly described by numerous writers, among whom Captain Joshua Slocum, Richard Henry Dana, and Charles Darwin are among the best known. Dana, in his preface to *Two Years Before the Mast*, expresses a certain doubt about the need for his book: ". . . there have been so many stories of sea life written, that I should really think it unjustifiable in me to add one to the number without being able to give reasons in some measure warranting me in so doing." I feel somewhat the same in attempting, for example, to give an impression of the notorious Strait, which Captain Slocum, passing through at this same time of year, in 1896, took more than two months to navigate. He was alone in a small sloop, the *Spray*, and his perspective was somewhat different from that of an adventurer like myself, who gazes fearlessly upon these ferocious waters—they are calm at the moment and were calm yesterday—from the window of my room in the Hotel Cosmos. And this, I suppose, must be my justification, that mine is a fresh approach.

Punta Arenas, first of all, is a center for the scattered oil, coal, and ranching industries of the region, is developing a silver-fox farm, and is also a free port; these are the reasons for its surprising size and relative prosperity. It is a bare, airy place—for the prevailing wind out of the southwest is almost constant—and pleasant enough during the summer season, though unless one is here on business it hasn't a great deal to recommend it. Like many towns in South America, however, it can boast an interesting regional museum; this I visited on the afternoon of my arrival. The museum, maintained by Silesian missionaries, has fine collections of preserved fauna, including the eskimo curlew, now extinct; this bird once migrated as far as Patagonia from its nesting grounds in Canada. (The Punta Arenas specimen is rather startling at first, until one sees that it was given bright blue eyes by its unknown taxidermist.) There are also two enormous cougars, nearly the size of lionesses; my impression had been that the mountain lions of South America were much smaller than our own. But the most interesting displays are of the artifacts of the Fuegian Indian tribes, among which only the Alacalufes of the outer channels of Chilean Magallanes, to the southwest, still exist. Like the Yahgans, who inhabited formerly the eastern channels and south shores of the main island of Tierra del Fuego, the short-legged Alacalufes pass the great part of their lives in their rough canoes and go virtually naked in a world of sea and granite celebrated for wind and cold. The Yahgans, in fact, were described by Darwin as the most primitive people on earth, and his own descriptions tend to bear him out:

> While going one day on shore near Wollaston Island, we pulled alongside a canoe with six Fuegians. These were the most abject and miserable creatures I anywhere beheld. On the east coast the natives [i.e., the Onas] . . . have guanaco cloaks, and on the west [i.e., the Alacalufes], they possess seal-skins. . . . But these Fuegians in the canoe were quite naked. . . . These poor wretches were stunted in their growth, their hideous faces bedaubed with white paint, their skins filthy and greasy, their hair entangled, their voices discordant, and their gestures violent. Viewing such men, one can hardly make oneself believe that they are fellow-creatures, and inhabitants of the same world.

According to Darwin, the Yahgans subsisted on shellfish, carrion, and fungus except on special occasions, when they enjoyed the flesh of captured enemies or of old decrepit women in their own tribe. Unlike most Indian tribes, they were brutal and treacherous even before they were disillusioned by the white man, and, throughout their brief recorded history, rewarded all efforts to better their lot with theft and massacre. Darwin's party returned to their homeland three Fuegians previously taken to England for the edification of the royal family; after three years' exposure to civilization, two of these reverted almost immediately to their former ways, making off for parts unknown with all the belongings of the third, a man called Jemmy Button. Some hope, however, was held out for the latter: "Everyone must sincerely hope that Captain Fitz Roy's noble hope may be fulfilled, of being rewarded for the many generous sacrifices which he made for these Fuegians, by some shipwrecked sailor being protected by the descendants of Jemmy Button and his tribe!" But unhappily, as I was to learn subsequently in Tierra del Fuego, this modest ambition proved to have been in vain.

While in Punta Arenas I was taken some miles out along the coast to see an extraordinary rock garden, Las Robles, developed by members of the Campos-Menendez family, who were very hospitable to me in Punta Arenas and in Tierra del Fuego. Garden flowers of all colors, in a variety and profusion unimaginable in this climate, have been encouraged to grow on a steep bank of the Strait protected from the prevailing wind. The interest and beauty of the place were much increased by an adjoining garden of regional plants and trees, including the thorny *calafate*, the common shrub of Patagonia, and the two varieties of "beech." (These are *Nothofagus pumilio* and *N. antarctica*, both called *roble*, or oak. *N. pumilio* looks rather like the North American live oak but is actually identical with the Australian beech. This is the common tree of the Fuegian rain forests, and the fact that it is indigenous only here and in Australia gives one a strong sense of time and change on the earth's face.) There were also wild anemones, verbena, a variety of ferns, the *Fuchsia magellanica*, and the faithful *diente de león*, or lion's tooth—the common dandelion.

The weather today is back to normal—this is to say, blowing

a gale. (Despite traditional reports to the contrary, the wind blows hardest here in summer. This is very fortunate, for this wind, in combination with the intense cold of winter, would make life in these regions almost insupportable.) The color of the Strait is largely white, and the small cargo sloop, the *Gaviota*, on which I had hoped to cross today to Tierra del Fuego, will not venture out. In consequence, I took a walk this morning out onto the sandy point for which the town is named; Captain Slocum, in fact, referred to it unabashedly as Sandy Point. The beach is dark and gravelly, littered with garbage, and in this respect, as well as in its wintry aspect and the sharp bite of its summer wind, is rather like its northern counterpart at Point Barrow. As far out as binoculars can reach, the Strait is alive with birds: large white-fronted cormorants, black-mantled kelp gulls, the small brown-hooded gull, South American terns with crimson bill, and the hulking cinnamon skua; I last saw this bird, or rather its near relation, in the North Atlantic in November. A small flock of the white Magellan rock goose passes along the beach, and there are ducks bobbing far offshore. Beyond them, slicing downwind on long, stiff wings, sails the black-browed albatross; this majestic bird is the first albatross I have ever seen. I search also for the Magellan penguin and for the small diving petrel, but they are nowhere to be found in the rough water.

Behind the beach, in a bleak lagoon, more terns, gulls, and skuas face the wind, and with them on the mud flats a large flock of white-rumped sandpipers and some snowy plovers; both these latter species, like the eskimo curlew and other shore birds, migrate here from their nesting grounds in North America. On the beach itself lies a varied sea wrack. There are shells of mussels and limpets, both of these uncommonly large, a pretty striated snail, a round white clam, some dead isopod crustaceans, strands of the mighty sea kelp, bits of petrified wood, a dead cat, and a dead dog. And toward the end of the morning there appeared a school of large swift dolphins, hunting along the beach. When swirling through fish, these animals would surge half out of the water; they are called Commerson's dolphins, I believe, white beneath, with a white oblong patch behind the dorsal.

Though the wind was as stiff as ever, the Strait had grown much calmer—presumably the tide was now running with the wind rather than against it—and I kept searching the far coast for a sign of the *Gaviota*. But there is no sign of her, and I shall be here at least until tomorrow. This, of course, is one of the drawbacks of travel in out-of-the-way places, that travel is at best uncertain and one is often stranded for three or four days at a time.

February 5.

The winds in the Strait of Magellan are extremely unpredictable. The early morning was calm and windless, and then suddenly, without warning, a wind was skipping across the pier where the *Gaviota* was unloading her bales of wool. In a matter of minutes the harbor was seething with a short, high chop. After taking aboard some barrels of wine and pickled food, we set off in this weather for Porvenir, on the Chilean coast of Tierra del Fuego. The *Gaviota* is equipped with a slow motor, but, once clear of her berth, she hoisted a heavy mainsail of brown canvas. Though we were running under power before the wind, the sail immediately bellied taut, increasing her speed to a respectable eight knots and serving as a steady sail as well. For the first two hours she spanked along like an *America*'s Cup contender, only to plough to a near halt when, quite as swiftly as it had come, the wind dropped out again; an hour later, near Porvenir, the wind returned, stronger than before, but by the time we disembarked, it had collapsed.

As one crosses the Strait, the snow-touched peaks of the Brunswick Peninsula are dominant in the west, and to the south, Dawson Island and the mouth of Useless Bay. Albatross wheel across the wind, wings stiff as boomerangs, and the strange diving petrels flee our bows, fluttering away across the chop. Overhead, the faint shrieks of a tern, which two skuas are pirating of its catch; it is amazing how agile the dark, bulky skuas can be. (This species, unlike most, is scientifically well named: *Megalestris chilensis* may be freely translated as "big Chilean pirate ship.") The swift tern cannot shake them off, and finally, so high now that it can no longer be heard, is forced to drop its minnow. The skuas fold their wings and drop like stones, but both swoop up at the last minute, having lost their catch in the rough water.

The *Gaviota* is besieged by a school of the flashing dolphins observed yesterday; they charge the bow, duck beneath, leap, whirl, swim upside down—I have never seen such a dolphin show in all my life, and they move so fast that, on the surface, they throw up a high, curling slice of water as they go. They stay with us for twenty minutes or more, fooling along the hull: though they circle the boat with ease, their flukes, even at close range, betray scarcely a motion. They move smoothly as projectiles.

The coast of Tierra del Fuego is dark behind cold white walls of fine rain; these are characteristic, apparently, of certain weather. The rains are separate and look like smoke, but are not the reason for the island's name. The fires seen by Ferdinand Magellan in 1520 were almost certainly signal fires of the Alacalufes, which were often built on mounds of earth in the crude hollow-log canoes.

Long strings of cormorants move up and down the coast, and a flock has gathered near the mouth of Porvenir Inlet. The inevitable German is aboard, this one a Chilean native, and he claims to have seen five Magellan penguins a few minutes before. These birds have eluded my binoculars, though at the moment he speaks of, I must confess, I had crept in out of the cold rain for a cigarette. The rain in Magallanes is as treacherous as the wind and falls often when the sun is shining.

Porvenir Inlet is a natural harbor and a pretty one, in terms of the barren landscape. The coast here is low and flat, and the mountains are visible far away in the background. The water is speckled with cormorants and ducks, including the great, heavy *pato vapor*, or "steamboat duck," which is flightless and moves swiftly over the surface, using its wings as paddles. (The two species of *pato vapor* are the least famous of the three types of flightless birds in this part of the world, the other two being the penguins and the rhea, or South American ostrich.) The crewmen of the *Gaviota* are firing at the birds with a .22, but they are poor shots; I am particularly glad of this a moment later when one of them, carried away, starts shooting at a dolphin. Shooting at live things with a .22 rifle—whether they are edible or even retrievable is a matter of no importance—is considered terrific sport in South America and, as the wildlife of the continent grows scarcer, will become more and more important in the inevitable extinctions.

I carried my bags up into the village and located some late lunch and a bed in a small *pensión;* though the place was without running water and featured a grim outhouse in the backyard, its cleanliness was exemplary for these parts, and the kindly owner, Señora Candellaria del Gallardo, should probably be congratulated; whatever else may be said, she has been of more help to wayfarers than Jemmy Button and his tribe. In the afternoon I inspected the huge bales of sheep wool awaiting shipment on the dock, then walked out along the harbor. Shore birds were everywhere—sandpipers, oystercatchers, Hudsonian curlews, the lovely red-breasted winter plover, and the ubiquitous *teros*, or lapwings. The latter, with their crest and striking pattern, are very handsome, but their loud, constant cries are the only voice in the bird world which I have found actually offensive—in fact, their persistence drove me inland. Climbing some low, bushy banks, I found myself in open country and walked out through the thinning shrubs of the coastline onto the Patagonian plain.

The flowers in bleak places always seem the most welcome of all, and today their colors are quite startling against the olive monotones which stretch away beneath the clouds. A yellow flower rises smartly in tall, bushy clumps, and there are white and bright blue flowers like asters, and the good old *diente de león*. Also, some delicate ground ferns and lichens, and a kind of red crowberry. All these are sheltered among low bushes, of which the most prominent is the thorny *calafate*. Fluttering busily here and there are song sparrows with orange napes, and a tiny black and rufous bird, unusually tame; this is the red-backed ground tyrant, one of the many flycatchers in South America.

The lapwings have followed me onto the moor, and their stridence is mixed with the gloomy honkings of the black-faced ibis, out of sight in some nearby gully; these birds, in chorus, sound exactly like a bored child playing with the horn of a toy car, and their odd noise, drifting downwind, is one of the atmospheric sounds of Patagonia. Sheep bleat somewhere, as if in answer to the ibis, and far off beneath a darkening sky a black horse trails slowly along behind a rise, pausing briefly to graze. It lifts its head suddenly into the wind and then moves on.

The following morning I arranged a ride with a delegation of *chilenos* bound for Río Grande, in Argentina, to witness a *gran match de fútbol*. (The main island of Tierra del Fuego is divided by a north-south line between Argentina and Chile; the latter country controls as well the smaller islands to the south of the Beagle Channel, including the Hermite Islands and Cape Horn. Staten Land, a large uninhabited island off the southeast tip, belongs to Argentina, and a few small islands at the east end of the archipelago are still disputed.) We traveled in the back of a large truck, some twenty strong, over the bed of which a tattered canvas had been rigged as shelter from wind and rain. There was nothing to be done, however, about the jolts of the dirt road or the carbon monoxide, both outstanding features of the ten-hour trip, and two young women promptly became sick; though the tailgate was near at hand, they did not avail themselves of the passing countryside but, with that odd passivity of peasant peoples, vomited dolefully where they lay. The Spanish are rarely sentimental about suffering, and, the occasion being a festive one, the girls' misery provoked friends and family alike to shouts and seizures of uncontrollable mirth.

The sun and rain came and went all day, flying before the wind. From Porvenir we went south through a hilly country of scrub beech, turning east again at the shore of Useless Bay. The country changed to flat, dry, short-grass plains, and the truck was barely able to remain ahead of the dust cloud in its own wake, which, driven forward by the wind, caught up with us regularly on the turns. To the southward, out on the great empty bay, the whitecaps formed in cresting banks, and beyond, in the far distance, the Andean peaks, approaching their southern terminus at last, rose sharply on the sky. The highest of these are Mount Sarmiento and, much farther east, Mount Darwin, both of them over seven thousand feet.

The dominant bird of the open country is the lovely *caiquen*, or upland goose; in this species the gander is predominantly silver, while his mate is a lustrous cedar brown. These birds are incredibly common in Fuegian Patagonia—we saw many thousands in this single day. Wild duck seem relatively scarce, however, and only a few kelp gulls, lapwings, and small carrion hawks, or *chimangos*, braved the winds of this open country.

The wind increased during the day, with gusts of rain. At noon, canvas flapping, we paused to air the women. We were now near the head of Useless Bay, among the outbuildings of a large *estancia*. From here we moved inland, and the quality of the countryside gradually improved as we crossed large sheep ranches in the direction of the border. The latter was crossed late in the afternoon, and shortly thereafter we drew up at the Argentine frontier post, by the wide bay of San Sebastián, on the Atlantic. Here the wind had reached its peak, and while I struggled with the door of the customs shack it literally spun me in my tracks. Toward sundown, however, it relented somewhat. We were now in the heart of the sheep ranges, and on both sides of the road the animals moved away from us, drifting off across the blowing grasslands with their soft, rolling canter. Large flocks of geese rose, silhouetted, and dropped gently down again, and a large black-breasted hawk—the Chilean "eagle"—sailed out across a bluff to peer and slide away. The bluff sloped gradually, climbing to the cliffs along the coast; we were on the road to Río Grande now, the ocean a brittle froth out to the eastward. Between breaks in the cliffs the gravel beach was visible, and beyond it a wide stretch of rocks and pools uncovered by the tide. As in Porvenir, the shore birds here were common, and one huge flock of sandpipers danced ahead of us down the coastline, their white undersides flashing like fine confetti as they banked. Cape Domingo, falling steeply to the tide rocks, and ahead the twilight glint of buildings; a little later, honking and tooting at the baffled *argentinos*, we careened down to the mouth of the Río Grande, into the little town of the same name.

Río Grande owes its existence almost entirely to the sheep ranches, or *estancias*, which surround it; many of the seasonal herdsmen and shearers live in the town, bringing a certain income, and small freighters come here with food, gasoline, and other supplies, taking away raw wool and mutton. The freighters anchor in the river mouth and at low tide are high and dry on the cold mud flats. The recent development of oil in Tierra del Fuego will certainly increase the size of Río Grande, but for the moment it sadly lacks accommodations for the traveler. Its tiny "hotels" are scarcely deserving of this name, and as the same is true in Porvenir and in Ushuaia, on the southern coast, the hospitable *estancias* are besieged by stranded wayfarers; a night's lodging can generally be obtained, but one will not be truly welcome, understandably, unless the visit has been arranged well in advance.

In Buenos Aires, happily, I had been introduced by Peter Deane to Señor Carlos Menendez Behety, who was kind enough to give me an invitation; I arrived at the Estancia María Behety just at dark. Because of the uncertainty of travel in Magallanes, I was already four days late, and, standing there on the doorstep with my motley bag and knapsack, caked with dust, I was not all that might have been wished for as a guest.

The main house of the *estancia* is large and handsome and surrounded by lovely gardens; this island in the sea of grass is protected from the wind by a wall of tall white palings which surround it. Down the hill lies a complex of ranch buildings, which were shown me after dinner by Señor Menendez's nephew, Jaime Speroni. There are stables for horses and for breeding rams, corrals, great shearing sheds, storehouses, electric plant, mess hall and dormitories for shepherds and shearers, the house of the *capitaz*, or ranch foreman, and so forth, all of these luminous in the bright darkness. In these latitudes, so near to the Antarctic, summer darkness is never total; there is only a deep shadow on the land, and the sky reels with explosions of southern galaxies. I took a long look at the unfamiliar stars, the brightest group of which forms a gaunt pattern which gives a three-dimensional sense of the Crucifixion. This is the Southern Cross.

The Estancia María Behety, which includes 50,000 hectares, or well over 100,000 acres, of land, was established in the last part of the nineteenth century, when it was called "La Segunda Argentina." Together with its neighboring ranch, the Estancia José Menendez ("La Primera Argentina"), it comprises the largest family holding in Argentine Tierra del Fuego. The next in size is the Estancia Viamonte, adjoining José Menendez to the south; this ranch, established just after the turn of the century, is owned by the Bridges-Reynolds family, who also have another large property at Harberton, on the Beagle Channel. The Bridges family moved north from their mission settlement at Harberton, while the Menendez came originally from Chile. Though the two families differed somewhat on their policies toward the Indians—a Menendez foreman of the early days is said to have put a bounty on dead Onas, whereas for many years this tribe supplied both ranch hands and shearers at Viamonte—there was also a good deal of mutual respect, and eventually they joined forces to construct the first bridge over the Río Grande. It seems appropriate, too, that *The Uttermost Part of the Earth*, by Lucas Bridges, and the *Pequeña Historia Fuegina*, by Dr. Armando Braun Menendez, remain the most authoritative books on the history of the region.

The Río Grande lies a few miles southward of the ranch buildings at María Behety, under a steep, dry bluff. With Jaime Speroni, I went there the morning after my arrival, crossing the rolling plain on horseback. The day was bright and cold, and the wind, buffeting over the treeless land, seemed strong enough at times to snap a rider right out of the saddle. *Caiquen* geese were everywhere, and forlorn-looking sheared sheep with a red smear of paint across the rump, and here and there, cut down by the inevitable .22, the remains of a goose, gull, or chimango, feathers bending in the wind. (That afternoon the Menendez children and their cousins were kind enough to take me for a tour along the seacoast. Among other things, we saw a Magellan penguin, and I am sorry to report that this attractive bird was destroyed by a fusillade of .22 fire almost before I could admire it in my binoculars. Three *caiquenes* also bit the dust and were left where they lay. The *caiquen*, it is true, is destructive to sheep range, for not only does it eat great areas of grass—five *caiquenes* will eat as much as a single sheep, according to Carlos Menendez—but its guano "burns" a good deal more. Nevertheless, the indiscriminate shooting of a few birds is useless, and probably the solution lies elsewhere. The geese may have prospered unduly due to man's persecution of a coyote-sized red fox native to Tierra del Fuego, which attacks lambs as well as *caiquenes*; it is doubtful, however, whether its sporadic kills outweigh the damage caused by the excess geese. Interference with the balance of nature, as well as the senseless killing so common on this continent, were primary factors in the decimation of wildlife in North America and are making their mark here, a half-century later. To the credit of the Menendez, however, it should be said that the disappearing guanaco receives full protection on María Behety, a precocious step by local standards.)

The Río Grande, like other streams in Tierra del Fuego, has been stocked with brown and rainbow trout, and here the latter reach the size of salmon; fish of fifteen pounds or more are not uncommon, and much larger individuals have been taken. The river today was roiled and swift, running low between its banks, and from a gravel bar ahead of us a pair of blacknecked swans rose up in slow motion against the wind and moved powerfully away upstream. These beautiful birds are native to Patagonia, but of recent years have apparently declined in numbers.

Downstream, by the river bank, stood a lone beech, the only native tree on the *estancia*. The aspect of the land is bare but it is not barren, and its very bareness, when the sun is bright, is stirring. Formerly the earth of the open range was honeycombed by burrows of the *tucu-tucu*, a tailless rodent like the guinea pig, but these animals have been virtually eliminated by the myriad hoofs of sheep and horses—María Behety supports sixty thousand sheep, a number of horses, and a few wild guanacos—and now the land is ideal for riding. The earth is grassy and resilient, and on the homeward ride, downwind, we cantered easily along for miles. The ride was immensely exhilarating, and it seemed to me at that moment that, without a horse, one could not get a true sense of Patagonia.

There are neither trains nor buses in Tierra del Fuego, and, except for scattered plane flights between Río Grande and Ushuaia, one must depend for transportation on the hospitality of the frontier. In my case this courtesy was extended by George Blackwell and the men of the Tennessee-Argentina Oil Company, with whom I spent a most agreeable morning before leaving on a truck bound southward for Ushuaia. Oil has been found in quantity in Chilean Tierra del Fuego, and the Tennessee-Argentina Company now has a twenty-five-year lease on the Argentine side, where it has already brought in several wells. The personnel here are tough and friendly, and I'd like to say that, despite an indefensible tendency to avoid my countrymen when traveling (doubtless related to what Maugham has described as the hatred of one tourist for another, though these drillers and construction men can hardly be classed as tourists), there is a special kind of American honesty and "openness," an ability to laugh at oneself, which can be extremely refreshing after a long time without it.

The truck left in mid-afternoon, crossing the Río Grande and passing almost immediately the large freezing plant and warehouse used by the *estancias* in the area. To the east rose Cape Peña, where once, long ago, the forceful Scot known as "the King of Río Grande," leading a raiding party, slaughtered some fourteen Ona caught on the beach while sealing. (Seals were once common at Cape Peña but, like the small South American sea otter, are now scarce on the coasts of Tierra del Fuego.) The day was dark, and as we bounced southward on the rutted road, patches of scrub beech on the accumulating foothills broke an oppressive landscape, gathering in small woodlands behind Viamonte. Between the hills ran long, winding open valleys known as *vegas*, and in some of these were narrow, rapid streams. The *carancho*, a large dark caracara, replaced its smaller cousin, the brown *chimango*, as the country changed, and its presence suited perfectly the ominous terrains.

We entered unbroken forest, wind-bent and sad with its thick wisps of "graybeard," or *Usnea* lichen; the trees carried also on their outer branches a round, parasitic cluster very similar to mistletoe. Then the road emerged on the east end of Lake Fagnano, a body of water in the Fuegian foothills of the Andes which extends from this point more than forty miles to its western extremity in Chile. The edges here are clotted with forests of dead trees, victims of flood caused by earthquake. The wind today had diminished very little, and the lake was rough and desolate. Between here and the island's eastern point, a hundred miles away, the glaciers and mountains are still largely unexplored; this is also true of some of the larger islands of the archipelago, to the southwest.

On the south shore of the lake we met Oliver and Betsy

Bridges, bound homeward from Ushuaia; they had a welcome fire and water boiling, and in this strange place I delivered a note from mutual friends, Ted and Dorry Blacque in Bolivia. With the *chileno* truckdriver and an Argentine passenger, I accepted their kind invitation to stay to tea and to stop off at Viamonte on my return.

Climbing the lumber road into the mountains, the truck passed a few woodsmen's huts and camps; the driver invariably honked the horn, as if to give these lonely men some reassurance that an outside world still existed. The trees increased rapidly in size as we gained altitude, some of them reaching one hundred feet or more; the curious thing here is the amount of deadwood, which makes the forest floor almost impassible. Darwin, who imagined that Tierra del Fuego consisted entirely of this forest, was decidedly oppressed by it:

> On every side were lying irregular masses of rock and torn-up trees; other trees, though still erect, were decayed to the heart and ready to fall. The entangled mass of the thriving and the fallen reminded me of the forests within the tropics —yet there was a difference: for in these still solitudes, Death, instead of Life, seemed the predominant spirit.

At dusk the mountain crags were gloomy in dying clouds. Darkness came on swiftly, and the snow on the sharp peaks and distant glaciers became dim and amorphous. In the close forest of the ravines the truck ground and slipped and stalled on the steep, rough road; we inched along, hour after hour, crashing and lumbering through rain pools. Then the descent on the far side began —the mountains are not high here, but precipitous—and after midnight, a little numb, we careened into Ushuaia. The Gran Parque Hotel—as hostels go, the showplace of the town—was dank and crowded, but at last provided cots for myself and an Argentine companion in the dining room. (The following night I was lucky to get a bed at all, but lay down finally on a pallet placed next to the bed of no less a person than the genial *patrón*:

the little room, having no window on the open air, was a little more close than I would have liked, but I was no less grateful to him for all of that.)

The settlement of Ushuaia on the Beagle Channel in 1869 was the white man's first successful foothold in southern Tierra del Fuego, all prior attempts having ended in famine, or massacre by the Yahgans, or both; the most disastrous episode, at Wulaia Harbor ten years earlier, had cost the lives of every member of the missionary party except the ship's cook. The chief instigator of this massacre, apparently upset that he had not been accorded the special privileges due him as interpreter and world traveler, was Jemmy Button, on whom Darwin and Captain Fitz Roy of the *Beagle* had based their hopes for improvement of white-Indian relations. In 1871 Deacon Thomas Bridges of the Tierra del Fuego Mission Society brought his young wife to Ushuaia, and the town has since become the government seat of Argentine Tierra del Fuego.

These facts and many others are available in *The Uttermost Part of the Earth* by Lucas Bridges, son of Thomas Bridges and uncle of Oliver Bridges, whom I first met on the shore of Lake Fagnano. The book includes excellent photographs of the Yahgan and Ona Indians, whose painful redemption at the hands of the white man was concluded within half a century by their almost complete extinction; the warlike and troublesome Onas of the north were swiftly reduced by the ranchers of the Río Grande region and by savage inter-family vendettas, but the fatal agent in the destruction of both tribes was the diseases of their saviors, notably measles. The seven to nine thousand Indians thought to inhabit Tierra del Fuego at the time of the settlement of Ushuaia were reduced eighty years later to fewer than two hundred pure-breds; today not more than one hundred Alacalufes eke out an existence in the Chilean islands, and the Yahgans and Onas, a handful of old people excepted, are gone.

Thomas Bridges spent his life among the Yahgans, and his journals conflict with Darwin's account on several points—for example, that their speech was ugly: on this point Darwin must have confused them with the Onas. The Yahgan tongue was fluid and complex, and Bridges constructed a remarkable Yahgan –English dictionary which was subsequently "borrowed" and pirated by the notorious "Dr." Frederick A. Cook, better known as the man who laid false claim to having discovered the North Pole: Cook attempted to publish the dictionary as his own work, but was apprehended in time. Nor was it true, apparently, that the Yahgans were cannibalistic. Occasionally they put to death old people of the tribe, but this ceremony, known as *tabacana*, was apparently a kind of euthanasia, or mercy killing; to judge from the terrible circumstances of their existence, compounded by a unique degree of brutality and treachery, *tabacana* might more charitably have been applied at birth.

The original mission buildings at Ushuaia have been replaced by stores and houses—Ushuaia, like Punta Arenas, is a thriving free port—and by the edifices of government, including an Argentine naval air base; until recently it was also an important penal colony. It has the finest harbor on the main island, and the most beautiful, located as it is beneath the striking peaks called Mount Olivia and the Cinco Hermanos—five sharp spires on a single rise, east of the village. Across the channel looms Navarin Island and, to the west, the Andean snowfields of Hoste Island. But Ushuaia is best known for its location: if Punta Arenas is the southernmost city in the world, Ushuaia, more than one hundred miles nearer the Pole, is the most southerly settlement of decent size. (The Chilean settlement called Puerto Williams, across the channel on Navarin Island, may eventually appropriate this claim.) It lies just north of the fifty-fifth parallel, about fifty miles north of the outer Hermites and Cape Horn Island.

The famous Cape is rarely "doubled" any more, and in fact is scarcely ever seen, except by whaling crews, the rare planes to Antarctica, and the few hunters who pursue the last sea otters in the channels of the outer islands. The winds and seas of what are called the "Roaring Forties"—from 40 to 60 degrees south latitude—remain as formidable as ever; conflicting with strong currents, they combine to make Horn Island one of the least hospitable spots on earth, "a taste of hell," as an old seaman in Dana's account refers to it. There are no boats available in Ushuaia, the sudden winds make a trip by small plane dangerous, and finally, the Cape lies in Chilean territory; continuing disputes about jurisdiction of the eastern islands make frontier crossings complicated. In short, I could find no one in Ushuaia who had the slightest interest in taking me to see it.

In what may have been some subconscious attempt to get as far south as possible, I walked across a sort of causeway and down the rock beach of the outer harbor. Sea ducks, cormorants, and winter plovers came and went, and among the gulls was a species new to me: the small gray-headed gull, with crimson beak, much the prettiest gull I have ever seen. Floating in the harbor mouth and wheeling back and forth like clumsy albatrosses against the dark mountains which soared out of the sea was another species new to me, that huge soot-colored petrel, the giant fulmar; I shall not think of Ushuaia in the future without remembering the impression made by this great somber bird.

The following day I started north again, this time with a couple named Menon met through the courtesy of the Governor, Captain Ernesto Campos (met in turn through the courtesy of Señor Menendez; one passes from hand to hand in Tierra del Fuego). The weather had changed for the better, and the trip north through the mountains was quite different from the night ride of two days before. The Campos children were also in the car, and we moved leisurely, pausing for lunch at the pass high above Hidden Lake and Lake Fagnano. Here Señor Menon and the Campos boy got out their .22s, but we confined ourselves, for want of anything more lively, to shooting cans. At one point we crossed the Río Hambre, and it occurred to me how many names in this part of the world convey the low opinion held of it by the first travelers. In addition to "Hungry River," a few that come to mind are Port Famine, Mount Misery, Fury Island, Useless Bay, Last Hope Bay, Cape Deceit, and Desolation Island. On this bright, still day of summer, however, there is little to complain of: we stop here and there to drink the clear water of the lakes and streams, or pick wild mushrooms and *calafate* berries. Some of these damp, wood-fringed valleys look rather like the spruce muskegs of Alaska, and the open *vegas* are reminiscent of Montana. And yet these parts are all but uninhabited; it is incredible that a spectacular lake like Fagnano, surrounded by snow peaks and reputedly full of fish, should be deserted, without sign of life, on a fine midsummer day—but only until one stops to think about it.

The wood road to Viamonte roughly parallels the trail north laid out originally by the Onas and by Lucas Bridges, who in 1899 became the first white man ever to travel overland from the south coast to Río Grande. Thomas Bridges' life among the Yahgans was paralleled by his son's dedication to the Onas. These nomad families were not, anthropologically, Fuegians, but were related to the "pampa" tribes, particularly the tall Tehuelches of mainland Patagonia. Unlike the stunted, near-naked Yahgans and Alacalufes, whom they terrified, the Onas were tall and well made, and wore moccasins, a guanaco robe, and a peaked cap made from the soft gray skin of a guanaco's head. They were expert hunters and woodsmen, carrying large bows and fine arrows, and their fascinating customs had many traits of the Indian's affecting nobility, but, like the Yahgans—and unlike most Indian tribes of the Americas—they possessed an incorrigible treachery which even Bridges' indulgent accounts cannot quite put aside; throughout the early years, while the Onas still constituted a potential threat, he remained aware that even the closest of his Ona friends might murder him without a qualm if it seemed expedient to do so. As in many tribes of North America, they killed one another freely, expecting no better in return, and a lack of unity among the Ona groups—the northern or plains people, the mountain people, and the "Aush" of the southeast—

prevented an effective resistance to the white man. Many were killed, and others were taken prisoner and removed by the hundreds to the Chilean Islands, where they died off, and still others died in the recurrent plagues. The last community was the one which attached itself to the new *estancia* at Viamonte.

Viamonte looks very much the same today as it did when the main house was first built, in 1907, and Lucas Bridges' younger sister, Bertha, now Mrs. Reynolds, still comes there to visit. The house is attractive, looking out across a field of planted cedar to the ocean, and I was happy to spend a few fine days there on the way back to Río Grande. Each morning I took a horse into the woods of scrub beech and out across the *vegas*. One *vega* contains a large, shallow lake, alive with *caiquen*, brown pintail duck, and white-rumped sandpipers. Small bands of feral horses sail, tails high, across the open ridges, and everywhere the silent, grim *caranchos*: "their vulture-like, necrophagous habits," Darwin writes, "are very evident to any one who has fallen asleep on the desolate plains of Patagonia, for when he awakes, he will see, on each surrounding hillock, one of these birds patiently watching him with an evil eye; it is a feature of the landscape of these countries, which will be recognized by every one who has wandered over them." Rabbits, let loose upon the land some years ago, are very common, and one afternoon I helped the Bridgeses with the sad job of releasing trapped rabbits inoculated with myxamatosis. We put these doomed creatures down likely burrows under the beech roots, to infect their hosts, while the watchful *caranchos*, as if anticipating death, prowled back and forth over our heads or flopped among the branches, long heads craning.

One afternoon at Viamonte I walked out for nearly a mile on the remarkable shelf which the Atlantic lays bare here at low tide. The hard gray clay of the beach is littered with boulders, inexplicably sculpted; some are rounded, like stone wheels or pedestals, with rims on their upper edges, and others are oblong sections with strange channels, lying in lengths like fallen columns. There is the effect of broken statuary in a vast ruin once inhabited by giants. The sand supports a variety of algae, green and red and brown, including that great kelp *Macrocystis pyrifera*, prostrate in the shallows, held in place by taut holdfasts of intertwined "roots." This is the world's largest plant, attaining a length of more than two hundred yards; its lily-like fronds can rise to the surface from a depth of one hundred fathoms.

To the surface of the smooth green algae clings a tiny clam, blood-red in color; there are also a white clam, a blue snail, and a small snail with peppermint stripes, two species of mussel, a striated shell of the murex family, and a smooth univalve which grows quite large and is eaten by the local people. No crabs of any kind were visible in the tide pools—one cannot stay out on the ledge too long, for fear of being trapped by the sudden rush of the incoming tide, and I could not look too carefully—though there were small rock fish or "blennies" of some kind. Sea anemones apparently occur here, though I saw none. Cormorants and the antarctic duck swam in the leads, but the most striking bird, in appearance, voice, and numbers, was the oystercatcher common on these coasts. This species has a lovely, wistful call; I am trying to remember that call, and how it rose and fell against the distant thud of surf, but of course it is already gone.

My host, like his uncle and father, was born in Tierra del Fuego, at Ushuaia—his kind wife, Betsy, is an American—and though the members of the family rarely winter here, but go to Buenos Aires, they all have a deep loyalty to the island and dispute its reputation. Oliver Bridges points out that the wind, though fairly constant, is broken by the beech woods and in any case is much less violent than in parts of mainland Patagonia; the rain, which is heavy in the mountains and especially in the southern islands, is very moderate at Viamonte and throughout the plains. The winters, though very cold, are windless, and the salt air diminishes the snow, so that altogether, in his opinion, Tierra del Fuego is a far more hospitable land than the old accounts would lead one to believe.

Personally, I am partial to bleak places, and since the weather held fair throughout most of my stay here, and the wind was intermittent, his point of view seems very understandable. In its rigorous way, Tierra del Fuego is a varied and beautiful island, far more beautiful than those parts of Patagonia closer to the temperate zones. The Onas who once occupied this land, their primitive natures notwithstanding, gave many instances of their love for it, including the tendency, noted earlier, to die swiftly when taken away. Lucas Bridges describes a touching episode:

> Across leagues of wooded hills up the forty-mile length of Lake Kami, now Lake Fagnano, Talimeoat and I gazed long and silently towards a glorious sunset. I knew that he was searching the distance for any signs of smoke from the campfires of friends or foes. After a while his vigilance relaxed and, lying near me, he seemed to become oblivious of my presence. Feeling the chill of evening, I was on the point of suggesting a move, when he heaved a deep sigh and said to himself, as softly as an Ona could say anything:
>
> "Yak haruin." ("My country.")

The plane going north from Río Grande skirts the coast: to the westward the land flattens in a broad treeless plain with large pale lakes. Due east, three hundred miles away, lie the Falkland Islands, known to the Argentines, who still claim them, as the Malvinas. We cross the great bay of San Sebastián and the long sandspit of its cape, passing northward to the Strait of Magellan.

The Strait today is bright blue in the sun, like a broad avenue of color between the dry, barren, cloud-patched coasts of Patagonia. Below, Cape Virgenes, at the Atlantic entrance, and just inside it, inside a sort of hook, what must be the broadest beach in all the world.

The coast here is bare and gravelly, without roads. From here to the Río Colorado the land is of round gravel, a porphyry shingle in some places fifty feet thick; at the Santa Cruz River this shingle is said to extend all the way westward to the cordillera. A few small streams, and along their banks a sparse growth of dark green; behind the beach, spotted here and there, are the dry beds of ponds, and a live pond, farther on, has the tracks of animals branching out of it like spider legs in all directions. The sheep—if that is what they are—are invisible, however, as are all signs of man. Now, below, the green windy waters of the Río Gallegos; on the far bank the cliffs climb into the badlands of northern Patagonia.

These Patagonian deserts in the east have a burned, demonic aspect. The sulphurish ponds, margins white with encrusted salts, increase, if anything, the aspect of desolation. A windy day and a broken sky, and now and then, where the sun pierces, a pond glints evilly in an otherwise dark landscape. The clouds do not seem like clouds at all, but like the fumes of subterranean fires. Off to the east gleams the aquamarine of Bahía Grande; the sand and salt deserts contrast sharply. Behind the coast, just south of the junction of the Río Chico and the Río Santa Cruz, is a wasteland of twisted gullies and canyons and broken hills, but farther north the country levels out into the same cold upland desert plateau that one sees to the west, below the mountains. Cumulus clouds scud across the land, trailing black shadows. The isolated port of Saint Julian, tucked into the desert coast, flashes a moment on the sea horizon. The land grows higher, with a scattering of strange dry ponds, like stains of acid.

Below lies the province of Comodoro Rivadavia, and then the plane drones out again across the open water—the Golfo San Jorge. The ocean is dark and choppy under a high haze of wind clouds. Some time later we moved inland once more, over hundreds and hundreds of miles of barren . . . the Chubut River and, east of it, the Golfo Nuevo. Again, the ocean and, in a distant haze, the cliffs of the far shore.

Sliding in off the Gulf of San Matías, the plane casts a tiny shadow on a changing land. There is a scrubby vegetation along the coast, and on the north side of the Río Negro some evidence of man. The improvement is marked, but Darwin was able to write of this place: "The country near the mouth of the river is wretched in the extreme. . . . Water is extremely scarce, and, where found, is almost invariably brackish. The vegetation is scanty; and although there are bushes of many kinds, all are armed with formidable thorns, which seem to warn the stranger not to enter on these inhospitable regions." Nevertheless, signs of cultivation increase steadily north to the Colorado, where a few trees occur along the bank and in isolated groves. This is the edge of *la Pampa*, the land of the horse Indians, including the Tehuelches of Patagonia and, later, the Araucanians. The latter were a sedentary tribe of Chile until the advent of the horse, when they became fierce hunters of the plains; roaming most of Patagonia and the pampas, they made life miserable for the colonists on both sides of the frontier. (The colonists, of course, responded appropriately. Darwin exclaims over the fact that all Indian women over twenty were killed on sight, to which his informant responds, "Why, what can be done? They breed so!") The Tehuelches are now gone, but the Araucanians, like the Apaches in North America, were never effectively conquered, and still maintain certain rights and privileges in the Chilean lake districts.

The plane descends slowly, coasting out across the clay islands, like delta islands, of upper Bahía Blanca. On all sides now, the pampa extends away—huge pastel plains, shimmering in the heat, with their solitary cisterns and windmill pumps, and remote houses in little groves of eucalyptus, like citadels, and fat, slow rivers. The pampa is scarcely colorful any more—the *gauchos* with their *bolas* and *criollo* dress are of the past, and the ostriches and other creatures are following them. It is a civilized land, stretching north from Bahía Blanca to the River Plate.

NOTES ON THE CITIES

This book concerns the hinterlands of South America, and the large cities, therefore, have scarcely been mentioned; despite the homage paid them by the travel companies, they are probably the least interesting aspect of this continent. Many of the smaller cities, frontier towns, and villages referred to in these accounts have a strong regional flavor, and a few—Cochabamba in Bolivia and Tingo María in Peru are two which come immediately to mind—are really very lovely. But of the capitals I traveled through, the only one which seemed to me worthy of a visit on its own merits—in the sense that Paris or Florence or Prague or San Francisco deserves a visit—is not the "Rio" or "B.A." of the travel posters but the former capital of the Incas, the mountain city of Cuzco, in Peru.

Lima was the first large city I came upon, and perhaps because I made good friends there who were generous with their time, I enjoyed it very much: it is an open, airy place, with several interesting churches and museums (especially the private Larco Hoyle Museum of Inca and pre-Inca artifacts, including a room of marvelously graphic and often very comic pornographic ceramics), and at the edge of the city one can climb desert mountains or go swimming in the sea.

Santiago is urbane and pleasant, with its lovely wooded hills rising suddenly in the center of the city like giant rock gardens; Chileans strike one as more friendly and open than most Spanish Americans, and the girls of Santiago may be the prettiest in South America. (There are a great many very pretty girls in South America, most of them, unfortunately, afflicted with a traditional ignorance and a passivity of demeanor which, in combination with the whole continent's alarming ingestion of food, makes their beauty static and short-lived. A partial exception might be made of Brazilian women, but then Brazilians are lively and erratic and, with their generous admixture of many bloods, less inhibited than Spanish Americans, who tend to cling to the old ways as proof of Iberian heritage.)

La Paz, too, is a sunny, pleasant town; like Lima and Santiago, it benefits from its small size, natural setting, and the open nature of its city planning, rather than from its architecture, which is unexceptional. But its Church of San Francisco seemed to me the most rewarding of all I saw in South America, and its National Museum is most interesting, with extensive Inca, pre-Inca, Indian, and natural-history exhibits, and a clutch of pre-Inca mummies, laughing and howling silently in the cellar.

South American architecture, in the main, has a quasi-modern, monolithic deadness which submerges the few historic remnants. The heavy hand of dictators—one thinks of the monuments to Mussolini which disfigure Rome—must be bad for creativity, if the heaped-up pretension of Buenos Aires is any criterion; Buenos Aires at its best resembles Paris at its worst, reminding one—despite the noisy Latin jangle of its sidewalks— of the lugubrious bourgeois citadels in the neighborhood of the Parc Monceau. But then, I was stranded for two long weeks in Buenos Aires, and I may very well be prejudiced. To anyone who should find himself in that position I can recommend a first-rate zoo and botanical garden and the famous Natural History Museum in nearby La Plata.

While in Buenos Aires, I traveled to Punta del Este on the

coast of Uruguay and, though I passed twice through Monte-
video, formed no opinion of it. Punta del Este is the chief summer resort of the continent, on a pretty pine coast south of the
peaceful Uruguayan pampa, and its interest for me was much
enhanced by the presence off its shore of the Isla de Lobos,
where sea lions in great numbers gather on the rocks, as well as
a few remnants of the much persecuted southern fur seal; on one
bright day, fishing for anchoa, I was lucky enough to see a solitary elephant seal sprawled on the beach like a dead whale. I
spent a happy week in Punta del Este, the guest of Argentine
friends, Jean and Tony Deane, whose lovely house was set off
by a fine swimming pool. The acknowledgments with which this
book begins can in no way repay the kindnesses received in time
of need from these people and many others, in various localities
in South America.

São Paulo, in Brazil, where I paused for a day to visit the
fine snake farm at Butantan, is perhaps the most truly modern
of all the cities that I saw; it is not a handsome place, but there
is a sense here of experiment and life which is well suited to this
huge new nation. The modernity of Rio de Janeiro, on the other
hand, struck me as illusory, though with its harbor, airport, and
ocean beach all but surrounded by the city, and a setting almost
legendary, it seems a living prototype, a working model, of
cities to come. One thinks, What a beautiful city, but it is not
the city which is beautiful. The arrangement of cones and headlands, of beaches and blue bays against green mountains, makes
one envy the first navigator to enter the harbor from the sea.

I arrived in Rio in time of Carnival, and I swam at Copa-
cabana Beach, which is infested, I'm sorry to say, with some sort
of aggressive sand worm. The Carnival, like Rio itself, is colorful
and flimsy and very good fun for a very few days. In 1960 rain
fell much of the time, causing the cheap gilt and paint of the
outlandish costumes to run away down bare brown dancing
legs, but this factor in no way discouraged this frenetic people,
and as for myself, I was often to be seen, tall, fair-skinned, and

soberly suited, bringing up the rear of an oblivious, swaying line and reeking happily of the watered perfume which young girls squirt at passing merrymakers: the wild TUM-ta-pa-ta, ta-pa-TUM-ta-pa-ta, ta-pa-TUM of the brincar rhythm, resounding above the car horns day and night, stays with one for weeks afterward.

En route to Mato Grosso I traveled to the celebrated new capital of Brasilia, in the state of Goiás, which our illustrated magazines, with their false wonder and their art shots taken at night, have shown to us as the ultimate realization of twentieth-century advance. But Brasilia was a political inspiration, erected too fast and at appalling cost in an economy which, as yet, cannot afford it; the heavy, modern-type edifices do not soar in confirmation of the government's ideological barrage but stand mired in the raw, red clay of a drab landscape, different but not original, and tricked out in desperation with non-integral architectural gimcracks. I saw Brasilia, it is true, during the rainy season, some six weeks before its official inauguration, and doubtless it will look better when the oppressive litter of construction has been replaced by grass and floral borders; it will look better still when the poverty and famine has been relieved in the country's northeastern states, where the money used to fly in to Brasilia vast quantities of cement might have been better applied. But despite its grand design and modern technics, a cathedral shaped like a sombrero and an immense man-made lagoon, Brasilia is less inspired than pretentious, a brave new city cunningly disguised as a World's Fair.

5· MATO GROSSO

OF ALL THINGS IN NATURE, the one that most abhors a vacuum is a cartographer, and the most dread vacuums in all of mapdom, aside from the Seven Seas, are the interiors of Australia, Siberia, and the Estados Unidos do Brasil. A good map of Brazil's interior will show, nonetheless, any number of locations of apparent importance—the same importance, to judge from the print, as that awarded such places as Baltimore and Beirut—when in fact, of course, even the great cities of the region—Manaus, Cuiaba, Goiania, and, as of the moment, the new capital, Brasilia—are probably exceeded in size, if not in population, by a suburb like Greenwich, Connecticut. And this is true even though the interior of this one country is so enormous that it might almost be called the interior of South America.

The interior may be taken to include four of the large inland states, or all that country lying north and west of the fifth, Minas Gerais: "General Mines," which is rich in farmland as well as in minerals and jewels, lies directly behind the small, populous states of the Atlantic coast. Of the four states in question —Pará and Goiás in central Brazil, and Amazonas and Mato Grosso in the west—only southeastern Goiás could remotely be called settled, and even this is a phenomenon of the last three years: new villages have sprung up, and old villages become towns, as a result of the decision to transfer the nation's capital from Rio de Janeiro to a barren Goiás plateau. The construction of Brasilia is still in progress, having begun three years ago from nothing: for reasons quite apparent when one looks at it—the location has no visible advantage, scenic or otherwise—this neck of the woods has never before been frequented by man.

The nearest city to Brasilia is Goiania, a hundred miles away, and the road between them is also new, the first leg of the much-publicized Brasilia-Belém highway, which slices through sixteen hundred miles of jungle to the port at the mouth of the Amazon. (Goiania is southwest of Brasilia, while Belém lies to the north; why the highway should go to Goiania before turning around like the curve of a fishhook and starting north again is the kind of logical question one soon learns to avoid asking in South America, for fear of the confusion on both sides which the answer might bring.) It starts off past the first of the myriad billboards—Mercedes-Benz—which soon will block the new city from view, and continues on across impoverished plateaus cut by ravines. The grassy land, grown up in varying densities with shrubs and tree scrub, is rather lifeless in appearance; the absence of birds and animals is marked, with only a rare kestrel or caracara on a low treetop. The most notable feature of the landscape, once Brasilia has been left behind, and perhaps before, is the number of huge anthills like irregular reddish cones, some of them of the volume of an oil drum. There are also ant nests fastened to the limbs of the scrub trees; occasional trees are bent by their huge fruit.

The road descends gradually, and near Anápolis the land rapidly improves. There are sloping fields of upland palms, quite startling here, and the *ipé* tree with its bright yellow flowers, and a lumber tree called the *peroba*, and jacaranda. The ravines and roadsides are a lustrous green, and flop-eared Brahma cattle wander through the brush. Then, in a valley, a pattern of baked roofs: these tiles, with the prevailing rufous clay, make the color red characteristic of towns throughout South America, and Anápolis, when it appears, is no exception.

An hour beyond Anápolis is Goiania, the capital of Goiás; Goiás is still the frontier state of Brazil, and its central plaza has a statue of a *bandeirante*, or pioneer. At Santa Leopoldina, a hundred miles away, the country's roads to the northwest come to an end on the banks of the Araguaya; beyond lies the northern Mato Grosso, all but unpopulated.

In Orizona, a village some hours east of Goiania, lives Clayton Templeton of the New Tribes Mission, whose acquaintance I had made a few months earlier on the *Venimos*. I left for Orizona the next morning on the five a.m. bus—the five a.m. bus is the only bus all day—and dawn came eventually as we lurched down the dirt road. Against a black-silver sky the silhouettes of exotic trees stood stark and unfamiliar. Here and there swayed a tall, solitary palm: this tree, leaning against an early sky, is the loneliest tree imaginable.

Then it was day, and everything was unmysterious and plain. The road trails on across dull country, a brushy open cattle range. We passed lone huts, and once a herd of cattle with its *vaqueros* on sheepskin saddles. Peering darkly from beneath broad felt sombreros, these cowboys in low boots and homespun clothes, mustachioed, with thin, dirty beards, are the picture of banditry, lacking only the cartridge belt slung across the chest and the villainous smile. Occasionally the bus crashed through an adobe village, the driver leaning on its wild country horn, but the chickens, aged, and low-slung dogs looked bored when they bothered to look at all. Pedestrians in the provinces of South America, both animal and human, are apt to be more sophisticated than the drivers; the latter, because vehicles are still relatively uncommon, consider themselves a race apart and are determined to draw attention to themselves, whatever the risk to life and limb.

Four hours out of Goiania the bus humped to a halt in Vianápolis, and here, while changing vehicles, I encountered Templeton, who was making the same transfer, but in the opposite direction. There was nothing to do but return with him to Goiania; from there we went on to Anápolis for the night, going back to Orizona the following evening.

While renewing acquaintance, I told my friend of a violent argument I had gotten into with a man in Brasilia, to which his response was an inquiry as to whether or not I carried a revolver. "If not," he said, "you're the only man in the countryside outside of the very old or very poor, and Clayton Templeton, who doesn't." He went on to say that he had never seen or heard of a fist fight in all his ten years in Goiás: all disputes, even the smallest, are settled here with knife or pistol, and not uncommonly both. He recommended that I obtain a gun and carry it at all times in the interior, and while at first I thought he must be exaggerating because of his own uneasy position (as a Protestant preacher in a fanatical Catholic backwoods, he has had his life threatened more than once; only two weeks ago three men stopped him in the street, and he came away from the discussion with three red marks on his belly where a a stiletto had emphasized their points), I realized very shortly that he was not.

In Goiás, for carrying a weapon where people can see it and beware, one is speedily arrested, while a concealed weapon is considered inoffensive. Similarly a Brazilian here who commits an offense of any sort, whether or not he means to confess, hightails it from the scene of the crime: should he wait on the spot to give himself up, he is considered to be a flagrant offender and may be jailed indefinitely, or until time of trial. On the other hand, if he waits twenty-four hours before turning himself in, he is usually set free until his trial comes up. This sort of justice, like the law against exposed weapons, seems eminently logical to the people of the interior. Every man carries a long knife beneath his shirt and if possible a revolver as well; foreign guns, less apt to explode in one's own face, are very much in demand, and among these the favorite is the Smith & Wesson .32, or "smitch." (The word "smitch" has acquired a local connotation of superior quality, and is sometimes used as a general adjective: a thing is either "smitch" or it is not.) The law being the graceful thing it is, both knife and pistol are used on one's opponent without the smallest hesitation, especially under the influence of the local white lightning, a cane alcohol called *pinga* (in Spanish America, *kachasa*); listening to Clayton, I recalled the advice I'd gotten in Belém, three months before, from a man well traveled in the back areas of Brazil. "Brazilians are all right," he said, "most of the time. But they can't handle their own *pinga*, and when they're on it stay the hell away from them—they all got knives."

Murders are common and usually go unpunished, unless the bereaved take the law into their own hands; otherwise, after a few weeks' cooling period in jail, the murderer is often shown the door. If he has money, he may be home for dinner on the day of his arrest, and if he has a lot of money, the chances are that he won't be arrested at all—assuming, of course, that he is not a skinflint. The late Colonel Fawcett remarked on this legal phenomenon, and things have not changed much since his day. (I don't mean to single out Brazil in this regard. Money pretty much has its way throughout all of South America, to a degree quite startling even to a mind grown hardened to the spectacular graft and corruption in the United States. One wonders at times why the Communist Party hasn't made more progress, Church or no Church, because it is the peasants who are getting it in the neck. But one forgets about the appalling ignorance which stands in the way of constructive resistance, an ignorance which the Church itself, with its use of mystique and sacrament, tends to perpetuate—I hesitate to say "encourage," but the fact is that in backward countries or communities ignorance appears to be the Church's handmaiden; at the very least, the two are often seen in company.) The only murderer Clayton knew of who was punished by the community was the husband of a woman we talked to the following night, at the Anápolis station. This fellow, having killed his eighteenth victim, was adjudged to have gone too far and was hunted down in the woods and killed by a committee of his townsmen. Two weeks ago, near Orizona, a man killed the killer of his son and is now temporarily in jail; Clayton saw the body of the dead man, the second one, that is, which contained, in addition to four bullets, fifteen stab wounds. And a girl who worked formerly for the Templetons is at present in the hospital in Anápolis, also with four bullet wounds, administered by her husband. But in view of my own role here, the story I found most affecting concerned a journalist in Goiania, who wrote in his paper that the local *jefe* of the electric works had the *fuerza* turned on especially, during a shortage, in order that dental work might be performed on his own mouth. The charge was true, but nevertheless the *jefe* felt affronted, and shortly thereafter the journalist was seized in a café, dragged into the street, and executed. No one preferred charges, nor did the man's newspaper consider the item newsworthy. As in the Wild West, which is much admired here (I've heard the term used as a single word, "wildowest," an adjective meaning "authentically western," I suppose: a very "wildowest" holster; and some of the younger men in the villages wear their sombreros pointed in the front, gunslinger-style), the man with power, political or otherwise, is the law, and the policemen are philosophers. Clayton, a very mild man, would carry a gun himself were it not for the fact that using it—in the unlikely event that he used it effectively—might compromise his evangelical aims. Nevertheless, he intends to get one to keep in the house.

The Templetons live with their four children—a fifth is studying in the United States—in a large former store, one room of which has become a simple chapel. The place is somewhat in a state of siege, since worshipers of the enemy faith keep threatening to tear it down. At least, they threaten to attack the roof, from the top of which, at appointed hours, two loudspeakers carry music and the Baptist message to the Catholic townspeople; the people, with their roofs of tile and thatch, are defenseless against exposure to the Word, and this mild infringement of what we would think of as their rights (forgetting for a moment that they *have* no rights) may annoy them as much as the outlandish dogma. Apparently, however, they enjoy the musical fare, which includes numbers like *"Brilhando, brilhando . . ."* ("A sunbeam, a sunbeam, Jesus wants me for a sunbeam . . ."). And something of the message, in addition to the kindness so pronounced in both Templetons, has made "believers" of forty-eight Orizonans in the two years the mission has been here, despite considerable social and ecclesiastical pressure in the opposite direction. For the first three months Clayton preached to a room occupied only by his family; there then came to hear him a solitary prostitute—a beautiful woman, Clayton says—but her interest would have to be called ambiguous, for a month later she committed suicide. A start like this would have defeated most men, but Clayton kept at it, and the people came to him one by one. At first they fled every time the Protestant Bible was read, and the children were instructed by their priests to avoid the Templeton house at peril of their souls, for it was inhabited by demons, but gradually even these obstacles were overcome. As I walk around the village with him, it is obvious that the great majority like him, however leery they may be of what he stands for.

Orizona is a typical red-clay-and-adobe-brick village of the provinces, with its full complement of dejected dogs, thin chickens, roving hogs, and vultures; these compete for existence under the hot sun with human beings who are less indolent than worm-ridden, less unambitious than without hope—their contentment is resignation. Change is suspect, and everything is taken at face value. A team of twelve great oxen screeches into town ("screech" is not used here to denote excessive speed, but rather the actual noise made by a wood axle turning against a cart bed—the local belief is that this hair-raising noise keeps flighty oxen calm) pulling a ridiculous little cart of logs; they were hitched up to impress the people who do not have twelve oxen, and the people are, quite sincerely, impressed, as they will

be again the following Saturday. These same people, resigned
for centuries to the status quo, have always built their tiny
houses with the shutters swinging in, thus cramping their small
interior when the sun is shining and insuring rain on the floor
when there is rain; Templeton's efforts to discourage this struc-
tural aberration have been met with the stiffest sort of resistance, though one man who finally tried one window with the
shutter swinging out is now ecstatic over the newfangled arrangement, and wants to convert even his doors.

One afternoon Clayton's son Vance took me on an expedition into the countryside; we were joined by a missionary who
may be called Harry Croft. Croft had worked formerly among
Indians on the Tocantins River but had to give it up because of
chronic dysentery. He is a quiet, gentle man, still young, but
there is a terrible air of defeat about him, and a dazed, suspicious
glance from his bent head, as if he thought that at any moment
one might crucify him. He watched with a strange intentness,
even relish, as a big drunken, unshaven *vaquero* in a floppy sombrero pitched out of the roadside brush, dragging and kicking at
a bleeding steer which had been ringed cruelly through the nose;
when the steer refused to go farther, the man drew a pistol
from a green embroidered holster at his belt and shot it neatly
in its tracks. Later the steer was butchered and lay on the roadside weeds in great rolling islands and puddles of joints and en-
trails, attended by flies and ants and a pack of cadaverous dogs.

We went on, up a marvelously eroded road, like a deep
trench in the red clay; on both sides of the road were deep
canyons of erosion, in the clefts of which tall century plants
bloomed like huge asparagus. The banks of these canyons are
full of burrows, and these are inhabited by small parrots; at our
approach the parrots tumbled out and went squalling away
down the canyon. From the top of the road, one could look
back on Orizona, nestled in the broad fronds of its banana trees,
under its yellow spires. Around it and beyond lay the green, rolling open range of Goiás.

After supper one night we walked down through the village to talk to a farmhand and his wife; in kerosene light, the family sat on the doorsill of their hut, still and neat as a row of birds, their feet bare on the clean-swept earth of the floor. They talked shyly with soft, vague gestures. The woman seemed twice her husband's age, as women do here; on the man's salary of forty cents a day there isn't much to eat, and most of what there is is given to the man, to keep his strength. Many of the women in the villages have goiters, due apparently to a lack of iodine in the diet. The only women who eat quite well are the prostitutes, who are numerous even in this village; the poverty and an excess of women give them little choice about their line of work, even if they wanted one.

At another hut, the following day, I watched an old woman carding cotton and weaving it into string; this is a soothing process and endlessly amazing. A simple grace prevails here, in the postures of children waiting for nothing in the doorway, the young girl breast-feeding her baby, the old man in the corner with hands folded in his lap—the grace of people who have never gone anywhere and will never go. Only their grief is ungraceful, as perhaps grief should be: the villagers crowded and gawked around a dead baby done up in a little pink casket, its purple-gray tiny fingers twisted together in the clasp of prayer, and wild flowers stuffed in around it. All must have seen dead babies a hundred times before, and will see a hundred again—there were two in Orizona just today—and still they come and gawk. And yet it is hard to comprehend that something which has never lived can die—one stares at it with a certain awe, moved and revolted, and the revulsion has nothing to do with the spectacle itself. For some reason, I associated the dead baby with a little boy I had seen earlier on the far side of the village, at the Templetons' Bible class. This boy wore striped shorts cut from an old pair of pajamas, and his head had been shaved bald to rid him of vermin, and his older brother, who was singing next to him, rested his arm on the bald head. They were singing a song about trains and God which involved saying "toot, toot" as a kind of chorus, and the bald boy's "toot, toot" was said with great eagerness, so that his head would pop out from beneath his brother's arm, but it was always a second or two behind the others' and very wistful. It may well be that I was in a vulnerable frame of mind, but in any case I found him heartbreaking. Every time he said, "toot, toot," he would glance wide-eyed around with his sharp little face, like a nervous weasel, and on one of these occasions he caught me smiling at him. I have never seen a smile like the one that appeared on that ugly little face in all my life—he was beside himself with excitement. He just knew I liked him, that was all, and that was plenty, to judge from the reaction. And it is the implications of this need of his that upset me, that caused me to make the arbitrary association between this child and the dead baby, as if their fates were identical in the end. It was a confusing day, during the course of which my soul was prayed for, and my safety, and the hope was expressed that my stay in Orizona would prove a blessing to me—I kept thinking of Albert Camus, with not quite such sympathy as usual, and without coming to any conclusion, either.

That evening, under the bare, weak electric bulb in the whitewashed room where Clayton conducts his "meetings," I thought about the advantage held by the Catholic Church here, if only in the pomp and trappings of their services: all that ruby and gold and candlelight and satin must seem exalted after the bareness of a thatch hut (just as, to one sated by the glut of American *things*, the austerity of a Fundamentalist service seems preferable). Clayton uses only a bare table—there is no symbol anywhere in sight, not even a cross—and accompanies hymns on a small harp not unlike a zither, pausing now and again to speak or let one of the congregation read a prayer; on this particular evening Margaret Powell, a missionary on leave from the Caraja Indians of the Araguaya River, gave an interesting talk on mission work with that tribe, the women of which she referred to invariably as "ladies." I sat in the rear, observing the congregation; most of the people were women, and there were also some uneasy young people, a number of children, an idiot, and a few dogs. It was hard to know what to make of the whole business, except that the Templetons took the villagers and their poverty seriously, and the villagers knew it.

On Monday afternoon, after three pleasant days in Orizona, I returned to Anápolis with Clayton and his son, preparatory to flying up in a missionary plane to the settlement on the Araguaya; we traveled by bus to the station at Eginereu Teixera and along the roadside saw two of the small *ema*, or ostrich, about the size of a thin turkey. Later, from the train, I glimpsed a bird which I feel certain was the white-tailed kite, a lovely pale hawk which I had seen only once before, in California. Shortly thereafter the train came to a long halt because a freight train ahead of it had jumped the track. This is not a serious calamity on this line: the trains do it as regularly as toys, and for very similar reasons. It is simply a matter of bringing up a repair crew from somewhere or other and going to work with big jacks and rerailers. After a few hours we walked down the line and observed the work (we also observed that, where the wheels had jumped, no one had bothered to spike the rails to the cross-ties; the rails had simply splayed under the weight), enjoying the cool night air and the smell of cigarettes and damp earth and smudgepots. Nobody was in much of a hurry, and we completed the hundred miles to Anápolis at two a.m., about twelve hours after we started off. Clayton says this is only slightly worse than average, worse because there were two train crews to botch up the rerailing instead of one; ordinarily it is the train which one is on which jumps the track.

At the airstrip, early the next morning, George Glass, the missionary-pilot, asked me to lead him and the Templetons in the prayer usually offered in these planes before a flight over the wilderness. I refused, rather too abruptly, saying I did not feel qualified, and afterward felt a sudden sense of being cut off from

the others and at loose ends, so to speak. How serene these
people are—as if religion were a state of shock, deep, peaceful
shock, that good men like these are driven into by the spectacle
of reality. Or is it that we, on the far side of the same abyss,
do not wish to relinquish our tiny identities to a higher power?
At least, I don't, and I'm just as aware as the next man that tem-
poral ambitions are insane—not because we are immortal,
though, but because we are so mortal, and because our ambitions will amount at best to a hill of beans.

A ground fog was spread out below, airy as carded cotton
(my amazement at carded cotton was apparently still with me
today), and the ridges of the *planalto* jutted out of it almost
angrily under the early sun; the clouds spun away down to the
eastward, a white river. The shadow of the Cessna on these
clouds was ringed like a bull's-eye in an extraordinary round
rainbow—we were traveling in a halo, but, to my relief, nobody
remarked on the implications of this. Slowly the fog was burning off, and some large coffee plantations rose on the slopes below. There were miles and miles of them, and in an intervening
valley the Rio das Almas—River of Souls—flowing subterranean
in the valley fogs. Then we slid slowly down across the low,
flat country to the north of the *planalto*, and the *campos* grew
gradually more wet. Even the forests reflected light as we crossed
that angle of the sun. Here and there a lonely hut and yard—
what possesses a man to trek out here so far, when so much wild
land lies so much closer to the roads?—and an occasional small
band of pale cattle. The stream courses were jungly and palm-
strewn. In time the land changed to open swampland—this is
still the rainy season, and the rivers are in flood—gleaming below
in the stagnant places with all the turgid browns and purples
that one sees at the edge of an oil slick. From the southwest the
Araguaya wandered toward us, unassertive in this seasonal world
of water: we crossed its eastern fork and moved out over the
Isla Bananal. The sun's reflection crossed with us and knifed
through the forest: because the ground is wet, the sun appeared

to illumine the forest from below. On a rise at the river edge stood the hut of a Javahe Indian and a corral. This tribe is semi-civilized—that is to say, in peaceful contact with their white brethren.

George Glass dropped the plane low over the jungle, and we careened across the treetops, over creeks and swamp and tangled, evil sloughs. Then there appeared a broad flooded savanna, spotted with low trees and squat dwarf palms and an occasional pair of large white storks, the jabiru, or *tuiuu*, with its black head and cleaver bill and a scarlet slash across the neck; there were also egrets and caracaras and a flock of dark ducks— they looked long-legged and long-necked, like tree ducks. Deer —fat copper-colored deer—in ones and twos. A pair, the buck beautifully antlered, stood half submerged in a shallow pool, like moose.

Glass swung the plane across the river—we were now on the western branch—and we flew a while on the Mato Grosso side before crossing again to the island and dropping into the rough jungle airstrip at Macauba. The mission settlement at Macauba lies at the north end of Bananal Island, near the junction of Goiás, Mato Grosso, and Pará; from here the latter state extends northward across the Amazon. The huge island itself is formed between two branches of the Araguaya, which join again not far from here, some two hundred and ten miles north of where they parted. The Indians of the island are the Carajas and their sub-tribe, the Javahes; they are river Indians, and their villages, or *aldeas*, are scattered along hundreds of miles of the Araguaya. One of the largest of the *aldeas* is the one at Macauba; there are about eighty Indians here, a certain number of whom ran out through the jungle to greet the plane at the airstrip.

The Carajas, like most of the jungle tribes, are short, but they are handsome and friendly and are readily distinguished from Indians of all other tribes by the circles under their eyes —a small, exact black circular line the diameter of a quarter, tattooed under each eye, on the cheekbone. Some of them wear other facial marks as well—red and black stripes across the face—but the tattoos are disappearing among the young as the Carajas grow civilized. And all but the small children, in this missionary village at least, are clothed; most of the men wear shirts and a brief kind of shorts, and the women calico. The Indians also have elaborate, if scanty, costumes of bark cloth and feathers, but these are now saved for ceremonial occasions; some of the children, however, are clad in a necklace-bib of beads, and both children and unmarried boys customarily wear thongs at the ankle and below the knee, and a large bracelet or gauntlet at the wrist. Otto Austel, the young mission-ary who came out to the airstrip with them, was dressed in blue sport shirt, brown trousers, checked socks, and black shoes. All these people, regardless of race, color, or creed, were delighted to see George Glass, who, as the pilot of the rare plane bringing dis-traction to Macauba, is invariably the hero of the hour.

The Indians led us to the settlement on the river bank, where the *aldea* is split in two by the small white buildings of the missionaries; out on the river a Caraja in the dark, rakish log canoe of the Amazon basin slid past with the current. The In-dian huts are made of palm fronds draped on a pole frame-work; the fronds come from the *babassu*, which supplies as well the material for their weaving, the edible palm heart, and an oil from the *babassu* nut for use on skin, hair, and comestibles. The earthen floors are loosely covered with palm mats, and fires, pots, piles of fruit, baskets, squash and manioc, fish, mortars and pestles, chickens, dogs, and babies comprise the greater part of an organized litter; on the poles hang clothing, more baskets, arrows, bows, an aged rifle, perhaps, and one or more *araras* and parrots. The brilliant *araras*, or macaws—the rare hyacinthine, the scarlet, and the blue and yellow species of this great noisy long-tailed parrot are all found here—are usually moth-eaten in ap-pearance; taken from the nest at an early age, and a symbol of Caraja wealth, they are plucked too regularly by their owners for feathers to use in arrows, earrings, caps, female loincloths, and male wrestling belts, and for supplementary decoration of bows, lances, gourd rattles, dolls, and war clubs, and for their striking "sunray" headdress. Feathers are used lavishly on the costumes and artifacts of their long festival, or *ijaso*, and on those to be sent off upriver, where tamer Carajas, with inferior workmanship, are starting a thriving tourist trade; already the airport shop at Goiania is littered with feathered trash, some of it no more Caraja than the feather duster. The Carajas are thought to be the most colorful tribe in Brazil, and before too long their craft will be as popular with Brazilian tourists as the Navaho blanket in the United States—unless the poor birds give out, which some of the prized species show every symptom of doing in this area. The pink feathers of the flamingo are considered the most valuable, but these birds, like the plumed egrets, are becoming difficult to obtain, and already the chicken is putting in an appearance in some of the poorer work.

Tattered "sun" headdresses were still visible in some of the huts, but the *ijaso*, lasting about three months and celebrating an obscure fish, had recently come to an end; the village, in fact, was rent at both ends by the wails of mourners. "My child is dead, is dead by witchcraft"—this is the ritual chant and is vented for hours at a time, usually by an old woman facing the hut wall in one corner, whether or not the family is mourning a child or even a death. Witchcraft and medicine men are very important in the life of the Carajas and constitute the chief obstacle which the missionaries must deal with in their work of illumination.

If anybody is equipped for this work, however, it is Otto Austel, a young man who has spent several years with these people, has studied them with the close eye of the anthropologist—he has a complex file on Caraja mores and customs—and speaks their glottal tongue very efficiently. In regard to his work, Austel sadly concedes that the exposure of a primitive tribe to missionaries, however successful—because of the care, generosity, and devotion of the missionaries, the tribe is almost always benefited at the outset—is followed more often than not by its extinction, through the subsequent exploitation, mixed breeding, alcohol, and disease that arrive not with the advent of the Word but with civilization. He is trying to persuade his mission to work with tribes already laid open to civilization, who actually need help more than those unreached; help, however, is secondary in the end to the salvation of souls ("Do you know that three out of every four people in the world have not heard that God loves them?"), and the missionaries eventually move on to more dramatic work, leaving the now vulnerable tribe to the tender mercies of the traders and settlers. How long the Indian soul stays "saved," under the circumstances, is a question difficult to answer, but a missionary I talked to elsewhere told me of a tribe on the Tocantins which, over the years, has had a succession of faiths, both Catholic and Protestant, squabbling over its souls and can no longer tell one from another; as a result it has become cynical and indifferent to the lot, assuming that the missionary of the moment will in the end forsake them, like all the rest. And whatever the reasons, the Indians of South America (the large agricultural civilizations of the Andes excepted) continue to decline in number: in 1845, one hundred thousand Carajas were thought to exist, but a half-century later these had been reduced to about ten thousand, and today there are two thousand at most, the Javahes included. This ratio of decline is probably about average for the jungle tribes of South America, many of which are already extinct.

According to Austel, however, the Carajas are presently holding their own and even perhaps increasing. Formerly they were nomadic beach families and groups, depending almost exclusively on fish, which are shot with arrows, harpooned (in the case of the huge *pirarucu*), and poisoned with barbasco; they also hunt wild pig, turtles, and birds, though the latter are killed primarily for their feathers. But nomadic hunters who "gather" to survive are always limited in number, and the missionaries have encouraged the Carajas toward vegetable plantations. This group, at least, grows its own manioc, squash, corn, sweet potatoes, and bananas, supplemented by the fruit of such wild trees as the *caja* and the *jatoba*; they have made a beginning at raising their own cattle of the scrubby Brahma cross which does well in the lowlands.

The first afternoon at Macauba I went to see the Indian plantations and the jungle. The forest, even the river forest, of Goiás and Mato Grosso is not true rain forest, for the trees here are not enormous, nor do they form a solid canopy above: they are woods, as the name "Mato Grosso" suggests. (*Mato grosso* means "thick woods," but this isn't quite correct, either, since much of the state, like Goiás, is wild, grassy range country, supporting scattered shrub and bushes.) A hundred miles to the northward, in the state of Pará, the trees on the river banks are already tall, spreading gradually to unbroken rain forest where the Araguaya joins the Tocantins. Nevertheless, the jungle here is impressive, and some of the *piqui* and *jacoba* trees are very large indeed. There is also a variety of palms, including the *macauba*; the lumber tree known as "cedar," the *landi*, which is hollowed out to make canoes, and the rare Brazilwood tree for which the country was originally named. On the ground, in open places where a rock of volcanic aspect protrudes through the thin soil, there is a pretty weed with small purple flowers, like clover; though the plant is not insect-eating or otherwise endowed, its leaves are sensitive to the slightest touch, which causes the whole plant to fold in upon itself, swoon dead away. It comes around again in a little while, but the most delicate passage through it of a cat would leave a clear wake of bent brown stems among the green.

The bird life, as on the Amazon, is complex and colorful, and the air is never empty of bird sound, interweaving in a kind of counterpoint the chant of tree frogs and cicadas: a black bird with a bright reddish beak had a sudden strange melodic ring, and I noticed especially a dark, striking blue and green parrot, a dark flycatcher, white-bellied and scissor-tailed, another dark flycatcher with a white head stuck onto its body like a ping-pong ball, and an emerald-backed and rufous-bellied bird, white-chinned and long-beaked, luminescent as a hummingbird. This bird, I believe, is one of the motmots.

But the remarkable thing here is the variety of biting insects, and especially ants. There are large black flat-headed ants, and large black ants with both pincers and tail sting (these are apparently cannibalistic, and can be seen on all the trails, sometimes three together in silent, murderous struggle), and leaf-cutting ants, and small black ants, red ants, and white ants: the red ants include the fire ants, a few of which, at the suggestion of my missionary companion, I placed experimentally on my hand. Immediately, with a rare unison of ill temper, and little bodies all doubled up with the effort, they drove their stings into my skin, producing the sensation which gives them their name. Later we opened a large termite mound under attack by fire ants: the latter roamed up and down the exposed tunnels, seizing up and making off with the larger bodies of their pale relatives. A kick or two delivered at the base of the mound brought the fire ants out of the holes in awesome swarms; they resembled a red foam, tumbling over one another and pouring down and around the sides of the mound in search of the tormentor. They then fanned out into the grass, and we retreated.

There were also an imposing blue hornet—"Now that one's got quite a sting to him," Austel said—some bees and ticks, and the remorseless mosquitoes and *borrachudos*, the tiny black *pium* fly which leaves a dark pinpoint of blood at the surface of the skin.

Of poisonous snakes the island has very few, but the *onca*, or jaguar, is common here—Tom Pope, Austel's affable partner at Macauba, saw one on the river bank only a few days ago —as are deer, capybara, and peccary. Another common creature, in its black, white, and red-throated varieties, is the piranha, and my experience at Macauba strongly supports the prevailing theory that this fish almost never attacks except when there is blood or other wound fluid in the water. The whites and Indians swim readily in the river, and come back to the same place to catch piranha: experimenting, I caught a pugnacious, toothy specimen of two pounds or more in the exact spot where I had dived five minutes before, and a moment later caught a second, smaller one. The following afternoon we went swimming again. The Austels' little boy, with the other children, remained in the water after the rest of us had come out. He had a cut, nearly healed, on one thumb, and suddenly we heard him scream. He was rushed from the water with a bleeding hand, the thumb severely bitten by a piranha.

There are two Caraja *aldeas* near Macauba, and we visited these one afternoon in the mission launch, a long, outboard-powered craft built by the Indians. One *aldea*, consisting of three huts, lies on a high sand beach on one of the river islands, and the other, slightly larger, across the river on the Mato Grosso shore: behind the latter low mountains rise out of the wet savannas, the Serra de Araia, and faraway to the west, toward the Xingú, another sierra which I would have identified, according to my map, as Fawcett's Serra de Roncador if I had not read in Peter Fleming's *Brazilian Adventure* that this range does not exist. This village is the only settlement of Carajas in Mato Grosso and exists in the shelter of a nearby frontier settlement of Brazilians; this region of the Mato Grosso is ruled by the fierce Kayapos, of whom the Carajas are terrified, and who fight instead with the Brazilians and with another people of this region, the notorious Xavantes (this "x" is pronounced "ch," and so is the "t"; hence, "Cha-van-chees"). The Kayapos and Xavantes are alike in that both were driven from eastern Brazil into Mato Grosso; the Xavantes, in fact, are the unconquered element of a peaceable tribe of the Tocantins called the Xerentes. They are also alike in that they are shot down frequently by the frontiersmen of Mato Grosso, where in 1953 the ambush and massacre of twenty-two Xavantes—just after this band had been peacefully "contacted" by Brazil's dedicated Indian Service—has undone years of painful effort. An Indian raiding party wiped out an entire family of settlers only a few years ago, and skirmishes continue. The fine Brazilian law (sponsored originally by General Rondon, who traveled this wilderness with Theodore Roosevelt) prohibits the killing of Indians for any reason, including self-defense. (I say "fine" because it is precocious for South America, where the majority of governments, officially or otherwise, still exterminate Indians who become a nuisance.) But the law is not always observed in Mato Grosso, despite the fact that the crime of killing an Indian is far more serious than the crime of killing a Brazilian; the latter, to judge from attitudes in Goiás, is scarcely considered a crime at all.

Otto Austel, who is devoted to the Indians, is also sympathetic with the settlers of Mato Grosso. They are the pioneers, the *bandeirantes*, of Brazil, yet apparently they receive little or no cooperation from the government, being treated as squatters and even outlaws—which of course many of them are. This morning on the trail we talked to a handsome booted Brazilian who is a wanted killer—though it must be remembered that the term "killer" in these parts describes a fair percentage of the male population and lacks our own pejorative connotation. In any case, the settlers move civilization forward at great risk and hardship, only to be ousted by the "owners," who take over the land once the coast is clear. The settlers then move farther into northern Mato Grosso, which is still all but uninhabited.

The frontier settlement across the river, with its traders, its alcohol, and its Catholic priest, is rather troublesome to Macauba, since the Carajas have the traditional small tolerance of their race for alcohol and wander readily from the paths of righteousness. Usually, however, it is outsiders who cause trouble. One night while we were standing on the bank an Indian from across the river appeared in his canoe and announced his intention of killing his wife, who had fled to her family on the

Macauba side; he wanted her back, dead or alive. Being badly outnumbered, he lay smiling oddly in the stern of the canoe until such time as he was invited, or became drunk enough—he had a bottle of *pinga* in his hand—to venture ashore. The invitation would have to come from the female head of a household, who would then carry his rifle for him and lead the way. The rifle lay in front of him in the canoe. It was plain that he meant to come ashore sooner or later, and the *aldea* was very uneasy. It was decided to invite him, and an old woman took up the rifle. At this point Austel and Pope, who let the Indians settle their own affairs whenever possible, decided to intervene. Austel, who knew the man, approached him as he came ashore. Hugging and cajoling him, he confiscated a stiletto and, after a brief struggle and last snort, the bottle. Then he took the rifle from the woman, promising to return all these things whenever the man should decide to leave. At this point Pope placed a very large arm, both comforting and restraining, on the man's shoulders; he stayed with the Indian until later in the evening, when the man sobered and was persuaded to depart.

The village is most upset, however, by even the faintest prospect of attack upon them by the Kayapos; even in their own accounts of famous Kayapo-Caraja battles the Carajas invariably lose, and they see no reason why things should be any different now. Actually, a modern skirmish would be most unlikely: though there are periodic alarums, probably baseless, there has not been a battle for years. The Kayapos do not use canoes and would have to swim across to Bananal, fully armed, eluding the vigilance of the numerous and noisy *araras* and dogs: should they have to retreat, they would be wiped out in the water. On the other hand, the Kayapos fight to gain prestige and welcome a disadvantage. Unlike the Xavantes, who in war are said to admire stealth and treachery above all other virtues, they rarely attack when they have the upper hand and prefer open combat, declared in advance.

One night George Glass showed the Indians colored slides,

including several photographs of themselves. The latter they took in their stride, giggling a little, and they gazed admiringly, for the first time in their lives, at pictures of cities, of the sea, and of an ocean liner, all identified for them by Otto Austel. But curiously—and this was somehow moving—they were affected most by pictures of wild animals and birds, the egrets, ocelots, and monkeys with which they were familiar. Several men jumped up and pantomimed the bow and arrow, aiming at the screen, and the rest called softly their strange cry, which can be heard great distances through the forest—coo-ee-e—or hooted their rich, infectious laughter, like the joyous hooting of Negroes.

The following night two Indian men demonstrated under the moon the dances of their festival. They wore costumes of straw surmounted by very tall eyeless masks worn like hats, so that the figures seemed huge and faceless, blind. Straw scraping and bare feet slapping on the bare mud, gourd rattles in their hands, they tottered and heaved in time with each other, up and down, up and down, bumping and shuffling and uttering unearthly groans, the steps changing with the several changes of costume. They represented spirits, both beneficent and malign, and the huge apparitions are designed to frighten the women of the tribe and keep them in their place. While few Indians still take the spirits seriously, the men are as foolish about their lodge and its rituals as are our American "joiners," and their taboos are more severe: women who venture near the costume lodge are punished by multiple rape, and a dancer who lets his human identity be known may be put to death, though he is let off if his sister will offer herself to all the medicine men. (The now extinct Onas, thousands of miles away in Tierra del Fuego, had an almost identical custom of male lodges and ritual dances, with the same purpose; nosy Ona women, however, were put to death.)

The dancers this evening were both converts to Christianity, and while Austel felt certain that the tribe now takes the whole business as a joke, one had to wonder. If the odd, fervid groaning and shuffling of the straw giants in that jungle clearing, against a dim palm hut and black wall of trees, stirred a certain primordial dread and exaltation in a hard-eyed modern like myself, what must it do to people who until quite recently lived in the world of darkness and inarticulate fears which these figures represent? The Indian superstitions, after all—and I hope my friends at Macauba will forgive me—are no more incredible than the miracles they are asked to accept instead, though the airplane and penicillin have made the evangelists the greatest medicine men who ever lived.

Leaving Macauba, George Glass flew eastward to the village of Gurupí, which lies on the jungle highway north to Belém. We crossed the north half of the island, glimpsing a few whirring bands of parrots, the tireless *urubus*, and the sharp white outlines of egrets and storks. There was also a solitary deer, frozen in a swampy pool. Javahe huts appeared, and then the dull coils of the *branco menor* of the Araguaya, stuck on the flat, flat land. The far side of the river here is similar to the island, a great meadow with soft woods and streams, very peaceful in appearance from four thousand feet. But the plane slid down for a better look, and then the chaotic tangle could be seen in the vines and trees, and the meadow became marshes and morose bogs. This is the country of the savage Canueiras, who are said to kill whites and strange Indians on sight. Though Glass has flown this route before, he has never seen a trace of these Indians, and we watched avidly for a clearing or hut or trace of smoke. And then we saw something—a crude plantation hacked out of the jungle at the edge of a slough. Behind it, deep in the trees, a large hut stood almost hidden, and at the plantation edge, two ragged shelters. But the hut was well thatched, obviously inhabited. Several times Glass buzzed it closely with the plane, but nothing moved. The lifelessness, indicating flight into the trees, as well as the hut's location and the absence of visible trails, strongly suggested Canueiras: a lone Brazilian settler would be adventurous indeed to invade Canueira territory, and certainly he, or his family if he were absent, would come out and wave at a low plane. But there was nothing, only a breathless stillness, silence, palpable above the dry hum of the airplane, as if the jungle here were petrified. And it occurred to me that the dread Canueiras, terrifying to the Javahes, kill on sight not because they are warlike, as are the Kayapos, but because they are terrified themselves. Nevertheless, I kept an attentive ear on the plane's engine, not being anxious to terrify them further by a forced landing.

"Wait until I tell Otto about this," George said; he went on to say that Tom Pope wanted to try to reach the Canueiras, and I could not help but think how similar Tom seems to the five men who approached the Aucas in Ecuador, as described by one of their widows. How moving that account was, and yet exasperating: the faith which carried them far beyond the limits of courage and adventurousness, which made them, in the most literal sense, damned fools.

We took on gasoline and a breakfast of coffee and bananas at Gurupí, where a giant frog sat in a post hole near the airplane. Then we flew south, climbing up out of the lowlands and striking a violent rainstorm: the squalls of rain stood like pillars of pale marble across a ruined landscape. The squalls surrounded the plane quite suddenly, and a clatter of hail seemed to beat it toward the earth. But the plane fought clear after detouring to the westward; already we were over the rough cattle range of Goiás. A large ostrich, large as a deer from above, passed between two trees. Yellow bell flowers of the *ipé* tree speckled the harmonies of green, and tall *buriti* palms, with their short fronds, stalked down the grassy water courses. But the marks of this country are the huge smooth black boulders surging from the earth, some flat in the grass, others looming out above the trees in the small woods, like backs of wet elephants. Ahead, the low mountains of the *planalto* formed in the clouds:

Glass gave me the controls of the plane, and I steered her south uncertainly toward Goiania, unable to get that one hut in the Canueira country out of my mind.

March 12.

Today it is raining across Goiás. The small transport out of Goiania taxis roughly over fields of clouds, sinking down again into the swirl just east of the Araguaya. The plateau is broken by remarkable ponds, a series of them, identically shaped, like tears, and then the Araguaya, narrow and turgid here, winding off northward through the rain to Bananal, the Tocantins, the Amazon, and the sea. This is the Serra das Divisões, which forms a sort of east-west continental divide: there are many streams, their headwaters often but a few miles apart, yet those on the north side of the plane will end eventually in the Amazon, those to the south in the Paraná and Paraguay and, eventually, the River Plate.

The plane careens into the airstrip at Aracaras, the very first scenic attraction of which, seen at close hand just as the wheels touch the mud runway, is the wreck of a plane very similar to our own. A minute later we are waved into place before the humble terminal by a ground man with bare feet. The next air strip, at Guaratinga, in Mato Grosso, has no ground crew at all, and its terminal building is a hut of daub and wattle. My memories of Guaratinga will be two—a pair of small owls looking like quail, which I startled from a bush by the runway, and the take-off procedure of the pilot, a gay, abandoned sort of fellow, who kept the clumsy two-engined plane less than fifty feet from the ground, buzzing and swerving, for several miles across the roughest kind of upland country. Terror was general among the passengers, but as I speak no Portuguese and the rest were country people, already bewildered by their trip, no one dared say a thing.

We are now well into Mato Grosso, on the *planalto*, and the nondescript mountains of Goiás have changed rapidly to buttes and tablelands, pinnacles and escarpments, the sort of formations one expects to be bleak and rocky but which, here, are wooded. This is the country of the Borora tribe. Though there are areas of scrubby highland where the red earth gleams through the thin foliage, most of the woodland is dense, dense as green sheep wool—*mato grosso*.

From the village of Poxoreu, nestled among buttes, we fly on to Cuiabá, the capital of Mato Grosso and the town from which Fawcett set off on his last, fatal expedition: a little to the north of here lie the headwaters of the Xingú and the land of the Xavantes. From Cuiabá, the river of this name flows southwest to the Paraguay, and our next stop, the village of Cáceres, is on the Paraguay itself: from Cáceres, the plane heads due south to its final destination at Corumbá, on the Bolivian border. (In Spanish, the names of these three last-mentioned places would be accented on the second syllable, but in Portuguese, they are accented on the last syllable except in the case of Cáceres, which is accented on the first: this is one of the least important reasons why the two languages, quite similar when read, are actually so difficult to reconcile. Brazil is the only country in South America which uses Portuguese, and if one's Spanish is precarious, as mine is, one should not risk losing it altogether by attempting to speak Portuguese as well. With the sole exception of *obrigado*, a useful word meaning "thank you," the thing to do is to go right on speaking your wretched Spanish as if you imagined it was the native tongue, thus keeping your opponent on the defensive. With a little sign language to help him out, the Brazilian will get enough of it to help you keep from starving to death, and his gargled response—the voice is that of a person angered while eating macaroons—will be a total loss in any case.)

South of Cáceres the *planalto* dies in a series of steep ridges, narrow to the base, like man-made walls; these sink in turn into a great *pantanal*, or marsh, which, surrounding the upper Paraguay, extends between three and four hundred miles north and south and nearly two hundred east and west: while most of it lies in Mato Grosso, it overflows into eastern Bolivia and northeast Paraguay as well. This would seem to make it the greatest fresh-water marsh in all the world (at least, I can't think of one larger, though I shan't lack for somebody who can). In any case, it is a remarkable place, so remarkable that its obscurity seems astonishing. A tourist bureau, I suppose, might hesitate to recommend a swamp, and especially a swamp which lies, it must be said, a considerable distance from the beaten track. Nevertheless, it is worth going out of one's way to see, for it is a natural phenomenon quite as beautiful as high mountain or rocky seacoast. Or at least it is beautiful in this season, when the waters are high enough to create the swamp but not so high as to make an inland sea. Because the *pantanal* absorbs a hundred streams, the water is kept moving: it is clear, a gleaming black, free of stagnant algae and miasmic slimes. The grasses of its savannas are a fierce, fresh green, as are the beds of floating plants, looking from the air like dense water hyacinth. The variety of grass is broken by shady islets of pretty trees, and neat canals running among the water plants, and ponds which open into lakes, and out of the lakes, farther to the south, the blue hills of low ridges —everything in harmony and in place, without the usual swamp clutter and decay, under the bright sun of the central continent. The *pantanal* is trim as a deer park and looks infinitely hospitable, though it is not: it is trackless and fiercely hot, and it abounds in insects, piranhas, and large caimans. Its high ground, in the dry season, supports cattle—the region produces quantities of the South American dried beef, called *charque*—but otherwise it is inhabited most notably by jaguars, and by a remarkable *tigrero* named Sasha Siemel, who hunts these animals with a spear.

The plane passes over one village, pinched between water and mountain; the pilot, who has been flying low, hurls the inhabitants a roll of newspapers. We are near the Bolivian border, and at one point cross an outcropping of dense, hilly jungle.

One wonders if any white man has ever come there, and if it supports a community of Indians. There is still so much in South America which nobody really knows: a completely unknown tribe was discovered in Brazil only a few years ago, and there may be others.

The Paraguay rolls north in big soft bends, sculpting the marsh inlets and canals. At Corumbá, the low bank rises to a bluff, and the pastel town, its cleanliness and bright demeanor quite as unexpected as the *pantanal* itself, gazes northward across a shining wilderness.

Corumbá lies only a short distance north of Paraguay, where I had never been, and I arranged with a pilot named W. Porto to take me down the river and out across the *pantanal* in his small plane. We took off at 6:30 one morning, before the heat. The day was perfect, clear and shimmering, and as the rains have been slight this year, the savannas were emergent everywhere, like tundra. There were flowering bushes and marsh plants, the flower colors predominantly lavender and yellow, but the flowers do not contribute much to the beauty of the region, as they do in barren places—here the beauty lies in the soft harmonies and stillness.

We followed the Paraguay eastward, cutting across the bends and diving low on the numerous flocks of wading birds. Of these, the most common is the white stork called the *tuiuu*, but there are also ducks, blue herons, white egrets, and a white ibis, and, trading back and forth between tree islands, bright flocks of green parakeets and parrots. A number of the red lake deer could be seen, including several fawns and one buck with lovely antlers, and on a dry knoll, a solitary rhea.

Near the river at Pôrto Esperanca we saw the marble quarries in the sudden hills; here the railroad crosses, en route from Santa Cruz and Corumbá to São Paulo. At Fort Coimbra, farther south, W. Porto deposited our two other passengers; these men were dressed in the low "accordion" boots and the combination money-and-cartridge belt characteristic of Goiás and Mato Grosso, and the gear they removed from the plane included a long-barreled revolver, loaded, and a long knife, which one man slipped beneath his shirt. Later I asked W. Porto why these men were armed, and he said it was just a habit, very "wildowest."

Fort Coimbra is a border station, a punishment post for Communist officers and other difficult people who are better off out of harm's way: the fort on the hill, overhanging the river, is a relic of old wars with Paraguay. Just south of Fort Coimbra, Bolivia has a small foothold on the river, extending fifteen miles or so to the Otuquis River; there is no port or road here, however, nor even a hut. Beyond the mouth of the Otuquis, known also as the Rio Negro, lies the corner of northeastern Paraguay.

We flew down the main river and out across the Bolivian *pantanal* of southeastern Santa Cruz; here, in the canals and river edges, floated the dark shapes of *jacares*—the black caiman. There was one group of six or more together, the largest of which gave a great thrash and sank away as we banked down upon them. Their size was difficult to judge, but the wading birds on the banks nearby provided a fair yardstick: there were three or four of these ominous crocodilians which, though not huge, could not have been less than ten feet long.

At the Otuquis the three countries meet—for Mato Grosso lies east of the Paraguay—and we swung down over the Paraguayan settlement of Bahía Negra, a collection of huts largely occupied, according to W. Porto, by Indians. One remarkable thing about this place is the sharp dividing line drawn by the rivers between open savannas with scattered wooded islands—Bolivia and Brazil—and the solid forest of carandá palms on the Paraguayan shore. We flew westward over Paraguay, and a little inland the palm forest turned gradually to mixed woods. This is the edge of the Gran Chaco, as it is called, a low forest which begins northwest of here in Bolivia and marches all the way across Paraguay and several hundred miles into Argentina. On the way back to Corumbá we remained to the west of the river, crossing the Otuquis and the state of Santa Cruz, and returning to Brazil again at a point of the *pantanal* where rock islands, some a hundred feet in height, jut out of the savanna. Beyond these lie several good-sized lakes, and beyond these the ridge of low mountains, with their red and black cliffs of manganese, behind which lies Corumbá.

March 15.

Travel west from Corumbá, across the Bolivian jungles to Santa Cruz de la Sierra, is decidedly a sometime thing. Once a week there is a train, but this week it left the day before I arrived. And each week there are several planes, but this week there are strikes. Most maps of South America, including my own, reveal a road to Santa Cruz, but in fact no road exists. Why a map should show a non-existent road is beside the point: one may as well ask why the two competing movie houses in Corumbá are presently showing the identical film, or why the Bolivian official here made me pay dearly for a visa stamp in my passport, when his colleague at Guaqui, only two months ago, required no visa at all, or why, in order to catch a plane leaving for Santa Cruz at eight in the morning, from an airfield less than four minutes from town, one must be picked up at the hotel at six. Though I should know better by this time, I questioned the logic of the latter, and immediately the whole airline office became extremely excited and upset, as if I were some sort of anarchist. "*Aduana, aduana!*" they all shouted, rushing forward to the counter. But in fact the customs, outward bound, is never more than a five-minute affair. The taxi drivers know this perfectly well, of course, and will appear at six forty-five if they decide to appear at all. Nevertheless, for fear of being stranded another four days in Corumbá—the same fear which permits the Bolivian consul to pocket my cruzeiros—I will rise on the day of departure at five-thirty and be waiting at the hotel door at six a.m., in need of coffee. By seven a.m. my bag will have been checked through customs, and I will then wait from two to twenty-four hours for the departure of the plane. (The departure depends less on the machine's state of repair than on the number of passengers: flights on this continent are stalled off for hours and at times canceled altogether, with the most absurd excuses, when the manager considers the number of passengers insufficient.) This protocol is invariable and inflexible throughout South America, where the punishment of airline passengers is, if possible, even more cruel and unusual than that inflicted in the United States—except that after a while the senselessness of it all is no longer infuriating. One becomes stolid and resigned as any dray horse, aware that an infusion of logic, honesty, and efficiency into this world would create a chaos impossible to imagine.

If one has to be stranded, one could do a lot worse than Corumbá, though Julian Duguid, the author of *Green Hell*, calls it "without dispute, the most unpleasant place I ever saw. A low range of limestone hills rears up out of the cattle-plains, and the sun devours the yellow streets. The whiteness of the houses is blinding, the heat comes up in a haze, and a vast, heavy stillness broods over the terraced town. By day the porous stone sucks in the hot savagery of the tropics, and breathes it out like an evil odor at night." Be that as it may, the town's location on a hill overlooking the Paraguay and the *pantanal* is striking, and, for my part, I found the heat moderate enough and the odors no more evil than those come upon elsewhere in this redolent land. I may have arrived at a more auspicious season, however, and doubtless Corumbá has improved somewhat in the last decades, though, as I recall, both Colonel Fawcett and former President Theodore Roosevelt had a good opinion of the place. The food is not quite what it might be—I don't believe there's a fresh fruit or vegetable in the whole town —and a huge moth with two white spots like eyes staring out

behind is a permanent resident of my wall, but otherwise
the place seems cheerful and prosperous enough. In addition to
the *charque* industry, there is also production of manganese and
marble.

March 16.

The *pantanal* continues westward from Corumbá into Bolivia, but there it shortly turns into low, smoky forest; a small
river winds, and the trail of another, marked by the break in
the trees. Then there is only a vast, unbroken green—this is the
"green hell" of Duguid's inspiration, a term applied by every
writer since to the particular jungle he chanced to visit. A species
of pale, boney tree stands higher than the rest and from the
air appears as a kind of lint on the broad mat. I wonder at first
why this low jungle—the north end of the Chaco—seems so
much more formidable than the rain forests of the Amazon, and
then I realize that there are no visible rivers or streams, no water
of any kind in sight, for miles and miles. This jungle desert is
inhabited by the Ayorés, a very fierce tribe much chastened in
recent years by the New Tribes Mission.

The land ascends gradually toward Santa Cruz, turning a
deeper green; the Guapay, or Río Grande, slides below, irregular
and ungraceful in its broad dry bed of parched backwashes and
ungainly islands. One by one, huts and roads appear, gathering
quickly and accumulating at last in the town of Santa Cruz
de la Sierra: beyond, the Andes rise in dusty silhouette out of
the heat.

6· BEYOND BLACK DRUNKEN RIVER

WITH ITS MUD STREETS, thatch roofs, and raffish waterfront, and its barefoot Shipibos with their nose ornaments and bright clothing, the Peruvian river town of Pucallpa is as colorful as it is hideous. The trading post for thousands of square miles of wilderness, it attracts a motley fleet of cargo craft and long canoes; these swarm like a hatch of flies on the broad brown Ucayali, drawn out of the water courses of the vast *selva* or Amazon jungle, which, lying there in steaming silence across the river, stretches away for twenty-five hundred miles to the Atlantic coast.

The cultural center of Pucallpa is the bar of the Gran Hotel Mercedes, which serves coffee and liquor and *gaseosas*, or soft drinks, from dawn until after midnight. From its open doors and windows a splendid view may be obtained of the hogs and vultures which pick over the orange quagmire of the street. Here, in January of 1960, I had first encountered Vargaray, an intense dark man with that South American badge of white blood, the mustache, and the man who first told me of the monstrous fossil jaw near the Mapuya River. The Mapuya does not appear on maps, but was identified as a tributary of the Inuya, which is in turn a tributary of the Urubamba; the latter joins the Tambo near Atalaya to form the Ucayali, which, flowing northward, joins the Marañon about five hundred miles downstream, forming the main body of the Amazon. The Mapuya is located in the flat rain forest, eastward toward the frontier of Brazil, and therefore seemed a most unlikely site for paleontological discovery; in fact, no man in the Mercedes had ever heard of fossil bones found in the open selva. Flood, humidity, and voracious ants were among the numerous factors presented to poor Vargaray to assure him that his fossil could not exist. But Vargaray became very angry when he was doubted, and his passion about the huge *mandíbula* was impressive.

The plot thickened with the appearance in the bar of a man named César Cruz. Cruz was brought forward by our genial host, Señor Fausto Lopez, as just the man to conduct a search party to the bone. A rancher on the Urubamba, he possessed all the necessary *canoas*, outboard motors, *mosquiteros*, guns, and men. Furthermore, he knew of a mysterious ruin on a more distant tributary of the Urubamba, the Río Picha, which no white man had ever seen. Cruz suggested that an expedition—which by now was considered a foregone conclusion in the bar—attempt to locate both *mandíbula* and *ruinas*.

The legends of the lost cities, and especially of the Inca El Dorado known as Paititi, die very hard indeed, in part because lost cities are still being found. The most famous of these, of course, is the Inca mountain town of Machu Picchu, which was found in 1911. Since then several other important locations have come to light, and almost certainly there are more.

Nevertheless, the great majority of those one hears about never existed, or if they did exist, their discoverers have not lived to tell the tale. Jungle legends are, in the main, absurd, and Cruz's story of the lost city on the Picha put me on my guard, especially since there was not the slightest question in the mind of anyone in the room, myself included, as to who was expected to pay for the Picha expedition. I explained what was true, that my sponsors expected me to go to Africa directly from Buenos Aires, where I was to arrive the following month. But, as I have said, there is no world beyond the selva, and my excuse was scarcely heeded; it had already been determined, in fact, that my friend the local Army *comandante*, Juan Basurco, would accompany me in the discovery which was to make all of us famous. At a loss, I let an ironic smile play about my lips, in the manner of one willing to go along with a good joke, and peered cynically about the room through my own cigarette smoke. No one took any notice of this, however. Details of the trip were now discussed, and Cruz added fuel to the general excitement with the statement that a Machiguenga Indian working on his cattle farm had actually been to the Picha ruin and could guide us there.

Cruz is a graceful, quiet man of medium height, very dark, with wary eyes pinched close to the large hawk nose of an Indian and a sudden smile which reveals three teeth of gold in the very center of his upper *mandíbula*. He speaks gently and has an infrequent, appealing laugh, and I took to him immediately. In the following days I had a few whiskies with him, and by the time I left I had contracted the jungle fever. Tentative plans for an expedition had actually been set up, and the journey to Africa postponed. In the early spring, when the rains had abated and the upper rivers would be navigable, I was to meet Cruz and his men at the headwaters of the Urubamba.

In the clear air above the Andes, flying out, I wondered if I had not lost my mind, if I were not, indeed, the greatest gringo idiot that had ever fallen into that nest of thieves. At best, the existence of the monster jaw was most improbable, and that of the Picha ruin beneath serious discussion. I could only console myself with the certain prospect of seeing the jungle at close hand at last, and this had become important to me.

The fossil jaw is there or it is not: the dearth of precedence in the finding of large jungle fossils and my own lack of educa-

The Upper Urubamba, from ruins at Machu Picchu

Hacienda Marquez, on Yanatili River (Black Drunken River)

The cloud forest at El Encuentro

Ardiles

Epifanio Pereira, at Sangianarinchi (note dancing frog)

Andrés Porras (right) and his friend
Señor Antonio Basagoitia

Toribio

Machiguenga campfire

Construction of balsa raft, Pangoa

Agostino

Mouth of the Pongo, lower end (*picture taken at 4000 feet by George Insley, missionary-pilot*)

Dawn on the Urubamba

Last resting place of the Happy Days, *Timpia*

Machiguenga chief, Timpia

Machiguenga woman, Camisea

Campa woman (note toucan), Inuya River

Campa hunters and drying arrow shafts

Indian encampment, Inuya River

Quebrada Grasa

César Cruz and author, with mandíbula, *Mapuya River*

Mission Conibos, Ucayali River

The fossil in police yard, Pucallpa

tion in the matter make it hard to advance any theory of proba-
bilities. The likelihood, such as it is, of the existence of the ruin
is based on the theory that the Incas retreated from the Spanish
down into the Urubamba Valley, to Machu Picchu and perhaps
beyond: the Picha ruins, however, would be at least two hundred miles beyond, at a lower altitude by far than any ruin found
to date on the eastern side of the Andean cordillera.

In Lima I called on Señor Rafael Larco Hoyle, one of Peru's
leading archaeologists and the owner-curator of the country's
finest collection of pre-Inca artifacts. Señor Hoyle assured me
that no ruin, large or small, had ever been found in the region
described or, in his opinion, ever would be. He cautioned me
strongly against believing any such tale, on a theory of his own
to the effect that even an honest man, after one week in the
jungle, contracts strange fevers and becomes a liar. This is a
charitable theory and may serve to excuse some of the jungle's
wild-eyed chroniclers; it remains to be seen whether or not I
come down with the disease itself.

On the other hand, a jungle veteran named Andrés Porras
Cáceres, who worked on the Ucayali around 1944, had heard of
a ruin in the Picha area. Before he could visit it, however, the
river man who was to conduct him there, one Alejandro Angulo,
was killed by the Machiguengas.

Andrés Porras is the brother of Alfredo Porras, a friend in
Lima whose interest and kindness have been instrumental in
setting up the journey. Andrés, in fact, decided to join me, which
is a great stroke of luck, for he has all the experience that I lack
and is a most agreeable man besides. During the winter, while
I was traveling to Tierra del Fuego and Mato Grosso, he and
Alfredo set up the details of the expedition. I returned to Lima
in late March and in the first days of April left with Andrés for
Cuzco, in the mountains, where our journey into the selva will
begin.

I dearly wish that there were another word for "expedition,"
since I could scarcely apply that term to any trip sponsored by

myself: one "mounts" a reputable jungle expedition and equips oneself with pith helmets, lean white hunters, inscrutable Indian scouts, and superstitious bearers who will go no farther. Furthermore, an expedition is backed by millionaires, museums, and foundations—either that, or the explorer (who in this case is invariably an author) sets off alone, or nearly so, and miserably equipped, into country from which, as he is told by old jungle hands in the early pages of the resultant book, he has not the slightest chance of returning alive. Since I am not an explorer, and since I have every intention of returning not only alive but sleek and well, none of these basic conditions can be said to apply to the outing I have in mind.

April 8. Cuzco.

Here is a rough outline of the journey: from Cuzco we proceed down the Urubamba—it is called the Vilcanota in these upper reaches—to Machu Picchu, and from there to Quillabamba. Beyond Quillabamba there is no scheduled transportation, but apparently there is a road of sorts to a point on the river at its confluence with the Río Yanatili, called El Encuentro. Here the Urubamba becomes navigable, and here we are to be met by César Cruz and three of his men with a small river boat and a canoe. We descend the Urubamba, including a famous rapids called the Pongo de Mainique, and eventually turn off westward up the Río Picha, in search of the ruin. We then return to the Urubamba and descend to the settlement of Atalaya. There we pick up Vargaray and head eastward again into the Inuya and the Mapuya, where we hope to locate and retrieve the famed *mandíbula*. We then return to the Urubamba and to Atalaya, from where we descend the Ucayali to Pucallpa. Whether or not we locate bone or ruin, we will have traveled close to a thousand miles on the jungle rivers.

This, as I have said, is the rude itinerary; we can't know more about it until we have spoken with Cruz himself. The last word from him was a cable from Atalaya to Lima which required four days to arrive (in the United States a cable is sent or it is not, but this system would offend every custom in South America, where inefficiency is an art nothing less than awe-inspiring) and signally failed to take into account a cable of questions and instructions sent off by Andrés a week before. This indicates that he failed to receive Andrés's cable—or rather, one *hopes* that this is what it indicates, the alternative being damaging to one's faith in the trusty Cruz. César's cable stated that he would meet us at El Encuentro on April 10, which would leave him so little time for the journey up the Urubamba that I wondered if he did not mean the *encuentro*, or confluence, of the Tambo-Urubamba, near Atalaya. But Andrés had been in Pucallpa two weeks before and had carefully established with Cruz's wife—Cruz himself was absent—that the *encuentro* in question was the one near Quillabamba. He did not feel there could be any honest confusion on the point.

In any case, Andrés and I will be at El Encuentro the day after tomorrow. As for Cruz, only time will tell.

Because we have no idea, owing to communications failures, of the completeness of Cruz's preparations, our three days in Cuzco have been largely devoted to minor outfitting—*curarina*, or snake medicine, malaria pills, meat sauce (for monkeys and other doubtful provender), machetes, and so forth. Fortunately Andrés was already well equipped with more basic material, including a pup tent, hunting knives, waterproof river sacks for our gear, a .44 Winchester carbine, and a portable radio. In addition, he has lent me a .38 revolver, as one is never certain what manner of unfriendly beast one may encounter in the selva.

While in Cuzco I had a look at several books of Peruvian exploration, through the kindness of Señor Benjamín de la Torre, and one of these, the *South American Adventures* of an Englishman, Mr. Stratford Jolly, directly concerned the Urubamba region. Mr. Jolly, in 1929, descended the Urubamba, though he was not the first Briton to do so: the previous year Mrs. Bertha Cox, an evangelist of sixty-five and "a courageous and very obstinate old lady," had made her way down the valley with an immense amount of luggage, after suffering incredible maltreatment at the hands of the settlers near the headwaters. Turning the other cheek, Mrs. Cox "gave the people who had treated her so abominably most of her chickens, in return for which they stole her dog, and followed the party for some hours down through the forests along the river-bank, in the hope that the canoe would upset and that they would be able to salve and steal the cargo." She survived her journey only through the assistance of "the rubber trader Peyrera, who was absolute king of the river below." Among the river people, this man had a very evil reputation—he was, among other things, a murderer—and Jolly himself was apprehensive. But he then received a message from the trader, who hoped to prove that "there were still decent people to be found, even in the inaccessible mountains of Peru." And in fact Jolly and his party were treated with utmost courtesy. With the help of Machiguenga Indians attached to Peyrera, both Mrs. Cox and Mr. Jolly were portaged past the Pongo de Mainique—an awesome place, to judge from his account—and arrived eventually at the settlements on the Ucayali.

The one other reference to this region I have come upon to date occurs in a work called *The Rivers Ran East* by an American, Leonard Clark: I came across this volume in La Paz. Mr. Clark, with a single Peruvian companion, descended the Andean rivers—the Perene and the Tambo, farther east—to Atalaya and Pucallpa, and his adventure, therefore, might be said to parallel closely the one which lies before us. (I hope, I must own, that all parallels have already been stated. In his very first hours in the wilds Clark is threatened by a huge rattlesnake, by a jaguar which approaches to a point fifty feet away, and by his own companion, who threatens to blow Clark's head off. From this point forward he is exposed almost constantly to assault by Indians, piranhas, crocodiles, vampire bats, and poisonous reptiles of "intense cunning," an "immense" specimen of which, in the climactic chapters, succeeds at last in burying its fangs in the author's throat. Since the wound adjoins the jugular, Mr. Clark is unable to bleed it, an irony which causes him to laugh; in a calm voice he informs his companion that he has four or five minutes to live, and it looks very much as if the constant prophecies of his certain doom are about to be borne out. But an Indian leaps into the jungle and gathers, prepares, and administers a potion unknown to science in the allotted time, thus sparing the author and his exciting story for the publishing firm of Funk & Wagnalls.) Despite the successful passage of Mrs. Cox and others two decades before the period of which he writes, Clark speaks of "the forbidden Urubamba" and the terrible savages who control it. Here, as elsewhere, he appears to have been the victim of considerable misinformation, a minor example of which is a report that in recent years a trader named Pereira was killed by Machiguenga slaves while attempting to establish a holding above the Pongo. The holding, of course, was established before 1920, and Pereira is still very much alive. He is said to be a most interesting man, and both Andrés and myself now hope to meet him.

Andrés once lived in Cuzco, and I have been here previously, which accounts for our failure to take advantage of its Inca splendors or the more vulgar monuments of the colonial Church. Also, Andrés has many relatives here, and these kind people, and especially his sister-in-law, Gloria Estelle Ladrón de Guevara León de Peralta, have seen to it that our every free moment was assigned to food and drink. Nevertheless, we took time to revisit the Inca fortress of Sacsahuaman above the city, and let the bare sun and distances of the sierra seep into our souls. Andrés, however, is bothered by the altitude, and the mountains themselves oppress him; he is anxious to get down into the jungle. I agree and am, in fact, nearly beside myself with anticipation.

April 9. Quillabamba.

Our last evening in Cuzco, with Estelle de León de Peralta and a friend from Lima, Celeste Allen, we celebrated something or other until very late, and as we had to rise at 5:30 a.m. to catch the *ferrocarril* to Machu Picchu, the expedition got off to a fairly painful start. But the mountain day was so clean and clear as to shock us back into awareness, and as the valleys of the Urubamba region are the loveliest I have ever seen, the journey was the greatest pleasure.

The ruins at Machu Picchu have been described in detail, ineffectually, by any number of writers, including myself (in Chapter III); one must see the place to comprehend it, and that is that. Like all the rest, I find it a formidable spectacle, unforgettable; in conjunction with Cuzco and its environs, with Ollantaitambo and the other mountain ruins, with the stark Puno and the clear, flowered valleys, it is the principal sight of South America and sufficient justification in itself for a visit to that continent.

This area of the Inca world, from Machu Picchu southeastward to Lake Titicaca, Tiahuanaco, and La Paz, is serviced with efficiency and, more remarkable still, a concept of hygiene bordering on outright cleanliness. The rare wayfarer who leaves Machu Picchu in the wrong direction—northward, that is, toward Quillabamba, rather than back to Cuzco—will notice a marked change in service the moment he sets foot on the crowded *ferrocarril* which proceeds down the valley. Andrés and I clambered aboard in the late afternoon, waving good-by to Celeste Allen and another excellent American named Colonel Tooey, who had accompanied us as far as Machu Picchu. Celeste, a very attractive woman, is a veteran of the jungle, and on the strength of some farewell *pisco* sours we were almost able to persuade her to accompany us; as it was, she located a bottle of Scotch somewhere in Machu Picchu, and we now carry it with us, to be drunk in her honor at the Río Picha if we find the ruin, at the Mapuya if we find the bone; failing both, it can always be smashed over the head of César Cruz. The car was scarcely out of sight around the bend when the track petered out entirely at a large hacienda of the montaña, or "high jungle," called Huadquina. Here we changed to a dirt road and the inevitable *góndola*, or miniature bus, with its protruding limbs, packages of food, and redolent good cheer, and journeyed on in the soft twilight toward Quillabamba.

Some parakeets seen above Machu Picchu were the first signs of the montaña, but other signs now began to appear. These were the red-flowered air plant bromelia, and the strange hanging nests of the black and yellow river oriole. The river itself remained turbulent and unnavigable, its brown color in vivid contrast to the white mountain torrents which dove into it at the mouth of each ravine. When the sun went down, the clouds of mist still drifted in the valley like dirigibles; the valley itself had gradually grown wider. By the time the *góndola* reached Quillabamba, night had come.

April 10. El Encuentro.

Quillabamba is the capital of the province of Convención, but its streets are of mud for all of that, and its best hotel and restaurant undistinguished to the point of simple filth; the hotel's communal toilet had a roof, however, and the restaurant personnel, though barefoot, sadly soiled, and otherwise informal in their appearance, were friendly and fleet of foot. After supper, attempting to locate a ride to El Encuentro, we walked a considerable distance around the town, which is perhaps not at its best beneath weak street lights.

Unhappily, we were to see it no other way, for long before dawn we were off in a market truck through the *montaña* valleys (though the mountains still tower around us, the altitude of the valley floor is now less than four thousand feet). The dirt road, often no more than a ledge, skirted the steep banks of the river below; the torrent could not be seen, but it roared from directly beneath us in a way which was very disconcerting.

The jaguar and the Andean bear, the driver told us, were common creatures of this region; a glimpse of either would have started the journey auspiciously, and I kept a sharp lookout ahead, in the yellow headlights. But we met instead with a strong smell of skunk, and an animal of this family, a mustelid called the *raposo*, sidled furtively, with neither grace nor speed, into some roadside weeds. This creature, rather than the jaguar or bear, was the first animal recorded by the expedition. There then charged across the road, missing first place by a matter of seconds, a diminutive mouse or shrew.

Like many places featured on jungle maps, El Encuentro marks only a geographical location and has no settlement of any kind. The road, in fact, comes to an end a few miles short of it, at the hacienda known as Qquellouno (a Quechua word for "yellow water"; there is a small stream of this color flowing through the hacienda, down into the Yanatili, which forms the *encuentro* with the Urubamba). Yanatili is also a Quechua word, slightly corrupted; roughly, the name means Black Drunken River. Though the torrent is dark gray, the name is otherwise a good one, for the river comes sprawling down out of the mountains in rolling curves, pitching beneath the footbridge by the hacienda at an awesome rate before losing itself in the brown Urubamba.

We arrived at Qquellouno just after light and a little later walked to the *encuentro*. The path rises steeply through a grove of cacao trees: the hacienda concentrates on coffee and cacao, though it also grows *choclo* (maize), yuca (manioc, or cassava), tea, and coca, the Quechua narcotic and source of cocaine. It enters the forest, then descends abruptly to the river once again. A blue morpho butterfly accompanied us part of the way, bouncing along just ahead of the Quechua boy who guided us; butterflies of numerous species, some a lovely fire color, were sunning their wings everywhere. There were also the inevitable files of marching ants—and I did not have to be told to run through them quickly, having learned this elementary jungle lesson in Mato Grosso. (One also learns quickly not to lay one's hand or lean casually on tree limbs, which are often spined and sometimes ant-ridden, or worse.)

The *encuentro* itself was lovely, reminiscent of a Montana mountain river, gravelly and swift, with a morning breeze and a wet sparkle in the leaves. But there were also incongruous cloud islands against the dark, thick mountainsides, providing that air of mystery and vague threat so common to landscapes in South America.

Cruz was not at the *encuentro*, and a Quechua who worked a *chacra* there said there had been no sign of him.

The path back up onto the ridge was slippery and steep, and the day, though still early—it was only nine—was fiercely hot. Our guide bounded ahead, and Andrés and I pursued him. Though in pain, we did not stop to rest, and I gradually became aware that we were indulging in some sort of competition, trying each other out, so to speak, though I don't believe that Andrés was aware of this. The competition was foolish; Andrés is nearly twice my age, and a man in his early sixties has no business hurrying on such a slope, despite the fact that his physical condition is far superior to my own. Andrés is an athlete and rightly proud of his condition: he does not smoke, drinks very little, and continues to surfboard, Hawaiian-style, in the long waves of the Pacific. A man's heart does not always pay attention to good intentions, however, and his very doggedness worried me a little. I remained ahead of him and, by feigning near-mortal fatigue, managed to slow him down. Not that fatigue was difficult to feign, for I was soon exhausted. When in good shape, I perspire very little, but now I was exuding a mixture of *pisco* and general effluvia which kept even the sweat bees at a respectful distance, and was in addition gasping like a *sungaro*, as the giant catfish of Amazonas are known. But to return to the competition: Andrés is a jungle veteran, hard as nails and anxious to instruct a greenhorn, while I am neither jungle veteran nor hard as nails, but stubborn. So I suppose, until we are broken in, we shall have to sniff each other out a bit, like dogs.

Actually, after five days together, we get on very well. This is a credit to Andrés rather than to myself, for I am somewhat unpredictable, given to long fits of speech and jollity when pleased but otherwise rather moody, while Andrés is cheerful by nature, I think, and, though talkative, very gentle and soft-spoken. The gentle quality of his voice, in fact, is one of the first things one notices about him. He is a very sympathetic man, in the Spanish sense of *muy simpático*.

Andrés's grandfather was a national hero of the Chilean War, from 1879 to 1883, and a former President of Peru; his cousin, Raoul Porras, is now Foreign Minister. Both Andrés and his wife are descended from Spanish and Inca nobility, and he is intensely proud of this; though he gets on well with everyone and prefers humble people to his own sort as a matter of taste, he is very conscious of his background and quickly establishes his identity with anyone who might not recognize who he is. If he is gentle, he is also quick-tempered; in Cuzco the other evening, jostled by a man in the hotel, he climaxed an exchange of views by announcing his identity. The other man, who clearly felt that he himself was the victim of the jostling, expressed indifference, at which point Andrés jostled him smartly once again. I was forced to seize my companion from behind and turn him away, in order to prevent bloodshed. Andrés is small but thick and powerful, an ex-boxer who once defeated a Peruvian champion, an ex-governor of the wild jungle state of Madre de Dios who was fond of emphasizing his points by discharging his revolver—the revolver I carry with me—within the confines of his office.

Cruz did not appear during the day, nor is there much hope that he will come tomorrow. Every man on the hacienda has a different concept of the country and its distances—not one has ventured even as far as the Pongo de Mainique—but all agree that Cruz has not allowed himself sufficient time to navigate the river, much less the Pongo, at this time of year.

We are occupying an open shed lent to us through the courtesy of the *patrón*, Señor Abraham Marquez; the room faces out on stone terraces used for drying coffee beans. Beyond, among the huts of the Quechua laborers, wander cattle, pigs, chickens, dogs, and ducks. There are also peacocks, and two of these birds are perched on the arm of a huge wooden cross which stands at the corner of the terracing.

In the afternoon the tropic rains came crashing, and the Indians scuttled to gather in the drying beans. Afterward the place stewed in the sweet odor of pig and chicken dung, and of the surrounding *selva cerca*, or near-jungle. Andrés is still optimistic that César will appear this evening, while I am already regarding covetously the heaps of coffee beans in the adjoining shed: these would make an excellent place to lay our bed rolls. But Gregorio, Marquez's suave *administrador*, has conjured up two slat beds and two mattresses, and we are to sleep in comparative style. At six it is already dark, and as these river haciendas—even a very stylish one like this—have none of the ordinary comforts like electricity, there is little to do by eight o'clock but go to bed. Outside, a rooster crows half-heartedly, and the air is filled with the ominous rush of the Black Drunken River.

April 11. Lugarte's.

Still no Cruz. We have now decided to make our way downriver as far as we can, in the hope of meeting Cruz en route. Marquez himself may be going in a day or two, for he has another holding at Siraiola (place names on the Urubamba refer not to settlements, as there are none, but to the confluence of a tributary river), but meanwhile we will try to obtain a *canoa* or balsa raft at one of the small haciendas on this upper stretch of the river.

Early this morning we set off in a truck with a group of Quechuas bound for Quillabamba; the truck left us at an arroyo above El Encuentro where one can cross the river in a sort of crate hauled on a cable. On the far side another road proceeds downriver for a few miles, and Gregorio assured us that a truck would be available to take us to the hacienda of a Señor Lugarte.

On the far side of the river stood two trucks, both of them broken down. We have been here now for about five hours, in company with peons more patient than ourselves, who would wait here until doomsday without complaint. One little boy of about ten is all swollen like a tick from malnutrition; he cannot walk, and his family has seated him in the hot sun, rather inexplicably, since they themselves have sought shelter in the shade. The boy has a little cup of filthy water which he keeps slopping on his swollen feet; struggling to extricate himself from his hot rags, he whines in pain. A man refills the cup for him, and later I do the same, but the family pays no attention to any of us; they squat in the shade, dull as stones with their blank yellow eyes.

At noon we recrossed the river and obtained a squalid meal in a local hut. In the hour we waited for the meal—a kind of bean stew with fried plantains and the inevitable yuca— Andrés consumed eight or nine oranges from the piles lying around on the mud floor. He kept reaching for more, less out of hunger than out of impatience and frustration about our journey, and as, under trying circumstances, the food habits of one's traveling companion can become a crucial source of annoyance, I tried, not entirely successfully, to keep his addiction from irritating me.

In mid-afternoon, convinced that no truck would necessarily appear, and anxious that Lugarte know our whereabouts should Cruz appear, or should Marquez decide to go downriver,

I set off on foot, accompanied by a small boy carrying a chicken. Andrés remained behind to guard the *equipaje*.

The walk down the valley was pleasant enough. *Loritos*, or parakeets, hurried in all directions, and the river banks swarmed with swallows, anis, river orioles, and other small birds unknown to me. We came on two dead snakes, one a sort of green racer, very pale—*culebra chicotillo*—and the other brown and large, bright-yellow-bellied. Neither was poisonous. The boy knew the names of all the trees, though he could not spell them; there was the *leche-leche* (literally, "milk-milk": my small companion fetched one a fierce whack with my machete, and a white fluid sprang forth), the red-trunked *sacahuinta*, the pale *ohe*, and the *palo santo*, or "holy tree" with its great gleaming leaves and infestation of biting ants. As usual, the ants were numerous and varied; we inspected two large ground species, a leaf-cutter with a broad head known in Quechua as *cuki*, denoting "mother-in-law," and another one, black, marching in long files, which the boy called *chaco*. He was awed by the *chaco*, saying, "This one attacks anything, *anything*, and kills it." I presume this is the famous army ant.

We were now well below the *encuentro* and could see in the distance three high cascades of great beauty, one below the other, at the foot of which, the boy said, lay the hacienda of Lugarte. We stopped to drink at a pretty stream and once picked and sucked a few red coffee beans from trees along the road. The distance to Lugarte's was said to be ten kilometers, or about seven and a half miles, but at dark we still had not got there. After a time we passed the hut of the boy's family, and a still smaller boy came out of it and joined us. He brought his brother a machete of his own length, which increased my guide's confidence enormously. Nevertheless, we had no light, and there were some spooky sounds abroad, including the echoing tom-tom of the giant frogs and the squawks of marsh birds. The older boy spoke ominously of the dangerous creatures of the night, including the jaguar, *el tigre*, and the large venomous snakes;

both boys were barefoot, and I must say I admired their *sang-froid*. The little boy would run ahead, and his high voice would come floating back to us, wistful and regular as a bird call: "Look, look, what's that? . . . No, it's nothing. . . . Look, look, what's that? . . . No, it's nothing. . . ." But after a while the suspense became too much for him, and he fell into line behind us. Here and there a dark lump would stir softly on the pale path ahead, and, a description in *Green Hell* of a huge tarantula seen under similar circumstances having come to mind, the first lump gave me quite a start. But apparently I am not fated for the horrors which befall my confederates. My serpents are not only non-poisonous but dead, and the evil-looking lumps on the night roads are harmless frogs.

It was nearly seven when we took a side path through the trees and came out at last at the edge of the mud yard of the hacienda. A single dim light was burning on the stoop. "*La hacienda*," my guide whispered, and before I could thank them properly the two children darted back into the forest.

On the porch sat a solitary man in jack boots, and an enormous boar—truly a monster, larger than a pony—stood stock still at the foot of the steps, the light reflecting from each bristle. Neither man nor pig took any notice of me. I approached the steps. I had walked at least ten miles and was dry and tired.

"Señor Lugarte?" I said.

"No," the man said. With the wan light and bleak mud, the silent man and the giant pig, the whole scene seemed theatrical, full of evil portent. But after a moment the man stood up politely and invited me to join him on the porch. We went through the usual elaborate courtesies of these countries, at the conclusion of which I wondered aloud if the hacienda truck might not be rented, to go and fetch Andrés. The truck, he said, was broken down. He then wondered aloud where I imagined I was going on the river and, when I told him, smiled unpleasantly. He was bald and smooth-faced, intelligent-looking, and his smile was chilling. He told me he had a hacienda of his own farther downstream. "You know," he began, "that even in the dry season the rapids at Sirialo, not to speak of the Pongo, are no joke. This is not the dry season, señor, and I must tell you that what you wish to do is very dangerous. I came myself past the *tumbos* of Sirialo today on the mule trail, and they are frightening—appalling." He smiled, and I did not smile back. He shrugged his shoulders. "In any case," he concluded in a manner which dismissed the whole subject as absurd, "your man Cruz could never make it up that river."

Señor Lugarte appeared out of the darkness, a small bewildered man who peered at me suspiciously. He could not seem to absorb the card of introduction I had brought from Señor Porras Cáceres: either he did not recognize the name or he was unable to read at all. He agreed unhappily that the *río* was very dangerous at the moment—*muy bravo, muy feo*—and was the highest, for the season, that he could ever remember. (Probably this is true: the floods this February on the Urubamba watershed washed away *chacras* that had stood for years, and all but destroyed an Indian mission at Camisea. In one bad night the river at Timpia rose thirty feet.) The two men decided that the river was unnavigable.

Though every other piece of information we had received had so far proved to be questionable or mistaken, I found this report extremely discouraging. If one could believe what one heard, one could act accordingly, but the absence of good information and the resultant uncertainty, in company with the unquestionable fact that César had failed to appear, were beginning to eat at my morale. Lugarte's Indian woman now appeared and served us a dismal supper—rice and yuca, garnished with a piece of meat so strange and foul that, try as I might, I could not get it down. The three took baleful notice of my defection. The radio was blaring senselessly (in South America radios are always played for all they're worth, and at full volume), and outside the musky yellow light in which we ate, the monster pig, still rooted to the spot, grunted spasmodically.

Señora Lugarte, if that is who this defeated woman was, was kind enough to give me a bed in a large loft with the smiling man, who was also a transient: a night's lodging, on the rivers, is offered to strangers as a matter of course. The sheet on the bed had seen a lot of service since last washed, but I had no sleeping bag with me and was glad to have it. The great part of the loft was devoted to drying coca, and the leaves gave off a sweet, reassuring smell, not unlike alfalfa. My companion, who still seemed to be smiling, had an Indian muleteer and servant; the servant slept, appropriately, I thought, on the floor beneath the foot of his master's bed.

April 12. Downriver.

A peon who came this morning from the arroyo said that Marquez intends to go downriver today; he must pass this way, as his *canoa* is located below Lugarte's. Therefore, he will have to pass Andrés, and I decided to await them here, rather than walk the ten miles back to no good purpose.

In the early hours I went out along the road, taking note of some unremarkable birds—doves, river orioles (known locally as *pustes*), parrots, anis, and finches, including a lovely species with a breast like deep red velvet. A rail squawked like a harassed chicken in a marsh made where the river had overflowed its banks, and a hawk screamed from the top of a tall white tree. The spiders and insects, however, are most interesting, even to a person like myself who has always preferred to disregard them wherever possible: one spider, gold-tipped and built like a spiny crab, is truly demonic. Then there are lavender dragonflies, the color of which is almost exactly duplicated in the flower-like leaf of a small tree. And the *mariposas* flutter and pose in every conceivable combination of pastels, from tiny violets and green-and-oranges to the huge cobalt-and-blacks and the rich blue morphos—Matisse colors, by and large, arranged strikingly, and sometimes with a flickering *trompe-l'œil* effect, on a jet black base. The narrow-winged helicon butterflies of this upper region of the Urubamba are more astonishing in their variety and colors than any I have seen in South America, or anywhere else, for that matter. (H. W. Bates observed 700 species of butterfly within an hour's walk of Belém, as opposed to 390 in all of Europe.)

In mid-morning Andrés appeared, but no Marquez. We left our equipment at some peon huts at the end of the road, a few miles below Lugarte's, and rode back with the truck to the arroyo; our idea was to return to Black Drunken River and find out Marquez's plan, as nobody else was the least interested in taking us farther downriver. I told Andrés of the discouraging reports I had received, but Andrés is a veteran of the great rapids on the Huallaga River, farther north, and believes these people exaggerate out of ignorance and fear. At the arroyo we met Marquez, Gregorio, and four peons coming the other way; we returned with them to the end of the road and prepared the canoe for departure.

To reach the canoe we had to descend a steep forested slope, carrying a 30-horsepower outboard motor, gas, tools, food, some bales of wire, general supplies for the hacienda at Sirialo, and our own rubber sacks. A path was cut through with machetes, and I am relieved to report that, during the course of this operation, I contrived to tread upon a snake. I say "relieved" because, to date, my experience has been so puny compared to that of other writers. Since the snake episode may be as close as I shall come to their experience, I may as well recount it in all its harrowing detail: I stepped on this snake despite the fact that two peons had already passed just in front of me, and I can't deny that it gave me quite a start, writhing up over a decaying log in the damp brown shadows. The Indian behind me said, "Culebra!" and the one in front turned quickly around and halved the creature with his machete. The snake was brown with yellow bands and a fat gray head, and a post mortem proved it to be harmless (or at least it was not a pit viper—it may have been one of the obscure rear-fanged species). It was at least sixteen inches long.

Marquez's *canoa* is typical of the rivers, big and deep and black, and hewn from a single log; incongruous in the stern, his outboard motor, with its dirty gasoline line and general air of sludgy incompetence, is typical also. It was not the machine for a leaky, overloaded *canoa*—in addition to the cargo, we were ten men and a boy—in a swift mountain river. But Don Abraham Marquez is a spirited young man and consigned us without further ado to the torrent; we moved upstream a few yards in an eddy until, gaining speed, we moved offshore on the eddy's curl, swung violently around, and started off down the Urubamba.

Almost immediately the motor stalled, just in the waves of the first river bend or *vuelta*, and a good deal of water slopped in. The boy, Ascensión, a beautiful child of twelve or so with an infectious laugh, was wide-eyed with alarm. "Are you afraid?" he asked me. I said that I wasn't yet, though I might be any minute, and he managed to smile.

The river varies from about forty to one hundred yards across with a current which, even in the wider reaches, must exceed eight knots; in the rapids and in the deep-water swirls of the bends it is markedly more swift. The motor is used only to steer or to try to gain the bank, and the latter recourse was attempted a minute later, when the second small rapid brought about a second important ingestion of cold water. The canoe was plainly top-heavy, owing to the fact that the excess crew were piled on top of the cargo; when we gained the shore at last, the heavier items of cargo were deposited on the bank, with Ascensión to guard them. Another of Marquez's peons was taking some mules down the jungle trail to Sirialo and would take Ascensión and the jettisoned gear along.

We took to the river once again. The canoe rode better now, but Andrés and I, sitting on its floor in the forward section, were several times up to our waists in water and spent most of the afternoon bailing. I wasn't happy about this, especially since we had yet to strike a true *mal paso*, as the danger points on the river's course are known; the river was swift, and turbulent at the bends, but it should not have presented a severe problem for a good canoe and good *bogas*, or boatmen. Unhappily, we had neither. Marquez admitted this himself a little later, when we had made camp for the night. He was amused by the inexperience of his men, some of whom had stood up and leaped around in the precarious craft at the first sign of trouble; in the frequent intervals when the motor was not working, those entrusted with the paddles had done everything in their power, or so it seemed, to keep the canoe broadside to the current.

I asked Marquez how many of the men had had experience on the river.

"Not one," he said and grinned at the hugeness of this joke. "Not a single one."

April 13. Sirialo.

Last night we camped on a broad river beach of gray sand where the white water of a tributary stream roared into the Urubamba. I went to sleep to the rush of the river, with only the thip-thip of hunting bats between me and Orion; we had reached the wild montaña and were well on our way. In the morning we would reach the Coribene and a village of Machiguengas presided over by a Dominican priest, Padre Giordia; this priest knew the river well and would lend us a *canoa* or balsa raft, with Machiguenga *bogas*, for the journey to the Pongo and perhaps farther. Furthermore, Padre Giordia had a radio and could advise the several missions in the hundreds of miles between this point and Atalaya that we were on our way downriver. They would notify César Cruz, wherever he was, to come to meet us.

But at four in the morning the bright stars disappeared and the rain began to fall. At five we huddled miserably in a steady downpour. The peons got a fire going, and we had a breakfast of lemon juice and hot water mixed with a kind of fine-powdered farina made of yuca and beans. By six we were on the river again, in a dim light, with water coming at us from every direction—from the air, over the bows, and through the bottom. A dull fear joined the farina in the pit of my stomach, for capsizing or foundering in this current would be no joke at all, especially when one was trying to protect camera, binoculars, notes, and other fragile essentials of the journey. Once again the problem presented by the river was far less serious than that offered by the crew. The spectacle of their cheerful and noisy incompetence, which threatened to drown the lot of us at any moment, was especially frustrating to someone like myself, who has had a certain experience of small boats: I positively itched to fire orders.

We passed down the empty, raining river without undue incident, however, having to repair to the bank but twice before reaching the Coribene mission; a solitary bigua cormorant perched on the snag of a drowned tree was the only living creature I observed, though one of the crew glimpsed a large *shushupe*, as the dread bushmaster is known, on a steep bank by the water's edge. Just above Coribene a group of peons at a small *chacra*, apparently surprised to see us, had cheered our doughty craft, but at the first huts of the Machiguengas, where the Indians on the pouring banks stood like statues in the rain, we were greeted with dismal silence.

At Coribene, Father Giordia succored us with coffee. He is an intelligent-looking man with white hair standing straight up on his head, and he voyages frequently on the river although he does not know how to swim. But he assured us that the river farther down, and especially the Pongo, was not navigable at this season, and that Cruz could not possibly come upriver, even if we were foolish enough to try to go down. Furthermore, his radio was out of order, so that he was unable to transmit any messages; the suspense as to César's whereabouts and intentions would continue.

I digested this spate of good news with some difficulty staring out across the thatch huts of the Machiguengas on the river slope below the mission; in the rain, they seemed to grow up out of the mud. The valley of the Coribene, climbing away into the mountains across the river, was obviously a lovely one, but I was in no mood to appreciate it.

The padre said that there was a foot trail through the jungle, two and a half days from Sirialo to the Pongo de Mainique; there, perhaps, Machiguengas attached to the hacienda of the lengendary Pereira could get us past the Pongo, and down to the next mission at Timpia, where Cruz might be waiting. But there was no trail of any sort from Timpia onward, and it was quite possible that Cruz had never come at all, or had come and gone. We asked again if we could not hire a few of the padre's expert Indians to take us on the river, and he said again that this would be impossible. At a loss for a solution, we rejoined Marquez and started off for Sirialo.

For, navigable or no, the river was navigated once again by Don Abraham Marquez and his merry men, this time with near-fatal consequences. The rough swirl at one of the final bends inspired some plain and fancy seamanship which left me gasping; even the indomitable Marquez exclaimed afterward, "That was an ugly one, hey, *señores*?" We careened to a landing in a canebrake, just short of a horrid pile of black rocks tumbled at the mouth of a thick, sulphurous stream; the black rocks formed the first real *mal paso* of the river and were therefore the point at which Marquez no longer considered the April river navigable. The canoe was hauled in among the rocks, and we forded the rush of yellow water, waist-deep, holding our gear on our shoulders. This was a bad moment, too, as my knees were still weak and shaking with cold and offered little or no control over my sneakered feet, which splayed wildly on the slippery rocks below;

one false move, I thought, and I would slip beneath the yellow waves, to be swept onward to the Pongo and points north. I froze momentarily, and Andrés, who chatters at these nervous moments—I tend to remain silent and morbid—sensed my alarm. His own assurance and encouragement stung me forward like a goad, and I came plunging out at last on the far side.

The hacienda at Sirialo is typical of these small river holdings: an adobe house, thatch huts for the peons, mud, chickens, pigs, a donkey or two, coffee and cacao trees struggling up out of the choking flora, mud, insects, a damp heat of imminent rain, more mud. The jungle rises up behind, looming forward as if ever on the point of obliterating man's intrusion in a wild maelstrom of green. The adobe hut itself had been invaded by jungle weeds, and on this dark day its half-built shell littered with boards and burlap seemed particularly uninviting. We stood dully, our clothes soaked and muddy, with nothing dry to change into, while the hacienda manager expressed his conviction that the foot trail to the Pongo gave out entirely a few kilometers below Sirialo. Marquez himself, exhausted and nervous from the passage down the river, had taken to the manager's bed. Left to ourselves, Andrés and I contemplated the insects and the mud, which was steaming now that the rain had stopped; our state of mind was so abysmal that it is difficult to describe without inducing it all over again, right here and now.

As of this evening, this is our situation: we are less than a day's canoe travel downriver, but returning upstream by the trail is a matter of three days, and any further progress would only increase the discrepancy. We are faced with the choice of an expensive retreat of at least ten days, to Atalaya via Quillabamba, Cuzco, Lima, and Pucallpa, or a desperate plunge down a river said to be unnavigable at this season. *Canoas* and balsas are apparently unavailable, even if a crew could be found willing to man them; the extent of the foot trail is a matter of general ignorance and dispute, though everyone, from the smiling man at Lugarte's to Marquez's man at Sirialo, agrees that it is *bruto*

—extremely tortuous. Even should we reach the Pongo and get past it, there is no assurance that Cruz will be waiting on the other side, or even at Timpia, some thirty miles beyond, and no means of advising him to do so. And in the hundreds of miles of wilderness between Timpia and Atalaya there is no trail of any kind.

The sensible course is a retreat. But the idea sticks painfully in our craws: the trip here has been made in such high hopes, and the return seems arduous and humiliating. We discussed alternatives this morning. We were spreading our dank gear and soaked sleeping bags on the muddy rocks and stumps when I suggested to Andrés that we might have to go back.

"I know," Andrés said almost gratefully. "I've been thinking the same thing."

He was grateful, not for the chance of retreat, of course, but because I'd finally voiced our mutual doubts; I was grateful in turn that he had not concealed his own misgivings under cover of mine. A smaller man might have said, Oh, do you think so? as if the possibility of turning back had never occurred to him. In any case, the moment the misgivings had been voiced, our morale rose again, and the idea of retreat appeared intolerable—as I have indicated elsewhere, both Andrés and myself tend to be pigheaded. This afternoon we made our way through the jungle to the neighboring hacienda, where a young man named Rosell heard us out with an indulgent smile: too many people had drowned just below his place, at Sirialo Falls—why, a bishop had died there only the year before—for him to consider a descent of the river at this season. Machiguengas might make it, he said, on a strong balsa: we should return to Coribene by the trail and prevail upon Padre Giordia to help us. As for the trail itself, it was impassable for mules beyond the Sirialo River, and human bearers were impossible to find.

But at supper Marquez was very discouraging about our chances at Coribene; he did not think that Giordia would risk his Machiguengas at this time of year, even if the Indians themselves were willing. It occurred to me in desperation that if I could prevail upon Andrés to dispense with some of his gear—thus dispensing with the need for mules, or for more than one or two peons—we could attempt a fast trip to the Pongo on foot, in the hope that we might obtain help from the Pereiras, or even pick up a balsa on the way. To my surprise (for he is over sixty, after all), Andrés immediately agreed: we would lay out our gear in the first light of the morning and pare our equipment to the bone. Whatever we left could return upriver with Marquez, to be sent eventually to Estelle León de Peralta in Cuzco. Far from being tempted to return ourselves, we were now repelled by the idea of wasting two more days in what would almost surely be a vain effort to get assistance from Padre Giordia; we planned to set off downriver on the trail as soon as we could get organized in the morning.

April 14. Rodríguez.

I slept happily last night on top of a bin of cacao beans, having first searched the shed with a flashlight for snakes, tarantulas, and scorpions. When I scrambled down at dawn, Andrés was already at work on his equipment but had managed to reduce his five large bags of gear by only one. He also planned to leave behind his sleeping bag, keeping only his poncho and a piece of canvas; by sacrificing the sleeping bag he felt justified in keeping with him such luxuries as a portable radio and a quart bottle of eau de cologne.

Andrés is in love with his equipment, which has seen him through many an adventure, but over the years he has accumulated quite a lot of it. The dates of his various expeditions are scrawled all over the stock of his carbine and the inner brim of his broad frontier hat, and in this sense he clings, through his equipment, to the past. He is unquestionably a jungle man of experience and courage, but he is nevertheless the only such man I have ever come across who is willing to burden himself unnecessarily. Had Cruz met us with canoes, as planned, his equipment would have been welcome, but it was now crucial that we travel light. I reduced my own gear to one sack, two-thirds full, and a small knapsack, and placed them next to his pile by way of contrast; I then suggested as gently as my irritation would permit that the refreshment to be gained from a heavy radio and a quart of eau de cologne would not begin to compensate for the possible loss of sleep he was risking by leaving his bedroll behind.

Andrés is a man who is not at home on the defensive and dislikes criticism almost as much as I do. Therefore he was soon irritable himself. Nevertheless, he sliced a little of the fat out of his sacks, and meanwhile Marquez had located for us a Quechua, one Zacharias, who for twenty *soles*, plus a twelve-*sole* bottle of *pisco* to be used en route as fuel (or a total salary of approximately one dollar and fifteen cents) contracted to bear a truly enormous weight for one whole day downriver. The enormity of his travail—two large rubber duffel bags full of heavy gear, plus a sack of canned goods and other emergency food—cannot be imagined unless one keeps in mind the steep, muddy trails full of slippery and sliding rocks, the stream crossings, the insects and clinging thorns, the fierce heat in the open swamps, and the promise of the long walk back over what, in any other part of the world, could only be called an obstacle course.

Nonetheless, Zacharias rolled the sacks up in his *qquepina*, the cloth sling of the mountain Indians, and we hoisted it onto his bent back. He set off cheerfully, the *pisco* bottle snug against his side, a wad of coca in his cheek, and his small mongrel, Tarzan, at his heels. Having thanked Don Abraham Marquez for his many kindnesses and said good-by, we followed him. Andrés was truly a hard-looking character, with his broad hat and rawhide chin strap, his carbine slung on his shoulder, his machete and packs, and, on his belt, his canteen, drinking cup, sun glasses, bullet pouch, and two hunting knives; if I had not borrowed a third knife and the revolver, he would have worn these too. To

Andrés's annoyance, I carried the revolver in my pack, not only because its holster would catch on thorns and bushes as we went along but because I felt like a damn fool wearing it.

By nine the day was already very hot. A short distance below the hacienda we had to ford the Sirialo River, just above its confluence with the Urubamba. Zacharias plunged across the current, barefoot on the boulders; Andrés and I struggled through with a little more difficulty. The packs upset our sense of balance, and Andrés once slipped and fell, though he recovered himself before water could reach his camera. Halfway across we came to a rock island; the water beyond was too deep to traverse with the gear. But there was a small hut across the way, and its owner swirled over in his canoe to fetch us.

The banks of the Urubamba, above the Pongo de Mainique, are a series of steep ridges broken by mountain valleys; there is no trail along the river banks, since these are too precipitous, and therefore one must climb the ridges, plunge down into the valleys, and climb all over again immediately. From the top of the first ridge, we glimpsed the dread *tumbos* of the Sirialo, which lie below the *encuentro*; perhaps because we were on foot, and far above, there seemed to be nothing very alarming about them.

On theory, we were bound for the hacienda of one Rodríguez, a man, so it was said, who might be helpful; he was supposed to live four or five miles below the Sirialo and to have some Machiguengas working for him. But as the day wore on and the miles moved slowly past, there was no sign of the good Rodríguez. Zacharias, *pisco*-crazed, got farther and farther ahead, while Andrés slowly fell behind. Whenever we stopped to rest, I could see that he was suffering. Once, offered a swig of the Quechua's white lightning, he accepted gladly, which was quite uncharacteristic. I felt a pang of conscience and began to worry.

The day had become frightfully hot: we were soaked beneath our packs. Andrés put up no resistance when, toward midday, I relieved him of his carbine. His pants were ripped and falling away at the knee, and though he did not complain, his face was gray. Shortly thereafter we came to the hut of a Rodríguez, though not the man we sought: an old woman there gave us lemon and water, and Andrés gulped at it like a man dying of thirst. He tried to pour some into his canteen, and his hand shook so that he slopped most of it onto the ground. His self-control was precarious, and for the first time since I had known him he actually looked his age.

By this time I was desperately concerned. I felt bad that I had taken him at his own estimate of his endurance, had encouraged him in his courageous decision not to let me continue by myself. He admitted now that he had felt a twinge of pain in his heart, and I got to the point where I had to consider what I would do should his heart give out. There would be no possibility of getting a body out of this valley to Quillabamba in this heat; he would have to be buried in the jungle.

But Andrés knew that we had gone too far now to turn back; retreating would mean a four-day walk, and he was not up to it. He felt that his trouble had stemmed from the straps on his pack which, in combination with the steep terrain, had made his breathing difficult. We decided that he was not to carry anything when walking, and that we would move more slowly. The woman gave us some fried eggs and bananas, and he felt better; afterward we rested in the hut until the heat had eased a little. A second peon was located who took over Andrés's gear and part of mine, and as it was only two hours to the right Rodríguez, we decided to move on, as we could accomplish nothing where we were.

At dusk we came out on the bank opposite the Rodríguez huts; their owner came across for us in his canoe. In this swift current the technique is to lead the canoe far upstream along the bank, make a break for the other side, and try to land as little below the target point as possible. Rodriguez and the boy in the bow were skillful, but even so they landed well below us and had to inch upstream along the bank.

Señor Rodríguez, a small dark suspicious man who later proved quite hospitable, denied any knowledge of available canoes or balsas with a vehemence suggesting that he felt himself falsely accused; he further denied that he harbored Machiguengas, much less the slightest inclination to take us anywhere on the river. Like everyone else, he spoke optimistically of hopeful prospects only a few miles farther down; if necessary, he swore, we could make it overland to the Pereira holdings in two days.

I have the impression that we make these people nervous, arriving armed as we do, on a mission so senseless as to make them suspect that it is actually something nefarious; they get our hopes up with their optimistic tales simply to get rid of us. It also appears that most of these people who have ventured down a short distance on the Urubamba are people of the sierra rather than the jungle. They fear the river, as Andrés points out, and know nothing about it, not even the actual distance to the next hacienda below. Beyond Rodríguez there are two or three small holdings; from the last of these to the Pongo de Mainique is a vast wilderness controlled by the Pereiras. Rodríguez could tell us this much, but he felt certain that we could obtain a balsa before we reached the Pereira country. He was not very convincing, and privately I felt that we faced the possibility of a three- or four-day march, with nothing we could count on at the end of it.

April 15. Ardiles.

Last night I slept badly on a hard cane mat laid on the mud, beset by chicken lice, small flies, and mosquitoes: Andrés, who had no sleeping bag, was given a kind of mattress, an ironic reward, I thought, for his improvidence, but one which came at a fortunate time, as he needed all the rest he could get. I awoke this morning rather low in my mind and taped a growing boot chafe on my ankle.

Our faithful Zacharias and his valiant Tarzan had departed in the early hours, bearing with them, as it turned out, the greater part of our emergency rations. Tired before we started, we soon set off ourselves, accompanied by two fresh bearers lent us by Rodríguez, and bound for the hacienda of César Lugarte—no relation, it was said, of the César Lugarte upriver. This Lugarte lived "three hours away, *señores*, walking slowly."

We reached our destination early in the afternoon. The march had required five or six hours over a path infinitely more tortuous than that of the previous day; once we paused to fire the .44 in vain at a *pava*, or guan, of which we saw several during the morning. Our feet were giving out, and we slumped exhausted on the bank while Lugarte peons on the opposite shore waved us back upstream; they were trying to indicate that they had no canoe and that we should cross at a point farther up where, an hour previously, we had been waved downstream. This latter intelligence, of course, was impossible to convey across the roar of the river, and so we simply slumped there, at a loss; we refused to retrace our steps over that terrible trail, for reasons which were becoming psychological as well as physical.

At last two young men came across the river on a small balsa to talk to us. One of them, called Ardiles, claimed to have a larger balsa farther downriver; to our surprise and pleasure, he agreed to take us down to the Pereiras'. He departed immediately on the trail upstream, to return in less than an hour with a *canoa*, in which he transported us to the Lugarte clearing across the way. One of our bearers, Alejandro, came along with us; he had decided to run away from Señor Rodriguez. In return for his services, we agreed to see to it that he got eventually to Lima.

Tomorrow we walk again, the usual "*cuatro o cinco kiló-metros, señores, nada más,*" but at the end of this walk, whatever its distance, there is at least a balsa. Ardiles claims that he is willing to take us into the jaws of the Pongo itself, and Andrés, who would now willingly risk his life rather than walk even one mile farther on this jungle trail, is all for it. (He may feel, of course, that walking is more dangerous for him, for his heart, than the Pongo could possibly be, and after yesterday I can scarcely blame him.) Though he feels better today, his legs are swelling badly, and he will soon reach the point where courage will not be enough.

We still have a few hours of daylight, and I have taken a bath in the river and washed out both sets of clothes. I am sitting now in the mud yard, observed by the silent Indian peons; their huts, surrounding us, are characteristic of the Machiguengas, high-peaked and closely made, with mud floor, thatch roof, and a kind of straw wall from floor to chin level. Chickens and dogs pick through the huts, and swarms of guinea pigs.

On both sides the mountain ridges hem us in, as if we were trapped in some sort of chute. And of course we are, for there is no turning back: we will soon have the Pereiras and the Pongo to deal with, and after that the open jungle, the unknown.

Of the Pongo de Mainique we have had only dark reports, and Ardiles himself, despite his avowed willingness to take us through it, speaks excitedly of enormous waves and falls and whirlpools, or *remolinos*. As for the Pereiras, they are as much a legend in the *montaña* as they were in the era of Mrs. Cox, and the truth is hard to come by. This much is probably fact: the patriarch, Fidel Pereira, is the mestizo, or half-caste, son of a Portuguese slaver and a Machiguenga woman. He was sent to the university in Cuzco, where he was a brilliant student, and was studying to be a lawyer. But during this period, for reasons disputed, he murdered his father and, fearing reprisal or the law, or both, he fled back into the upper Urubamba. There, in a wilderness to which he held no title, he has established a huge domain, and has gained control of virtually all of his mother's people above the Pongo, even the wild Machiguengas of the tributary rivers. The law has not cared to follow Pereira into Pangoa, as his home grounds are known, and Pereira himself, a single visit to Quillabamba excepted, has not left the jungle in nearly forty years. Some of his holdings he has parceled out among three sons, and there are several other children recognized as well. It is said on the upper Urubamba that his children by Machiguenga women number more than fifty, and that after his return from Cuzco he committed many other murders among his people, but these reports are as doubtful as the one that attests that the old man maintains potency to this day with a secret potion made of monkey milk.

April 16. Casireni.

Rudi Ardiles is a well-made young man with no front teeth and a thin mustache; under the circumstances, the mustache cannot be said to do very much for his appearance. Lugarte's *capitaz*—Lugarte himself is absent—dislikes Ardiles and says he is a liar of sorts and that on no account should we risk our lives by going with him through the Pongo; while it is hard to put one's finger on the liars in these parts, it must be said that Ardiles has a wild and shifty eye.

He appeared in mid-morning, and we set off immediately into the jungle. Toward noon we arrived at the clearing of our second *boga*-to-be; after a short argument this man was conscripted, and we celebrated the agreement over a bowl of *caldito*, the watery jungle soup in which, from time to time, one comes upon a piece of chicken. In the yard before us a large butterfly hunched along the ground, black as a burned cinder; it raised its wings suddenly, and the undersides were vivid yellow.

In a few minutes we were off again, Ardiles and the new man, Julio, forging ahead up a very steep jungle trail—at one point that afternoon the river was more than a mile below. Since Julio was, if anything, even less clean-cut in appearance than Ardiles, and since they had with them a good part of our gear, I attempted to keep up with them. It was impossible: the endurance of these people is subhuman. I got far ahead of Andrés and our faithful Alejandro, however, and for the next two hours, the difficult ascents and occasional cliff-hanging excepted, enjoyed myself very much. It was a sunny afternoon and, while humid, not uncomfortable in the shade, and I was able to absorb the atmosphere of mountain jungle as I went. As we descend the river the palms increase in variety and number— there are said to be over one hundred species of palms in the Peruvian jungles alone—and in one of these the ten to twelve thorny roots merge to form the trunk at least fifteen feet above the ground. There is also a tree with roots crimson in color; these roots are frequently exposed along the trail. The dominant tree, however, is still the tall white *leche-leche*.

There were new bird calls and many butterflies, a huge emerald and mauve cricket, and the largest black ant I have yet seen: this beast, an inch long, looked capable of killing one outright. The flowers, more scattered now, are nonetheless numerous and pretty: there is a violet-like species, and a blue-flowered vine, and a lovely orange bell flower. Some of the epiphytes and parasitic plants are starting to appear—one has clusters of tomato-colored berries. At the end of the trail, on the cliff overlooking the river, I came on a stone inscribed with a curious design, like a posed spider. Though not large, it was too heavy to add to our sacks, and I left it behind with regret.

The trail ended in the papaya grove of a Señor Olarte, presently away in Quillabamba; I was offered a papaya and a lemon by a peon and ate them greedily. Ardiles and Julio, with a boy from the Olarte hacienda, were repairing the promised balsa and have cut three new logs for it. The logs are trunks of the balsa tree, a species common on these upper rivers and the one from which the very light wood of children's model airplanes and other toys is derived: the trees are stripped of their green bark and lashed into place with liana vines. The machete is the only tool used by these people to construct what can be a very large and able craft. Ours is somewhat less than that, having a certain fly-by-night air about it: the poles of a first-class balsa are pegged together with hardwood spikes, cut usually from the black cortex of the chonta palm, while our poles are unpegged. Julio, in fact, made no secret of his contempt for our craft, which seems to me a rather unhealthy attitude.

I photographed the building process—the first photographs I have taken in some days, as the camera has been tied into a rubber bag while traveling, because of the frequent stream and river crossings and the rain. Unlimbering it has been more trouble than I have cared to take, perhaps because I dislike carrying a camera: it seems to me that one misses a great deal of *seeing* and *feeling* through thinking of one's experience in terms of light and angle.

The photographic duties done, I washed myself in the river, which was cold and roiled. Then, sitting on a rock, I washed out my socks and shirt, both in a state of dire emergency. After this, naked in the sun, I devoured a second papaya I had brought along. I rarely exult over food, which does not fascinate me unduly, but the excellence of this papaya can scarcely be appreciated by anyone who has not subsisted for a week on the white mealiness of boiled yuca.

When my shirt was dry I visited the balsa-builders: they were not finished, and we decided to put off our departure until morning. I returned to the hacienda, climbing up through large banana groves. There Andrés and Alejandro had arrived at last, and both of them were prostrate. I gathered that Andrés had had a bad time of it on the trail, and feel very guilty about it. Poor Andrés expected a calm journey by canoe, surrounded by all his beloved gear, and instead he has spent the last three days stumbling up and down these steep jungle valleys, with nothing certain at the end of it but another dirt floor and more yuca. His clothes are torn and his legs are swollen, and he carries with him a secret dread about his heart. But he scarcely complains, and, as the saying goes, I hope I am half the man he is when I reach his age.

We have now marched from above the Sirialo to well below the Casireni, a negligible distance on the river but a formidable route overland, burdened with gear. Actually we have walked little more than fifteen hours in the past three days, not counting delays and rests, but anyone willing to try this goat path in its present condition for five hours in the heat of a jungle day—anyone, that is, who is not of Quechua extraction and equipped with Quechua lungs, as all these mestizos appear to be —is welcome to do so, with my blessings. I can only say that Andrés Porras Cáceres, a very durable man, will not walk another step if he has to go through the Pongo de Mainique on a papaya rind.

It seems, at last, that our days on foot are over. I am tired myself, and my impressions of our route are blurred, for most of the time, trudging and clambering and sliding onward, I stared at the ground in order to find my footing. But there were some fine moments as well as painful ones—the cold water drunk face down in white mountain streams, the mysterious cries and bird calls, the light-dappled forest stretched high above the roaring river, the scarlet macaws—*bolivars* or *papagayos*— which followed us with their raucous screeches, the long files of leaf-cutting ants swaying along with their burdens, like an end-less thin green snake, the perched wood butterflies with the strange "eye" on the underside of their lifted wings, and the "eyes" themselves, staring owlishly from the jungle shadows. These details I shall remember longer than the muddy hillsides, the dry, rasping canebrakes, the palm thickets and thorns, the fierce humidity.

April 17. Pangoa.

In regard to weather, we have had bad luck on the river. Today it is raining hard again—it has rained hard at least once every day—and the brown river with its dark, dense green walls is cheerless. We shoved the raft into the current about 7 a.m., and at 7:02 were thrashing toward the bank again, perilously awash; we needed at least two more balsa poles, and Rudi and Julio went into the forest to cut and strip them.

By nine we were off again into the rain, and immediately the river seized us up and bore us remorselessly toward our first emergency, at a *mal paso* which the Machiguengas call Vacanique, or Cattle Drowning Place: we came over a shallow fall into a strong whirlpool, or *remolino*, and Ardiles's uncapsizable craft for a few horrid moments rode at a forty-five-degree angle. In the process waves smashed across the raft and bore away the largest of our sacks. The sack floated, and we retrieved it farther down, only to note for the first time that it had two capacious holes in it, in addition to my sleeping bag.

Bacanique was the worst passage of the day, though several others were a little tight. Had the sun been shining, the whole business might have been quite exhilarating, but the rain poured down and a cold wind was blowing up the valley, and the wildlife which might have stimulated us consisted of one orange serpent, drowned and belly-up in the swollen river. We paddled furiously all morning, not only to avoid the falls, or *tumbos*, and the *remolinos*, but to keep warm, for as a safety measure we were near-naked in our underpants. The raft was permanently awash, to a point above the ankles in the smooth stretches and above the navel—we were sitting—in the rapids. At midday the rain stopped at last, and shortly thereafter, exhausted by a *mal paso* called Quirimotini, or Place of the River Demon, we beached the raft on a gravel island and rested. A *pisco* bottle was produced, and a little water-logged yuca, and Julio supplied us with a big jawful of coca, the juices of which, when swallowed, produce a numb, pleasant sensation, a relief from both cold and hunger, and even a vague serenity of mind—one sees immediately why this plant is carried everywhere by the Quechuas, whose bleak existence might otherwise be insupportable. Our Alejandro is a Quechua, and the coca and *pisco* had a strong effect on him: manning one of the bow paddles when we took to the river once again, he failed to squat when we plunged into a rapid, swaying fearlessly until a shout brought him to his senses.

Just below Olarte's we had glimpsed two small haciendas: from that point onward we had traveled in Machiguenga country controlled by the Pereiras, though we had seen no sign of human habitation. Even the animals kept their distance, though after the rain had stopped, the birds began to move a little— we saw a few parrots and parakeets and a single flock of macaws. I questioned Ardiles about the trees, and he pointed out a hardwood he called *sandematico*, which he said was used commonly for *canoas*. Julio said that monkeys were common in these valleys—as a matter of fact, we ate one last night at Olarte's, an experience I don't care to repeat soon again—but we saw none, though we heard everywhere the small white *chito*, which sounds like a full-throated bird.

In a few hours on the river we had covered twice the distance made in all the past three days on foot.

In the early afternoon the hacienda of Fidel Pereira came into view, high up on a bank at a bend of the river. We wished to stop, but Ardiles, plainly uneasy, stalled around until the swift current had swept us irretrievably past. He repeated an earlier claim that the old man had become extremely difficult and kept an armed guard of Machiguengas to waylay trespassers, and said that we would be far better off in the hands of one of his sons, his own good friend Epifanio. Some Indians attached to Fidel Pereira came to the bank and watched us in silence until we disappeared around the bend.

Epifanio Pereira, a round-faced young man with a permanent vague smile and an air so innocent as to be rather disconcerting, greeted us cheerfully enough farther down the river at Pangoa; Pangoa, the monkey demon associated with the fogs on a nearby peak, is the name of the old man's former *chacra*, now worked by Epifanio. At the moment the hacienda consists of one very large high shed, open on all sides, under the eaves of which is a small loft in which Epifanio has his bed; below, there are a rough table and some bins of drying coffee, and around the edges the Indian fires. Spears, bows and arrows, tom-

toms, cane baskets, feather apparel, and other equipment of the Indians are strung from the cross beams, and there are, in addition, two small, low Indian palm-leaf huts. Two Indian women, an old squaw and a girl, were squatting over a fire before one of the huts, and two other girls were washing coffee beans in a log trough at the mouth of a small brook. Just after we arrived four men appeared out of the canebrake behind the hacienda and stood watching us with that implacable Indian silence; the women, on the other hand, would not look at us and kept their backs to us whenever possible. All of the Indians were dressed in the poncho-like *cushma*, a coarse cloth woven from wild cotton, with black, brown, and red stripes.

Ardiles had suggested that the friendship of Epifanio could be won by an offering of *pisco*, which is hard to come by in the jungle; we placed a half-bottle—we now have a single bottle left —at his disposal, and he drank it off, without apparent effect, almost immediately.

The sun came out in the middle of the afternoon, too late to dry anything; my poor saturated sleeping bag is all one man can carry, and I'm not quite sure where I'm going to lay my head. Not that I shall probably sleep very much in any case, for Andrés tells me I am subject to bodily harm. I have had a stupid dispute with Ardiles, at the end of which I told him that he was *sin vergüenza*: I should have known better, and I did, but I lost my temper. The expression, mild enough in translation—it means "without shame," or simply "shameless"—invariably produces an important reaction in Spanish countries, and especially, perhaps, in South America, in the wilder regions of which it is often more sensible to kill a man than to insult him. In any case, Ardiles feels mortally insulted and is openly plotting revenge.

Briefly, Ardiles, sensing our desperation, charged us a bandit's fee for his services; he excused it by saying that most of it would go toward paying two *bogas* for their dangerous work. If they did not receive very high salaries, they would not come.

But there was only one *boga*—actually, we needed three—and Andrés, Alejandro, and I did the work of the other. Therefore I suggested to Ardiles that the fee was a little high. He demanded the full fee, however, and since he has us by the throats, I had to pay it. But I also told him what I thought of him, to the dismay of Andrés, who was standing just behind him. "You've made a hell of a mess now," Andrés said to me in English; I can't recall ever having heard him swear before. Andrés was already seizing the arm of Ardiles, who was on the point of hurling the money to the ground; Andrés signaled to me to go away and let him handle it, and I am watching them now from the table. For the past two hours Andrés has not once let go of Ardiles's arm, and he has now got him to sit down on a log, down by the river. The Machiguengas and Epifanio (who is three-fourths Indian himself) are observing the whole business with a kind of wary calm, like watchful animals, and Epifanio is still smiling, if that expression of his can really be called a smile.

Andrés's heroic efforts have now brought about an uneasy truce, though Andrés himself is most unhappy about the present state of affairs. Ardiles has a code and pride of sorts, and it may be that the reason he is so angry is that he does not feel entirely right about his own position. Nevertheless, he is still talking wildly of revenge—quite seriously, according to Andrés. Ardiles is a Quechua mestizo who feels he has always been cheated and insulted by gringos—and his insistence on the word "gringo" was a factor in the dispute which caused me to lose my temper, though Andrés now assures me that the term applies to all fair-skinned people, not just Americans, and is not insulting in itself. Ardiles is anxious that I pay the penalty for all the gringos in his past. I'm not anxious to pay, of course. Andrés has warned me to keep my revolver under my head tonight, and I think I'll accept this advice, though I believe the whole thing will blow over. Somehow, Andrés has gotten the money into Ardiles's proud pocket, which is a big step forward. Andrés's position with Ardiles is that I do not speak Spanish well enough to realize what I am saying, which is probably true enough; also, I have contributed an apology to the cause. The apology was neither gracefully delivered nor graciously received, but, on theory, it permits Ardiles to have his pride and money too.

One reason Andrés is so worried is that the dispute occurred after Pereira had agreed to get us through the Pongo on a balsa. It now appears that Ardiles is Pereira's brother-in-law and could probably dissuade the latter from assisting us. Should Ardiles provoke a fight, we would be badly outnumbered; we cannot count on Alejandro, and our opponents, besides Pereira, Ardiles, and Julio, would include a number of Machiguengas, whose arrows, Mr. Jolly claims, can "bring down a hummingbird . . . at forty feet." But the alternative—Pereira's refusal, that is, to help us—wouldn't be much better, as we can go neither upriver nor down without his cooperation and, under the circumstances, would not be safe where we are even if we had enough to eat. Fortunately, however, Andrés has already suggested to Epifanio that he might be able to use his influence in Lima to help Epifanio obtain some sort of legitimate title to Pangoa, and as Epifanio already has the scent of our dwindling cash, he is, if anything, on our side, at least for the moment. We are all quite aware that he and his Indians could take our guns, money, and equipment by force, should they choose to do so, and possibly it is only the prospect of assistance with the land title which deters him. In any case, he is charging us the same high fee as Ardiles did, excusing this breach of his father's long tradition of hospitality with the confession that he owes so much money in Cuzco that he can no longer go there. We are taking the punishment lying down, and even smiling, for, as Andrés says, we have no choice in the matter and these people know it. Andrés is furious and swears that one day he will even the score.

Our dinner of banana soup went peacefully enough, and even Ardiles and myself managed to address each other in abrupt asides. Meanwhile, the Machiguengas have toasted my sleeping bag over their fire, a permanent installation centered between the burning ends of three large logs; the logs are inched forward as they dwindle. The Indians have relaxed somewhat, and some of them are giggling at our various eccentricities of dress and behavior; they are an open-faced and wide-mouthed lot, very appealing. One of their legends is that long ago their god took away their wisdom and cleverness because the child of this beneficent spirit, while entrusted to them, was swallowed by the river demon of the Pongo de Mainique. The wisdom was given to the whites, or gringos, who have put it to use in the manufacture of billboards and hydrogen bombs: one day, the Machiguengas hope, their god will relent, and their former cleverness will be restored to them, but for the moment they have resigned themselves to both ignorance and stupidity, a marvelous stroke of luck for the Pereiras and other *patrones* who have enslaved them.

Epifanio told us a number of Machiguenga legends and showed us a book of notes on the tribe that his father had compiled; a copy of these notes, which must be of great potential interest to ethnologists, is apparently in the hands of Padre Matamola in Quillabamba. Even Ardiles expressed interest, squatting next to Epifanio on a log bench, but the atmosphere is still strained. Later in the evening, when we lay down at last, Andrés had his carbine and his flashlight at his fingertips, and I kept the loaded revolver in my hand, beneath my head, though I took pains not to show it. There is a popular idea in South America that the British are frightened of cold steel, and in this regard I could easily be mistaken for an Englishman. I think that Andrés's idea of the difficulties is perhaps exaggerated, but I'd much, much rather be safe than sorry.

April 18. Pongo de Mainique.

The night passed without incident, and this morning the air had cleared to the extent that Epifanio took me on a guided tour of Pangoa; Ardiles came along, and so did Alejandro. We took one of the canoes downriver a short distance, to a point on the bank known as Sangianarinchi, or "painted stones"; there, on the smooth boulders by the river's edge, partly submerged at this time of year, are some extraordinary hieroglyphics and symbols of obscure origin, including a striking "dancing frog." *

Sangianarinchi is just below a former mission station of the *lingüísticos,* as the personnel of the Summer Institute of Linguistics are known throughout the jungles of Peru; this Protestant organization, as I have noted earlier, specializes in the transcription of the many Indian tongues into the written word and the translation of the Bible into Indian. The Pangoa station was run by a man named Snell, according to Epifanio. It has been abandoned for some time, for reasons which he did not make clear, and the jungle has reclaimed the clearing. The thatch roofs of the buildings are falling in, and the two rude crosses which still rise out of the growing tangle are precariously aslant, about to tumble.

At the hacienda, meanwhile, the Indians were assembling a balsa, using some logs already cut and dried as well as some green poles cut this morning; we returned in time to see two braves come sailing down the bank, clinging to slippery fresh poles gathered at a point upriver. These were soon notched and spiked and lashed together, and it occurs to me with rather a start that we are actually on the brink of "risking our lives," as Andrés remarked, unfortunately, I thought, in the Pongo de Mainique. But between risking his life and making his way back upstream on foot, Andrés would infinitely prefer the former, and though I am filled with a growing dread as we wait here, I must say I agree. One is through the Pongo, it is said, in fifteen minutes, though ideas on it vary so much that

* These drawings are not dissimilar to those found on rocks at the mouth of the Rio Branco in Brazil by Richard Spruce, a botanist who worked in the Amazon Valley at the same time as H. W. Bates, and whose text, like Bates's, remains a standard reference work a century later.

I wonder at times if anybody has ever been through it at all. Ardiles speaks loosely of waves twenty feet high, whereas Pereira claims that, in certain respects, the passage of the Pongo in the rainy season is less dangerous than in the dry season, when people ordinarily try it: his theory is that some of the dangerous rocks are covered over. I hope he is right, but I would have more faith in what he says if he were going to accompany us.

Whatever the truth of the matter, we are casting off at midday. I'm not at all sure we know all we should, and would feel much happier with a life-preserver. I asked Epifanio if he thought we would make it to the mission at Timpia before nightfall. He and Ardiles grinned at each other in a way I disliked very much, and Pereira said, "Maybe, if you go directly." This sounded pretty sinister to me.

I do not trust Epifanio, but he is an appealing fellow and I bear him no grudge. Standing there on the bank as we clambered gingerly onto our new balsa—in a desperate attempt to amuse myself at this ominous moment, I have christened her the *Happy Days*—both he and the unkempt Ardiles seemed genuinely sorry to see us go. Between them, they had all our money in their pockets, and no doubt felt that, in letting us disappear into the Pongo, they were killing the goose that laid the golden egg.

The *Happy Days* is comprised of four large balsa poles, with two much smaller ones along each side, and the usual cargo frame mounted in the center. It strikes me that about twelve more large poles would be just the thing, but apparently there comes a point—it is said to come rather often in the Pongo—when maneuverability is more important than bulk. In all, our craft is about eighteen feet long by four and one-half feet wide, very little larger than its predecessor but infinitely better made. Though rude in appearance, it has a nice feeling of solidity about it, and in calm water its deck is actually above the surface.

Our *bogas* are three young Machiguengas, dressed in *cush-mas*, with shorts beneath; they wear only the shorts while on the river. They have with them their hard black *chonta* bows and long cane arrows, to provide for them on the return trip through the jungle; they also have yuca, plantains, and a watery fruit called *limas*, in fiber bags. The three have been given Christian names—Toribio, Raul, and Agostino—but they do not speak Spanish. Our faithful Alejandro, a Quechua, manages to divine their intentions now and then, though when asked to interpret he only smiles gently, saying, "I don't know. Theirs is a different tongue." Alejandro is the fourth *boga*, kneeling clumsily behind the bow man, Toribio. He is dressed in his poor underwear, and he is a very ugly boy, with a head which could only look natural beneath the distracting headgear of the *puna*; his skin, when cold, is the nameless color of an old bruise, blotched with old healed sores of purple. His shoulders are narrow and his joints knobby, while his feet are short and thick as clubs; he has none of the grace of the Machiguengas, who slide into place like fishes. He has a low brow and exceedingly long lashes over small discolored eyes, giving him a lidded look, and he is not alert. Yet he is strong and faithful and has natural gentleness and manners. He also has a little plastic comb, his sole belonging, and with this he goes each morning to the river-side and carefully draws flat his coarse black hair; this is the sub-stance of his ablutions, and five minutes later his hair is awry once more, thus to remain for the next twenty-four hours. He was born in Cuzco, where he belongs, and wishes to seek his fortune in Lima, where he does not.

We had not gone very far downriver when we came upon a small *canoa* drawn into the bank; the Indians steered our balsa in beside it. Without a word, all three disappeared into the tangle. One reads of Indians being "swallowed up" by the jungle, and the phrase is a good one: one moment they were there, and a second later they were not.

Surprised, we sat stupidly where we were. In the silence

that followed we listened to a *chito* monkey and to the ubiquitous *pustes*. Andrés was openly apprehensive; we were not beyond the reach of foul play or "revenge," one form of which would be to have the Indians remove us downstream, thus, and suddenly desert us. A balsa cannot be poled upstream, and the trail, if one existed, not only would be difficult to find but would lead us straight back to the difficulties at Pangoa. Our emergency food was all but gone—we had two cans of peaches, a bottle of *pisco*, and Celeste Allen's ceremonial Scotch—and starvation in this jungle, for anyone but a native Indian, is a simple matter. In effect, our one chance would be to risk the Pongo and try to reach the mission at Timpia; undermanned and inexperienced as we were, this course would be all but suicidal.

Within ten minutes, however, the Indians returned. They brought with them lengths of strong liana, and these they secured to the cross-pole forward, then led back to the stern. To Alejandro they managed to convey the idea that from now on we could expect to use these lianas as a safety measure and should hang on for all we were worth.

A few of the *mal pasos* above the Pongo de Mainique are alleged to be worse than the Pongo itself, and while this is not so, at least in the rainy season, they are worse by far than anything to be found farther above. And no two are alike: the *encuentros* of the Yavero and Mantaro Rivers are very different in the type of maelstrom they create, and besides these there are such places as Bongoni (waves-next-to-the-land), Maranquiato (ravine-of-vipers), Shintorini (place-of-pig-transformed-into-fish), Patirini (where a bishop—*patirini*—was drowned), and Mapirontoni (place of many stones). These are but seven of the sixteen *mal pasos* between Pangoa and the Pongo which are recognized by name, and of all of them Mapirontoni, where gray waves leaped up in a narrow channel and crashed down across the raft, was perhaps the most spectacular. But there was something for every taste—swift rapids and evil *remolinos*, and water climbing the canyon face, tilting the raft at an uneasy angle, and holes-in-the-water where a boulder did not quite protrude, and rushing white wakes where a boulder did, and the inevitable *tumbos*—each *mal paso* drenched us. We wore only shorts and shirts, in case we had to swim, though I can't believe swimming would have helped very much in the *mal pasos*; everything, in the end, depended on the stoutness of the *Happy Days* and the skill of the Machiguengas.

Both of these seemed in good order, for though the dangers were far more serious than any we had encountered with Marquez and Ardiles, the actual emergencies were probably less. For the most part the Indians, squatting on their heels, worked deftly and silently, without the desperate shouting and confusion which characterized the earlier journeys; they spoke to one another softly, in little whoops, like children, and only in three or four places prior to Megantoni, as they called the Pongo, did their alarm get the better of them. Then they would screech at one another to paddle harder—*"Shin-tse! shin-tse!"*—and, when paddling was of no avail, would set up an unearthly howling, especially Raul, who emitted sounds of terror and psychic pain which were extremely hard on the nerves. On the other hand, a certain amount of racket comes naturally to these Indians in tense moments, and they continued to do their work very well indeed. We were racing along into a driving rain and wind when suddenly we dropped over a shallow *tumbo*, at a bend, and there, two hundred yards ahead, rose the sheer portals of reddish granite which form the entrance of the Pongo de Mainique.

At this the Indians howled anew and struggled desperately to bring about an emergency crash landing at a small beach of black sand lying under the steep bank on the left side. The bow man, Toribio, leaped for the beach with a liana, but he sank from sight into the torrent, and the line pulled free: I was certain in that instant that we had seen the last of him. But he popped up, mouth wide, and, as the current swept him down, caught hold of the stern as the raft swung around, for his tug had pulled her in toward the bank. The timing was miraculous, but, though Toribio grinned uneasily, the Indians otherwise took no notice of it. They tied the balsa to a stiff, scraggy shrub which is common on the banks in this part of the river, and Agostino and Raul went downstream along the sharp rocks, barefoot, apparently to peer into the Pongo.

There had been some idea before we left Pangoa that we would not try the Pongo until morning, on the theory that, in case of accident, we would not have the oncoming darkness to contend with. Now I was not sure how I felt about it: I was afraid, I knew that much, and more so because of this dark, gloomy afternoon of rain and cold, and I kept asking myself what in the name of God I thought I was doing here in the first place. On the other hand, there was no turning back, we were already trapped in the outer canyon, between cliff and torrent, and the side of me already frozen stiff and scared longed to be put out of its misery as speedily as possible, one way or the other. Andrés was shaking so with cold that he could scarcely talk; I imagine he felt as I did. As for poor Alejandro and Toribio, they squatted and shivered on the rocks, arms wrapped around their knees, naked and resigned as a pair of apes; their dark skin looked nobbly and dead.

I had in my shirt a little coca, presented me as a last-minute love token by Ardiles: I took a little and almost immediately felt better. At least I stopped trembling sufficiently to walk. I offered some to Andrés, but he refused it, saying it made him dizzy.

Now the two scouts returned, moving swiftly, and without a word untied the raft. A few moments later, much too hastily for my taste—it seemed to me that I had a lot of important questions about the Pongo, though of course our *bogas* could not communicate the answers—we were aboard and bearing down upon the Pongo, and at a speed which, had we had even the slightest control over it, could only have been called insane.

The word *pongo* denotes a ravine or gorge where a river bursts through the mountains, and the Pongo de Mainique, to the Machiguengas, is known as the Place of the Bears: the legend is that a river monster or demon in the form of a bear lurks in its waters, rising up now and again to do some drowning. The single *mal paso* on the far side of the Pongo is called Tonkini, or Place of Bones, which may or may not be an indication of the bear's success.

"The Pongo de Mainique," wrote Mr. Jolly, "is the worst pass on the river. . . . The approach was a magnificent sight. Gaunt rocks rose sheer on either side, with great white waves dashing high against them . . . The river thunders over huge boulders in a mass of foam and spray at a speed I estimated at forty miles an hour. The fall is from fifty to sixty feet. . . ."

My own impressions of the Pongo are less definite, owing to a certain nervous confusion; I can only say that if the conditions in the Pongo are as Mr. Jolly described them, then in portaging the rapids on foot—I insert this here with a certain calculating smugness—he and his party did the right and sensible thing. It is true that the approach is a magnificent sight, as the Gate of Hell must be, and the gaunt rocks and high waves at the entrance made a marked impression on me, to be sure, but after that I had but a tenuous grasp on my aesthetic vision. I don't say that everything went haywire, but my outlook was decidedly blurred, even when my head was not submerged.

Fear is very much like pain, in the sense that, in the intervals that one is free of it, one forgets how very disagreeable it is. I am not an authority on fear, avoiding the condition whenever possible, but I do know that its worst agony comes well beforehand, in the period of suspense; by the time the crucial moment arrives, a certain detachment—a fatalistic sense, a longing to finish the suspense, and finally a dull resignation—

has replaced the quaking. Stupidly, one plods to meet one's fate. In any case—and the coca may have helped a bit—I found myself able to absorb the experience more or less objectively. Here are my impressions, written down the following morning. I shall check them later with Andrés, who, as a dedicated believer that the rapids of the good old days on the Huallaga are worse than anything we could possibly come upon in these puny times, is sure to cut away the excess fat.

The *Happy Days*, then, rushed down upon the entrance and struck a white swirl under the great monolith on the east side; the Indians screamed, and the balsa yawed down into a kind of hole, spun around twice, and bobbed free again. The waves came at us from all directions, and we took several large ones full in the face; the next moment, to my astonishment, we had surfaced again and were sweeping along in swift, calm water. I had expected a maelstrom from one end of the Pongo to the other (one alleged veteran had told us that the waves accumulated all the way, reaching a terrifying pinnacle at the far end), and this breathing space came as a very pleasant surprise. Not only that, but it gave me a chance to look around, though I had to jar myself out of an odd state of mental suspension—perhaps the dull resignation I referred to previously —in order to do so.

First of all, the Pongo must certainly be one of the most beautiful canyons in the world; on a late afternoon of rain, it must also be one of the darkest. The sheer cliffs rise several hundred feet on both sides of the narrow cut, and the higher walls are overgrown with rich mosses and ferns and other denizens of shade and shadow. The rocks near the water, however, as well as the numerous caverns, look black, and the water itself, where it runs clear, is as black as in a fairy tale. The current bore us along in soft, slow ominous swirls—we were actually moving swiftly—passing us from one vague *remolino* to another. All this time the rain and wind swept at us up the canyon, which stretched away like a long avenue of high, dark battlements.

On the raft there was now that utter silence of simple awe, awe of the *mal paso* traversed at the entrance, perhaps, and even of the majesty of this forlorn place, which might be the rock garden of a giant, but mostly of the fact that we were now in it, irretrievably, with no place to stop or even to pause. (In the dry season, apparently, one can catch one's breath, take photographs, and so forth, at several small beaches and footholds which appear in the canyon, but this was not true on April 18, 1960.) And I remember a small yellow bird, like a yellow warbler, flicking along from moss to dripping branch; the bird seemed so heedless and natural in that world, as we were not.

I was sitting in the fore part of the raft, behind Toribio and Alejandro. Then came the small cargo rack, and behind it Andrés; I turned to look at him, and he peered at me noncommittally, like a beaver. We were just hanging on now, psychically as well as physically. Behind Andrés, Raul and Agostino commenced to moan, and I faced forward again: the channel was narrowing, and ahead the water had turned white.

The Indians were yelling something, and Andrés called to me, his voice a little strained. "Look out, now," he said. "Hang on with all you've got." I got a death grip on the lianas. Alejandro was staring forward at the waves, and even the back of his head looked surprised. The waves had not looked very high at first, but this was because we had seen only the crests of them; the waterfall between the raft and the waves had not been apparent in the rain. "Alejandro," I said. "Be ready, now." He nodded rapidly and flashed a kind of smile in a quick half-turn of his head. This was all he had time for. The Machiguengas were yipping and grunting, and Raul was making a special sound of his own that came from somewhere in his pelvis, a sound a man might make when, having been confronted with the imminence of his own death, he was then punched in the stomach. The next moment, forsaking their paddles, they howled as one and sprang for the lianas, for there was nothing more they could do: we seemed to slide sideways down the waterfall, and then we were looking up from the bottom of a hole, with the waves caving in on us from impossible heights.

I say "impossible heights" because, from a raft, any wave looks very large, and these waves would have been beauties anywhere. But with all due respect to Ardiles, they were nothing like six meters; a better guess would be anywhere from eight to twelve feet. And they had little force: at one point, when one swept across us, I was washed violently to one side of the raft, but I recall shouting to myself with relief how weak they seemed for their size. And of course they are not true waves at all, but only the upflung boil or chop of a great rapid.

Nevertheless, when that first big one loomed above our heads, I said to myself quite clearly, with a kind of startled exasperation, "Oh, come on!"—as if waves of this dimension had no business in a river, Pongo or no Pongo. After that, for an endless period which may not have exceeded half a minute, the Pongo went totally berserk. The raft spun and tossed, dove down and popped up again, tilted, leaped, and backslid, and behaved generally in what Mr. John Brown, the imperturbable British author of *Two Against the Amazon*, might have described as an eccentric manner. At the same time, it behaved very well, for it remained intact and at no point reached that precarious angle on the point of overturning which the Ardiles craft had achieved at Bacanique.

While in this world of water, both Alejandro and Toribio, floundering together like a couple of dogfish on the ends of their lianas, were washed back against the young *caballero* riding first-class. We were all piled up like maggots, and there was a good deal of vulgar clutching before things got straightened out. Then the waters abated and the two resumed their stations, as did Agostino and the hysterical Raul, and a good thing too, because this particular *mal paso*, the worst on the Urubamba, is followed immediately by its near-equal, a very large whirlpool on the right side of the river. (I have since been told that in the dry season this particular *remolino* does not exist.) The Indians paddled furiously, but the clumsy balsa slid implacable across the *remolino*'s outer rim. Instantly it was spun around and sucked toward the neat hole at the vortex; there came a horrid gurgling as the bow was drawn beneath the surface.

This, for me, was almost the worst moment. Alejandro and Toribio scrambled up the slope to a chorus of death cries from astern, and then the raft popped out, turned around, and tried it all over again, backwards. Again the good old *Happy Days* surged free, and this time, having made the complete circuit of the *remolino*, it skated out to the rim again: the frantic skill of the Indians drove it onward, into the open current.

It is just below this spot, as I recall, that a lovely waterfall feathers down the cliff face on the east side. Rather coolly, I thought—though, on reflection, I was probably trying to ease my nerves—I remarked on its elegance to Andrés. But Andrés only stared at me from behind the cargo as if I were some sort of madman. He had been calm throughout the passage, but later, when I asked him his opinion about the *remolino*, he said fervently, "I didn't like it."

Alejandro, squatting in front of me, could not get over his experience. He kept wringing one hand, eyes shining, as near vivacity as he may ever get. "*Ai-ee, qué rico!*" he repeated several times, rather inexplicably.

We went on down the black current, and in a little while Andrés called forward.

"I think they're saying that we're through the worst of it," he said.

"Good," I said. I was dying of relief and could say no more.

We went on in silence, through rapids and swirls that

could only seem negligible by comparison to their predecessors, and in a few minutes approached the lower portals of the Pongo. These are less imposing than the entrance, but they are mighty all the same and contribute immensely to the drama of the place. The rocks toward this end are rectangular in shape, as if cut by some mighty hand, and the moss on them, the ferns, and the lavender-red flowers of a vine falling down the face of the portal to the left give the whole place the air of an ancient landscape in the romantic concept.

I turned and looked backward, up the canyon. The dark walls were merging in the distance, closing us off, and beyond, the mountains rose and disappeared into the mists of the cloud forest; there somewhere lay the dank realms of Pangoa. For the Pongo de Mainique is the entrance to the Andes, in a way more dramatic than can possibly be described: the jungle on the lower side is quite different jungle from that above, only a few miles away. The river emerging from the narrow Pongo, through a cut perhaps twenty yards across, broadens out into a river of the rain forest, with its sweeping forks and river islands of gravel. The mountain valleys and shadows have disappeared, replaced by the flat *selva*, which stretches away indefinitely behind red, eroding banks. The swift white streams plunging into the river are gone too; in their place are quiet creeks and shady leads. Even the wildlife has taken on a fresh aspect: within a mile of the Pongo, we saw a *maniro*, a pygmy deer not much larger than a hare, and a pair of black ducks or small geese rose out of the river, large white patches vivid on their wings.

There were several tricky places, one of which, presumably, was the Place of Bones, Tonkini. But we were veterans now, with full trust in the *Happy Days*. On we drifted in a kind of growing realization, exultation.

Behind me, at last, I heard a sigh. I turned to see a new Andrés, grinning from ear to ear. "Now I feel at home," he explained. "Isn't it beautiful here? Flat, flat, flat! We're out of the Andes, and I'm glad. The mountains make me gloomy, and

I hate them." The change in his appearance was remarkable: for the past week he had looked old, and now he looked simply tired.

The Indians were grinning too, Raul with his black face tattoos and crude haircut, Toribio with his tight gas belly and thin legs of malnutrition, and Agostino, who in his way is beautiful. And Alejandro: Alejandro, in an access of belated nerves, was devouring one *lima* after another.

And I was grinning, at least inwardly. We were through the Pongo and we were an important step forward on our way, and at Timpia, not far below, Cruz might be awaiting us; in any case, there would be a radio there with which to reach him. And I too had had enough of the mountain valleys, the lowering clouds, the wary, nervous people. The weather was clearing, and my spirits were clearing with it: I felt a terrific surge of joy and life and felt like singing.

It was late now, nearly five, and darkness was not far away. In a little while the Machiguengas eased the balsa toward the shallow *encuentro* of a small river. We wanted to reach Timpia this evening, for in the jungle the custom is that people wait eight days and then go on; this was the eighth day since the date that Cruz had planned to meet us. Andrés pointed downriver, saying, "Timpia," and the Indians nodded and smiled. They understood that we wanted to go on, but Indians do not have our own exaggerated sense of time's importance, and they could not take our haste too seriously. They were tired, understandably, and they meant to camp here; that was that. The Indians of the selva come and go much as they please, having little or no concept of duty, and as each *vuelta* of the river meant a longer trek for them, through a wild jungle without trails, we would be lucky if they did not slip off during the night.

They drew the balsa into the mouth of the small river, and we camped beneath a yellow-flowered tree. Removing our soaked clothes, we realized how deeply cold we were: the last bottle of *pisco* was hunted out, and all six of us took deep swallows of it. The Indians, who had only their wet *cushmas*, built a fire and kept near it; over the fire they constructed their precarious grill of sticks and placed yuca and plantains there to cook.

Andrés was exhausted. He made his bed quickly on some branches cut with the machete and did not bother to eat supper. By six o'clock, when darkness came, he had turned in. Relaxed a little by the *pisco*, he spoke bitterly of the people we had had to deal with. "They are not jungle people," he kept saying, "but people of the sierra who have come down into the jungle. And there is an old saying in Peru: 'Never trust the people of the sierra.' These people have lied to us and cheated us, but wait and see: everything comes around in life a second time, and I am going to revenge us, wait and see. They have taken a year of my life, these people, and especially that business with your friend Ardiles." He looked up and shook his head. "I just don't think you realize what a bad spot we were in."

This was true—and I still don't quite accept it. I was in fine spirits, and I went over to the Indians' fire, where Alejandro loitered hungrily. One never touches the belongings of the jungle Indian unless one wishes to risk trouble, nor does one request food from them, according to Andrés, without insuring their contempt. But Agostino, the most civilized of the three, was quite aware that we were without food. Neither Andrés nor myself had felt like begging from Epifanio, and Epifanio had not offered anything but a few *limas*: we had counted on getting some supplies at Timpia. Whether because we had shared our *pisco* with him, or because we had been through the Pongo together—probably it was neither of these reasons, for the Indian is not sentimental—Agostino rose suddenly and thrust some yuca and bananas at us, silent and unsmiling.

We ate our supper in the darkness. Alejandro is no conversationalist, and my Spanish is poor, but we talked anyway because we were happy. Across the mouth of the stream a strange animal voice resounded, very loud and fast, "OCK, OCK, OCK, OCK, OCK," and then slowed quickly, "OCK . . . OCK . . . OCK," and, after a few seconds' silence, a solitary "OCK." The Machiguengas called this a *tarato*, and while Alejandro felt it was a monkey, I felt certain it must be a remarkable sort of frog or toad. We discussed this a little, and then it occurred to me—for the first time, I'm ashamed to say—to ask this uncomplaining boy if he could swim. He smiled sheepishly. "*Poco*," he said. "*Muy poco, señor*"—as if he were somehow at fault.

April 19. Timpia.

When I went to sleep the jungle sky was ablaze with stars —the Dippers and Vega and the Milky Way—but during the night it began to rain. I had given my tarpaulin to Alejandro, and my sleeping bag was soon soaked through. Toward four in the morning I got up and went to the fire, where the Indians, rolled up and headless in their *cushmas*, lay like mummies in the embers. They would steam and dry one side and, when done to a turn, roll over and offer the other. Even in this uncomfortable hunched act, they managed to maintain that economical grace of animals—and I say this with no condescension whatsoever, only envy.

There were two hours to go until daylight, and it seemed a good time to reflect on our position. We were not far from Timpia, a couple of hours at most, but I had no real hope that César Cruz would be there. We had a long way to go to Atalaya, perhaps two hundred miles, and more than twice that distance to Pucallpa, and we were all but broke. The balsa was ours, but the *bogas* would leave us at the first opportunity: we could manage the balsa here in the lower river, but the current below the Pongo was much slower, and Atalaya would be at least a week away. Furthermore, the haciendas below the Pongo were all but non-existent; we could not expect even the dubious hospitality of the upper river, for we were in the wilderness.

For the rest, we were short of bedding and spare clothes —Andrés's second pair of pants had been ripped to pieces on the march down from Sirialo, and by mistake I had left my own at Pangoa, drying on the eave poles of the hacienda. Our emergency food was gone, all but canned peaches and distilled spirits. We had the .44, but this is not as effective a game weapon as the shotgun Cruz was supposed to supply, and animals could not be counted on. And finally, Andrés's camera, on which we had depended for the colored pictures which might help pay for the expedition, had become saturated at last and was now defunct. I was wet and cold and tired from lack of sleep, and by dawn the great happiness I had felt the night before had slipped away, leaving a dank mood better suited to the morbid mists which shrouded the muddy river.

The Indians at first light rose from the fire and drifted silently away, up the small stream. They had left their weapons behind and presumably would return, but we were anxious to get to Timpia, and the suspense was disagreeable. Two hours later they returned, but now they indicated that they wished to go no farther with the balsa. As I have said, we could now manage the balsa without them, but we did not know the river forks and could easily go astray; besides, speed might be important. Unable to reason with them, we pointed angrily in the direction of Timpia, where Pereira had contracted to deliver us, and after a time, quite suddenly and quite mysteriously —so mysteriously that Andrés became suspicious—they decided to go along. We boarded the raft, and Andrés sat with his back to me, facing the two Indians astern, his loaded carbine across his lap. I thought and still think that he was mistaken about these Machiguengas, but probably he was wise to take no chances; he would not feel easy until this last thread with Pangoa, and the talk of revenge, was broken.

The rain continued through the morning, and another

lovely stretch of river slipped past us, all but unappreciated. At one point we started a heavy animal—probably a tapir, or *sachavaca*—from the brush at the river bank, but the visibility was poor, and we saw no game. The Urubamba curled away ahead of us, mile upon mile, with only an occasional small rapid at its *vueltas*. We came at last to the confluence of the Timpia, and the mission materialized in the mist, high on the bank of the tributary, about half a mile away.

The Indians beached the *Happy Days* on the sand bar of the Timpia delta, where we disembarked. Not wishing to leave them alone with the sacks, Andrés gestured to them to accompany us to the mission, but this they refused to do. He unlimbered his carbine, making it plain that we would not leave the balsa until they did; he then suggested that I make a show of taking my revolver from my bag and strapping it on. I did so, feeling very silly. Agostino now stepped forward, followed by Toribio, but Raul was still stubborn; he was giggling and seemed to me less larcenous than frightened. Finally he joined us, and we walked up the long sand bar of the Timpia, leaving Alejandro behind with the carbine to guard the raft.

The padres were happy to receive us and expressed astonishment that we had traversed the Pongo: they immediately sent their mission Indians down by canoe to retrieve our gear. One of these, having carried one sack up the steep bank, slung it carelessly to the ground, smashing the bottle of precious Scotch: I took this as an exceedingly evil omen. And indeed, Padre Daniel Lopez Roblés, the Spanish Dominican in charge of the mission, had no good news for us. First of all, his radio transmitter was out of order, so that we could not reach Cruz. And second, Cruz had never reached Timpia, assuming he had ever left Atalaya at all. Cruz is not highly thought of at Timpia, and there were even suggestions that he is a not quite trustworthy individual. Father Daniel, an agreeable and expansive man, has a tendency to jeer at things, and he jeered with gusto at the idea of Cruz's ruin on the Río Picha; he too has heard of it and confirmed that no white man had ever seen it, for the reason that it does not exist. The sole ruin below Machu Picchu that he was willing to recognize was one located a few years ago by two Englishmen and an American high up on the Mantaro. This is the Mantaro, called Mantalo on some maps, which joins the Urubamba near the hacienda of Epifanio Pereira, not the one which flows to the Apurimac from a point east of Huancayo. The Mantaro ruin, in a country of wild Machi-guengas, is all but inaccessible, and as only one party has reached it to date, and returned with unsatisfactory evidence, its very existence is still considered hypothetical. (I have since read an interesting account of the expedition by Julian Tennant, one of the young Englishmen involved. It contains a good descrip-tion of the lower end of the Pongo, which Mr. Tennant's party failed to ascend and declined to descend, possibly because an-other Briton, Professor Gregory, met his end there in 1935. It also contains the statement that Fidel Pereira's patricide was inspired by his apprehending the elder Pereira in bed with Fidel's sister, though Tennant does not reveal how he came by this lurid information. His book is called *Quest for Paititi*, which would tend to indicate that he was unaware of, or had not taken seriously, the claim of Mr. Leonard Clark that he had discovered Paititi, or El Dorado, a few years earlier.)

Andrés has had a good opinion of César Cruz until this time, based not only on my own impression but on what he him-self was able to learn of him in Pucallpa, but he now leans toward the opinion of the Dominicans. He feels that if Cruz had been acting in good faith he would have come as far as Timpia, even if, later, he had tired of waiting and gone back. Of course there may be good reasons why he has not done so, but for the moment the evidence is against Cruz, and it very much looks as if the expedition is to prove the wild-goose chase that everybody assured me it would be. The Picha ruin has been loudly discredited by Padre Daniel, and Andrés himself has joined the ranks of those who believe that the preservation of a large fossil in the rain forest is impossible. In fact, he says that all we can do now is to make our way somehow to Pucallpa and try and get our down payment back from Cruz. This would be cold comfort, as far as I'm concerned. On the other hand, I am certainly seeing something of the jungle, and this is what, I keep telling myself, I really wanted most of all.

Meanwhile, it turns out that Padre Daniel and his assistant, Fray Jaime Ayesta, are starting downriver tomorrow as far as the mission at the Sepahua. This will carry us past the mouth of the Picha, irretrievably, I'm afraid, but we have no choice. And there is a radio at Sepahua; if it works we'll be able to find out whether we're getting anywhere or not. At worst, Sepahua is a long step farther down the river. The priests have a large *canoa* with outboard motor, and the downstream journey will take little more than a single day, as opposed to three or four in the *Happy Days*.

April 20. Timpia.

As it turns out, my instincts about our Machiguengas' good intentions were probably right. The padre feels sure that their reluctance to leave the raft was caused by a fear of the mission instilled in them by the Pereiras, who do not like to lose slave labor to the Church. But it also turns out that Andrés's low estimate of our safety while at Pangoa may not have been as exaggerated as I've assumed. Epifanio has the worst reputation of the Pereira sons, and Padre Daniel speaks from personal experience: while he was in charge of the Coribene mission it was once invaded by Epifanio, who molested the Indian women and shot up the place with his gun. Fortunately he was too drunk to hurt anybody, but Padre Daniel told Epifanio that he would not accept confession of this sin, and that Epifanio must never return to Coribene. As for Ardiles, his complaints of mistreatment at the hands of a gringo he has guided through the Pongo are made extremely doubtful by the conviction of both Roblés and Ayesta, both of whom have worked in this region for eight years, that Ardiles himself has never been through the Pongo in his life. In fact there are not very many people who have, even in the dry season, and an interesting sidelight of the whole ill-starred voyage of the upper Urubamba is the possibility that, quite unwittingly, we may have had a more significant adventure than the ones we originally sought. Our sole idea was to get downriver to join Cruz, at which time the expedition would begin: knowing nothing of the Urubamba, and receiving only lies and misinformation from its inhabitants, whose ambition was to get rid of us, we looked upon the navigation of the *mal pasos* and the Pongo as a necessary ordeal of the journey, and one that such veterans as Ardiles and Pereira had negotiated a dozen times.

Having written this, however, I shall have to contradict myself a little. We received plenty of warnings, and we chose to diminish them, partly because of the agony of going back and partly because of Andrés's conviction that the Urubambans were scared to death of their own river, the dangers of which must certainly be exaggerated and which were not, in any case, to be mentioned in the same breath with those of the Huallaga, say, or the Pongo de Manseriche of the *alto Marañon*. But the bald gentleman at the Lugarte hacienda, Padre Giordia at Coribene, and Abraham Marquez, all of whom know something of the river and all of whom apparently wished us well, had told us that the river was presently unnavigable; Marquez went so far as to say that, if we risked the Pongo in a balsa with the river in this state of flood, he wouldn't give a *sole* for our chances. And these people were not alone: here and there on the river haciendas a peon had uttered a quiet, humble warning, like the *capitaz* who had told us to beware of Rudi Ardiles.

Against this advice we set our own stubbornness, and the experience of those steep, hot valleys of the *montaña* which would have to be retraced, and, finally, the easy assurances of Ardiles and Pereira. And we survived the Pongo without undue emergencies, which would tend to suggest that Ardiles and Pereira were right, and the others wrong.

The Pongo, from the vantage point of a small raft rushing through it, is a fearsome spectacle, no question of it. But—without meaning to set myself up as any sort of authority—it can probably be said that, given a good balsa which will not break up on a rock or cliff, and good *bogas* who will not panic, it can probably be passed safely at any time of year. Even a well-constructed balsa, overloaded or mismanaged, will break up in a hurry, but the most serious danger is of a *volteado*—overturning. This would not be difficult, even in a strong balsa, if the latter were permitted by the *bogas* to hang up on a rock or shallow shelf, with the other end sliding around and down into a rough pool below. We very nearly overturned, in just this way, at Vacanique.

I've said earlier that life preservers would be a comfort, and certainly one would do no harm. But in the Pongo, in the current of the rainy season, I no longer think it would do very much good. Sooner or later the swimmer would be caught in one of the big *remolinos*, and, even if it did not drag him down, it would keep him spinning merrily in his bright little jacket until he starved to death. (Andrés has been on a balsa that was stuck in a large *remolino* for sixteen hours, and there is a known case of a balsa and crew caught in one for twenty-four days.)

Whatever the dangers, the fact remains that trips through the Pongo are few and far between, and in some years there are none; and that such trips as there are are made in the dry season, from June through October, when the river is low and slow. Despite Epifanio's smiling assurances about the joys of April travel in the Pongo, the Dominicans know of only one doubtful passage through it in the rainy season: this trip may have been made at this same time last year by a Machiguenga who turned up at Timpia, having run away from the Pereiras.

If the priests are not mistaken, in other words, then Andrés and I are the first white men ever to travel the Pongo de

Mainique in what the Indians call "the time of waters." Since this feat was the one farthest from our minds, we thus become the greatest heroes *malgré eux* since the voyage of Wrong-Way Corrigan.

April 21. Timpia.

The padres are not ready to leave, and so we shall pass another day at Timpia. This will be the first place we have slept in more than one night since leaving Cuzco, and we have chosen the right place: Padre Daniel, with Brothers Ayesta and Ruiz, have been extremely hospitable and agreeable, and Ruiz has given us the first respectable meals we have eaten in twelve days. He has even contrived to make yuca presentable by slicing it very thin and frying the bejesus out of it.

Timpia is a village of about forty Machiguengas, high on a bluff overlooking the *encuentro* of the Timpia and Urubamba. The Indian huts, built up off the ground on poles, are actually derived from the style of the Piro Indians farther north: the excellent idea of the design is to keep the pigs, chickens, and four cows which roam the central yard from making themselves too much at home. The Indians grow yuca and bananas, and hunt and fish; they are civilized here, and the *cushma* has been largely replaced by calico and homespun. Our *bogas*, with their *cushmas* and face marks, long hair, and striking weapons, stand out from the rest like wild flowers in a bed of vegetables.

The three lingered at Timpia for a day, restless and wary. They left this morning, guided upstream as far as the Pongo by Indians from the village. Andrés was happy to see them go. He has been sleeping a good deal and looks much better. Since we left Pangoa, he has told me two very interesting things: first of all, it appears that Ardiles and Julio took a liking to the small machete Andrés carries, and, having used it in the construction of the first balsa, suggested that they would like to keep it. When Andrés made a point of taking this as a joke, Ardiles inquired, not quite pleasantly, what Andrés would do if they kept it against his will. Andrés told them that he still knew how to shoot. Clearly, this statement displeased them, and he hastily explained that, in the jungle, a knife of any sort is a very personal thing, and that either to sell one or to give it away brings very bad luck to both parties. Both Ardiles and Julio were Indian enough to take this superstition seriously, and no more was said about it, but the incident did nothing to increase Andrés's peace of mind.

The other thing was that Epifanio, by his own admission, was wanted by the law, not only in Cuzco, where he is seriously in debt, but in Quillabamba, where he recently slugged a policeman. Like his father, he felt quite safe in Pangoa, the implication to Andrés being that he could do anything he pleased there and get away with it. Obviously this was true, and Andrés's apprehension at Pangoa seems more natural to me all the time.

It is remarkable that a man of Andrés's age has borne that trip down through the montaña as well as he has. I suggested to him last night that, wild-goose chase or no, we had had quite an adventure. "Adventure!" he said. "My Lord! Look, in all the years I've spent in the jungle, I've never been through anything like the last ten days."

Yesterday, still in a state of nervous exhaustion, he had remained suspicious of our Indians. In the afternoon I went down to the river for a swim and had to carry the revolver to make Andrés happy; as it was, he wanted Alejandro to accompany me. But I refused this, wanting to be alone; we have all been at very close quarters, under strain, and solitude at that moment seemed badly needed. I also wanted to look at the *Happy Days*, tied to a dead stick stuck in the sand; unless an Indian made use of it, this would be its last berth, and after all, it had gotten us safely through the Pongo. And I let myself wonder if some such idea did not affect those Machiguengo boys: when I revisited the delta again today I found an Indian shelter of palm reeds and a cold fire on the *playa* beside the balsa. The *bogas* had gone a half mile from the village to spend the night there.

Raul, Toribio, and Agostino were not happy at Timpia. I watched them that first morning, when Padre Daniel made fun of their crude paddles for the benefit of the mission Indians; their faces, ordinarily cheerful, were set, unfathomable. It seemed to me that they felt uncomfortable in their wild dress and might have been made to feel inferior. They stood silently beside their bows and arrows rolled in neat bundles with the bowstring, while the mission children in their cheap factory shirts stood about them, gawking.

In any case, my heart went out to them, and I thought about them a lot today down at the river, where I walked around naked in the sun, feeling infinitely clean; their world was not the mission yard but the white trees and swift river, the tracks of a large ocelot or small puma on the sand near the shelter, the lost arrow feathered with blue and yellow macaw quills which I found in the cane behind the beach. I'm sorry I did not see them to say good-by, though this is a sentiment that they would not have understood. Our lives were preserved by the skill of these three smiling, graceful boys who, as a reward for building the balsa and risking their lives on it, may or may not receive from Epifanio a cheap knife or some cheap *pisco*. Today they are hunting barefoot through the jungle, moving back toward the strange world of Pangoa. They will be there three days from now, or thirty-three, for time means as little to them as their Christian names, Toribio, Raul, and Agostino.

April 22. Río Picha.

Yesterday I read my notes on the Pongo de Mainique to Andrés; he was generally in agreement on the various phenomena and added a few impressions of his own. For one thing, the Indians at his end of the raft were genuinely terrified, he felt, and gave way momentarily to panic; both were washed violently against him, and both failed to respond to his smile of reassurance. As far as they were concerned, the Pongo was no laughing matter, and they had no Western concept of the stiff upper lip to restrain them from howling out their dismay as loudly as possible.

Andrés too saw the bright yellow bird, but to him it was the bird which seemed out of place, rather than ourselves. The worst moment of his passage was when the balsa slid backward toward the vortex of the great *remolino*.

Having discovered the unique nature of our adventure too late, we are both stunned by the realization that we haven't a single photograph of the Pongo, nor even of its approaches. Andrés's camera, as I have said, is a casualty of the upper river, but my own still works in a sluggish sort of way, and, had we known what we were up to, we might have risked it. On the other hand, the heavy rain and the frequent waves crashing over the raft would have made its use impossible in the dark Pongo: my one chance would have been to go down with the Indians to the mouth of the canyon on foot and take a somber portrait of the portals. Also, we could have gone ashore below the Pongo and made our way back to photograph the lower end: this picture would have been less exciting, but it might have been spiced up a bit with a title like SPEWED FROM THE MOUTH OF HELL.

This morning we left early, emerging from the mouth of the Timpia before seven and heading down the Urubamba; behind us, at the *encuentro*, the good old *Happy Days* nuzzled peacefully against the banks, its lianas trailing in the current. We were now traveling in style, in a large motored *canoa*, with Padre Daniel, Fray Ayesta, Alejandro, and a Machiguenga *motorista* whose crucifix did not entirely obviate his black heathen tattoos. In addition to our own equipment, we carried some supplies for a new Dominican mission being established near the mouth of the Río Picha.

The *canoa* moved swiftly with the current, and yet I don't

believe we traveled as fast as we did on the balsa, without power, above the Pongo. The river has slowed drastically, and it is only the fact that our time is running out that kept us from continuing on the *Happy Days*, for balsa travel is incomparably more rewarding than travel by outboard, the growl of which tends to shut away the atmosphere of the jungle rivers.

There was a heavy fog on the river this morning, and the sun rose dimly behind the strange silhouettes of the forest—large *ohe* trees, and the *pona* and chonta palms, and the white *cetico* of the cecropia or fig family, with its great fingered disk of a leaf—this is the common tree of the river banks and islands —and a delicate elm with lavender leaves, the *bolaina*, and a tree with rich yellow flowers, and countless others: one can ask the names, but the names change with the locality and the tribes, even if one could spell them. The job to be done with this triumphant flora, still so little known, is enough to tempt one to become a botanist.

This stretch of the river is all but uninhabited, even by Indians. In the more than one hundred miles of river between Pangoa and the mission at Sepahua, there are only a few clusters of Machiguenga huts and two or three modest *chacras*. Nevertheless, wildlife, even birds, seems very scarce. A few small hawks, a kind of turkey vulture with a head yellow rather than red—we saw three of these on a sand bar—the blue-black and white swallow of the Amazon, a number of long-tailed blue and green parrots, a splendid blue and gold *guacamayo*, as the macaw is known in this region, and a flock of large, primitive gallinaceous birds, greeny-black with white crests and wing patches. The latter are called *pavas* or turkeys, though actually they are guans, resembling the chachalacas of our own border with Mexico. Two of these we were able to shoot for supper, as a consequence of their indomitable stupidity, including an ability to sit tight on their perches with outboards and small-arms fire crashing around their ears. In addition to the birds, we saw a magnificent specimen of the morpho butterfly cross before a sparkling waterfall, and two white crocodiles—strictly speaking, the white and the black "crocodiles" of the Amazon basin are caimans—which ran to the water with their quick, unpleasant gait at our approach. But the monkey, tapir, capybara, puma, jaguar, and other mammal members of the community kept their own counsel behind the still wall of trees.

The Urubamba is magnificent in this season, when the water is high without being in full flood. The small cliffs of rock, the waterfalls, shadowed streams, the red faces of landslide (the thunder-like landslides are a common sound on the rivers at this time of year), the ever-varying forest, the gravel bars and sand beaches, the canebrakes and palm thickets— these turn and blend and illumine one another at every *vuelta* of the river. And we had fair weather for a change, a cheerful sun which burned the mist from long stretches of calm, clean water.

We paused at the missionary station on the Río Camisea, then continued through the heat of the day to the mission at the mouth of the Picha. Here we decided to spend the night. It is on this river, of course, that Cruz claims a ruin exists, and, with the help of the pleasant sister in charge of the settlement, I made some inquiries about this mysterious place. Cruz had told me in January that the ruins were a few kilometers from the river bank, which places them far off the beaten track in a land where the rivers are the only roads: one wonders why they would have been built there, though the river might since have changed its course, a common phenomenon in this transient terrain. But an old Machiguenga who had been all the way to the headwaters of the Picha and who passed for the local sage claimed he had never seen a sign of ruins. If the Picha ruin is as decrepit as it probably is, the old man might not have recognized it even in the unlikely circumstance that he had stumbled over it back in the jungle, but the chances are he would have heard the legend, and he denied this. On the evidence, therefore—Cruz not being here to defend the minority view, much less transport us—we will have to forget the ruins of the Río Picha. The Indians disavow them, and this is not the kind of place where one can just go poking about the woods.

I discovered this latter fact to my own satisfaction late this afternoon, after a swim in the river. The pleasure of the swim was lessened somewhat by the memory of the two caimans of this morning; they were of the small, white species, alleged to be harmless, so I risked a quick turn and flourish in the shallows. (I'm not sure when piranha territory is entered, but this will become a consideration before long, and there are always the sting rays, electric eels, and the wretched *candiru*.) I leaped out with relief and was immediately set upon by insects of ground and air, a number of which hurried into my pants with me: the air has become decidedly more tropic, with a variety of soft, sweet smells, and from now on bugs will become an increasing menace.

Forsaking the river, I tried to make my way into the jungle, with the vague notion that I might come upon one or more of the elusive mammals, and possibly a snake or two; since my brother and I, as boys, harbored numbers of snakes, including copperheads, I have less fear of these creatures than of tarantulas, say, or scorpions, neither of which have the brains to run away. But the jungle turned out to be a thorn forest of bamboo, cane, and cat claw, growing densely around large *ohes* and another large species with a white-blotched reddish trunk, known locally as the *charapilla*. Stumbling along, supremely conscious of the din I was making in the airless silences, I was caught at from above, from below, and on all sides, and, having put everything for miles around to flight, I soon gave it up as a bad job and made my way back to the river. There the soft evening had drawn out the jungle birds. I saw all three forms of the brilliant *guacamayos*, including a small flight of the hyacinthine species, and a yellow-faced vulture, perched close at hand. There were a white and olive-brown swallow, two species of flycatcher very similar to the western and vermilion flycatchers of North

America, and a big jay I have heard often but never seen until today. It is blue and gray, with a black hood.

At the settlement the padres were building a chicken coop for Sister María. Andrés was listening to his radio, and Alejandro was occupied, as he usually is when not eating, in providing his huge mountain lungs with oxygen. A few Machiguengas loitered about, including one pretty girl who had recently let one of her twin babies starve to death and would have done as much for the other had not the Dominicans interceded. Her maternal negligence, cruel and unnatural by our lights, is by no means uncommon among the jungle Indians, who are more practical about such matters, especially when a shortage of food or even a simple disinclination to assume the burden make children undesirable. Behind her, the jungle encroached upon the little clearing and the two small open sheds, and charred skeletons of the *huacrapona* or *pona* palm, with its strange swelling half way up the trunk, stood black against the last light of the sky.

April 23. Sepa.

Today we made the longest journey of the trip, nearly one hundred miles of river between the Picha and a point on the lower Urubamba just above the penal colony at Sepa. In the morning we stopped briefly at the hacienda of Señor Antonio Basagoitia, who lives with his Machiguenga and Piro Indians near the confluence with the Mishagua; the Mishagua flows in from Madre de Dios, to the east. Señor Basagoitia is an old friend of Andrés from his jungle days. He was extremely courteous and kind and tended to bear out Andrés's feeling that the jungle *patrones* are of a higher and more hospitable sort than those of the montaña. We were given a fine meal of pork, eggs, yuca, and papayas, served up by a fetching little Indian whose name, appropriately, was Lolita, and Señor Basagoitia presented me with a curious wasp nest of wattle and daub as well as a pretty bracelet made by his Piros.

Señor Basagoitia is a friend of César Cruz and, to Andrés's surprise, spoke highly of him. Cruz visited Basagoitia during the winter and mentioned then that he expected to meet some people upriver, which would suggest that he took our project seriously. Basagoitia referred to Cruz as an *"hombre muy serio"* and said that his ruin on the Picha was more than a creature of Cruz's imagination, though it might well be a multiple hallucination: Basagoitia admitted that no white man had ever seen it. He said it was supposed to be about fifteen days up the Picha, that it was located in a kind of *pajonal*, or swamp, and that no Indian would go there willingly because a great pool in the place was said to have been used for human sacrifices.

Whether or not Basagoitia is an *"hombre muy serio"* is now the question. Andrés thinks he is, and, in any case, he is an *hombre muy simpático.* And I must confess that I wish Cruz were here and ready to go; at this moment he could take me in with even the weakest sort of argument.

We arrived at Sepahua (like Coribene, Timpia, and Picha, this headquarters of the Dominican missions is named for the tributary of the Urubamba on which it is located) in the early afternoon and were greeted on the bank by a mixed band of Piros, Amahuacas, and Machiguengas. These people were not, alas, in tribal dress and were thus more or less indistinguishable: the place looked less like an Indian village than like a kind of charity fresh-air camp, which of course it is. In saying this I wish to indicate no disapproval of Padre Manuel Diez and his cheerful staff of brothers and sisters, nor of the other good Dominicans who have kept our bodies and souls together for nearly a week: these are all good people doing a good job, however distasteful the effects of that job may appear to people like myself. It seems very sad that the individual characters of these Indians are disappearing so rapidly into the great blender of the white man, holy or otherwise, no matter how beneficial this may be to the belly and salvation of the individual brave: the people at Sepahua are no longer Indians, but ignorant and indigent Peruvians, and their cousins back in the small interior rivers, in their long hair and paint, make a far better appearance. In South America, with few exceptions, the tribe which permits itself to come into complete contact with the white man, on the white man's terms, has perhaps a half-century of existence left to it.

The beatification of César Cruz at the hand of Señor Basagoitia was tarnished somewhat by the people at Sepahua, who are more explicit about his vagaries than Padre Daniel: Cruz, they say, does not consider money in the bank a necessary perquisite for signing checks and is not known for keeping his word. He is a bird, as they put it, who never tarries in one spot very long, and is referred to here as "*nuestra Cruz*," in the sense of "the cross we have to bear." Since César was now on the suspect list once again, I questioned Padre Manuel about the fossil expert, he of the great jaw, Señor Vargaray.

"I know of him," said Padre Manuel. "You mean the man who has a *chacra* near Atalaya."

"That's the man, I think."

"I see," the padre said.

"Do you know anything about him?"

"Yes, I do," the padre said. "He's dead."

Padre Manuel was not certain that the defunct Vargaray was the man I counted on, only that a certain Vargaray of Atalaya had gone to his reward since January; as to how he met his end, the priest was uncertain, and the question remains up in the air—how the plot thickens!

We have arranged to go on downriver this afternoon in the mission canoe, in the hope that we will find Cruz at his *ganadería* tomorrow morning. But despite my hopes, Vargaray's fossil now seems very remote, and the one ignominious aim left to the expedition, as Andrés repeatedly assures me, is retrieving its money from César Cruz.

There is some thin satisfaction in the fact that Padre Daniel of Timpia, a born scoffer, displays us proudly to one and all as

Don Andrés Porras Cáceres and the American *ingeniero*, Señor Matthiessen (in order that my presence on the Urubamba seem no more bizarre than absolutely necessary, Andrés long ago hit upon the device of identifying me as an "engineer," and I am called by this title by one and all), who have passed through the Pongo in the "time of waters." And Padre Manuel, like the rest, has never heard of a trip made at this season, though he himself is a veteran of the Pongo. Padre Manuel, a tall bearded man who looks like Fidel Castro but is by no means as noisy, was aware of our coming long before we got here. He had known Andrés in the latter's term as governor of Madre de Dios, and when he learned by short wave from Padre Matamala at Quillabamba (who had learned it from Abraham Marquez) that we meant to descend the river, he radioed back immediately that we should wait at least two months. By this time, of course, we were on our way. Padre Manuel's transmitter was the first contact with the outside world that we had had since leaving Black Drunken River, and Andrés took advantage of it to send a message to his wife that he was still among the living.

We were given another meal at Sepahua, our last largesse from the Roman Catholic Church, and soon were on our way. I am bringing this journal up to date in the canoe, for the Urubamba has widened now into a flat, slow jungle river. The palms have increased, and the flowering trees: there is a variety of pea tree with red sprays of flowers, the *amasisa*, and the *bolaina* has become common. Pyramids of vines smother some of the larger trees, and the huge *lupuna*, or silk-cotton tree, with its magnificent wide-domed crown, is the dominant feature of this landscape.

But it is the birds that change the most. Parrots and macaws remain plentiful, but the hawks have increased in number and variety. There are a crow-sized bird, yellow fore and aft, with a brown mantle and pink bill, and a small, striking lapwing, and two large fantastical water birds—an ivory-crested white heron with a bright blue face which I have seen only once before, along the Amazon, and the great cleaver-billed white stork with the scarlet throat called the *tuyuyu*; it is called *tuiuu* in Mato Grosso, and is thus one of the few species known by the same name in both Brazil and Spanish South America. And finally, there are five common species which are also found in North America: the black vulture, snowy egret, roseate spoonbill, osprey, and spotted sandpiper. Spectacular as the spoonbill is, the osprey and sandpiper affect me more, reminding me as they do of my own North Atlantic coasts; it occurs to me now, after five months of wandering this continent, that I must start thinking about going home.

It is after dark when the lights of Sepa's penal colony gleam down the river. We decide to camp on the beach a mile above, and the beach is a lacework of tapir tracks, though the large shy *sachavaca* itself remains hidden.

Bats and a strange silver nighthawk flit nervously against the river's oily gleam. The moon rides in a spectacular night of stars, and as I lie here, on the cool comfort of the sand, writing by flashlight, the Southern Cross soars directly overhead.

April 24. Inuya.

A pink jungle sunrise through the early mist, and fair weather for the second consecutive day. We were on the river by 5:45, hoping to catch Cruz before he could take flight; the guard who ordered us to the bank as we passed Sepa thought we might find Cruz at his *ganadería*, as he had been seen at Atalaya three days before. (The guards inspect all passing boats, probably for escaped prisoners: escapes here are periodic, though the convicts almost invariably return gladly of their own accord if they are still able to find their way.)

About seven we swung in out of the mist and landed at the bank below Cruz's hacienda. Surrounded by his curious peons, the great man himself rose disgruntled from his breakfast, clad in a pair of weary pajamas. Dark-visaged as ever, he was not glad to see us and made no real effort to appear so, though once he flashed his sudden golden smile.

Cruz, predictably, took the position that the El Encuentro he had had in mind was the *encuentro* of the Tambo and Urubamba, near Atalaya. This is untrue, of course, but truth, as a thing open to infinite manipulation, has never been highly prized in the selva, whereas the saving of face is of the utmost importance: we did not bother to tell César that his friend Basagoitia had unwittingly betrayed him. We proceeded immediately to a reappraisal of the contract and worked out a new one acceptable to all in a few minutes. It was not quite satisfactory to Cruz, I suppose, since he would have got away with his advance if we had only perished in the Pongo, but I must say that he accepted his bad luck with grace. He says that he was in the Mapuya country on a lumber trip in early March, and that he has actually seen the fossil; he even has a rough diagram of it, though I could tell very little from this. The discoverer of the bone is an Indian, Juan Pablo, who works for a friend of Cruz, one Victor Macedo. As for Vargaray, he is very much alive—it is his father who has died—but Cruz claims that Vargaray has never seen the bone, and, whatever the truth of the matter, it certainly seems clear that Vargaray has been maneuvered out of the expedition.

Cruz is prepared to leave immediately in quest of the giant *mandíbula*, being fully supplied with gasoline, food, medicine, and *pisco*. The equipment, in fact, was all ready and waiting in a large crate, and I took this to be a sign of his serious intentions until Andrés pointed out—correctly, as it turned out—that Cruz must have heard, by the mysterious and infallible jungle grapevine, of our descent of the river and gotten himself prepared at the last minute. Now Cruz is rummaging furiously about, attending to last-minute details, while we inspect his hacienda: the place is typical of this stretch of the river, with the usual litter of chickens, half-breed babies, stumps, fire smoke, bananas, and yuca, and it is amazing how exactly it corresponds with descriptions of river haciendas of a hundred years ago. There are great wooden tubs of river fish, which his peons are scaling and cleaning: the silver *lisa*; the *sabalo*, which looks like a form of trout; a thin fish, the *chambira*, with two great teeth; and some small *sungaro*, a catfish which is said to reach a weight of over four hundred pounds. The cattle which he raises here are farther off, in some clearings up the river.

Andrés wishes to return to Lima for his thirtieth wedding anniversary, on April 30, and as he has no faith in the existence of the bone, much less in César Cruz, is considering leaving the expedition at this point and making his way home from Atalaya, which lies only a few miles down the river. But Cruz feels that we can ascend the Inuya and Mapuya and return with the bone in time to get Andrés on the weekly bush plane out of Atalaya to San Ramón in the mountains; from San Ramón, Lima is less than a day's distance. And as I would be sorry to have him go, I am also prevailing upon him to stay. My one misgiving is the fact that I would hate to have to rush, should something of exceptional interest turn up; also, César has offered to guide us far up the Inuya to the country of a very wild tribe of Amahuacas, but this would involve a round trip of twelve days, as well as a not inconsiderable risk to life and limb. Andrés feels that for the moment we have pushed our luck far enough, and, somewhat reluctantly, I have decided to agree with him. Since we are to confine ourselves to the *mandíbula*, he has now decided to come along; he still has a protective feeling about me and a conviction that, without his restraining presence, I would get myself in fatal straits in a matter of minutes.

Toward noon, turning eastward into the Inuya, we saw the Geoffroy's dolphin or inia, that gray-yellow river porpoise common throughout the Amazon; how strange it seems to find this animal more than three thousand miles from the sea—though of course there is a theory that all the dolphins and whales of the world were originally land mammals of the Amazon basin which returned gradually to an aquatic environment, and at last to the ocean itself.

We are traveling in a narrow canoe over forty feet in length, sharp-prowed and rakish and, like almost all Amazonian *canoas*, hollowed out of a single log—in this region, usually *cedro*, a large reddish member of the mahogany family from which Spanish or "cigar-box" cedar is obtained. Cruz has four men with him; I was about to say four Indians, since at least two are as Indian as any we have seen so far, but César, who himself is much more Indian than not, made rather a point of saying earlier that he had no *indios* on his place. (César is not a man too proud to contradict himself, and referred shortly thereafter to a Machiguenga working there, the man who had seen the Picha ruins.) One gets the feeling that an educated and intelligent mestizo like César Cruz has been forced by caste pressure into the position that only naked savages, or those under heavy paint, are to be called Indians, all the rest qualifying as Peruvians: a *peruano* is a man who speaks Spanish and wears clothes, and all mestizos are naturally anxious that this distinction be recognized, regardless of their immediate ancestry.

The Inuya River, which flows to the Urubamba from the east, is a river of the rain forest, brown and slow. Its flora and fauna approximate that of the Amazon, and many of its birds were already familiar to me: the snakebird, quite similar to the North American anhinga; the *chansu* or hoatzin, an archaic burnished-bronze fowl of the river brush which vents a fantastic huff and squawk when excited; two species of Amazon swallow; two Amazon kingfishers; and a number of others. There was the red-headed *soldado*, or cardinal finch, black above and white below, a bird common in aviaries (W. H. Hudson, in his *Birds of La Plata*, says of this species, "The song has little variety, but is remarkably loud, and has that cheerful ring which most people admire in their caged pets, possibly because it produces the idea in the listener's mind that the songster is glad to be a prisoner"), and a variety of other songbirds, swifts, and flycatchers. The hawks remain plentiful, including a sinister-looking black individual with a white tail band, and a species of miniature falcon. And finally, on that first afternoon, I glimpsed one furtive specimen of what looked like a wood rail, orange-buff beneath and straked gray above, with a long neck.

The flaming macaws, in pairs and in squadrons of twelve raucous individuals or more, continue to dominate the avenue of air above the two lines of trees; at times one sees them perched high in the great limbs of an *ohe* tree, from where they loose sounds which can best be likened to the most fiendish of children's noise-makers. Their cousins, the short-tailed fat green parrots with red patches and yellow tails, hurry in small bands across the river ahead, as do flocks of blue-green parakeets: for one brilliant instant the parakeets swarm in the red flowers of an *amasisa*. But the bird which has pleased me most is the large blue and black toucan. It flies in a truly comic way—it is the first bird I have ever seen which actually made me laugh —bounding and dipping, gliding and craning in a hesitant, prissy fashion, forever on the point of a fatal nose-dive brought on by the bulk of its great bill. One has the feeling that, should more than one toucan venture aloft at the same time, they would break every rule in the bird world by colliding.

Butterflies are less common than on the upper river, though I saw one superb cluster of green ones and yellow ones fanning gently on the hot clay bank; apparently, these groups are gatherings of males, of species belonging to the genus *Callidryas*. An inevitable solitary morpho flew nonchalantly on its way, like an awkward but happy child pursuing a high bouncing ball. Though the banks are cut everywhere with tracks, and the little *chito* monkey whistles far back in the forest, the mammals avoid us still: Cruz feels that, because of all the floods this year, there is water everywhere in the forest and the animals do not have to come to the river banks. The *lagartos*, or white crocodiles, are very numerous, as are the large river turtles called *taricayas*, which reach forty pounds and are said to be excellent food. Some of these are piled up piggy-back on the river logs, but they are wary and sink away when shot.

We paused to eat under the gnarled old limbs of the squat *shimbillo*, a river tree hoary with dead liana vines which much resembles the magic trees of fairy-tale illustrations. Late in the day, in a *shimbillo*, there sang a pair of black birds with red bills which I had seen once before, in Mato Grosso. I believe they are called barbets, and they have a remarkable clear wolf whistle of impressive volume.

Once we stopped at a small encampment of Indians high on a pretty shaded beach. These were traveling Campas, one of the great warrior tribes of Peru, and the braves were in *cushmas*, faces painted heavily with the orange of the *achote* berry. They had come to this region to cut the wild cane, *caña brava*, from which they make their arrows, and the new arrows, still unfeathered and untipped, were drying on the sand in conical stacks. From the Indians, Cruz's men obtained some pieces of cooked *sungaro*, giving raw tobacco in exchange. In addition to the fish, the Indians were cooking a large toucan. They were wary of us, though not unfriendly, and maintained a stolid silence as long as we remained.

At dark we arrived at a small lumber camp belonging to Cruz's brother-in-law. I swam in the river, and by the time I was dressed again César had prepared supper. We were in our bedrolls by seven o'clock, under a canopy of nine-fingered *cetico* leaves, like black flowers pasted on the shimmering sky.

April 25. Mapuya.

This morning we left behind Alejandro and two of Cruz's men, as well as some gasoline, green bananas, and other heavy supplies, the idea being to lighten the canoe for the shallows farther upstream and to increase speed. We get a different estimate of the time required to reach the original site of the *mandíbula* every time we pin Cruz down, the distance between this site, which I want badly to see, and the fossil's present location on the bank of the Mapuya requiring, according to his mood, from two hours to two days; like most of these people, he has a childlike trust in our naïveté—well-founded, in Andrés's opinion. Cruz is out for what he can get, according to the time-honored jungle law; he is still rankling over the idea that at the end of this trip he will owe us money, rather than the reverse. But meanwhile he is being very pleasant and spares nothing in the way of food, drink, and courtesy to keep us fat and happy. That he might try to hoodwink us, in other words, does not mean for a moment that he dislikes us. Having become hardened to this attitude, from the Amazon to Tierra del Fuego, I have come to the point where the fact that he might cheat us does not mean that I cannot like *him*. *Nuestra Cruz* is a bandit of a sort, no doubt, but he is a most agreeable one and would not harm a hair on one's head unless he was well paid for it. Meanwhile he is running a taut *canoa* and is a most excellent cook: after two weeks of yuca and plantains, his cuisine is the finest imaginable.

To vary his larder, César paused this morning at the canoe of a native game hunter, from whom he obtained a *pava*, or wild turkey, some *sajino*, or wild pig (this animal is similar to the peccary or javelina of our Mexican border states), and a large black spider monkey; the latter came swathed in palm fronds with a vague retinue of flies. The subsequent singe, shave, and shower that this hominoid underwent at the campfire, preparatory to being gutted, is the subject of an atrocity photograph so terrible that I'm not certain it should ever be developed.

Shortly we came to an encampment on the bank where the men had three wild pigs, shot this morning. This evidence of game confirmed the tracks which scar the banks, but our own bad luck in this regard continues to hold firm. All we could see were crocodiles, on which Andrés was venting a long-term

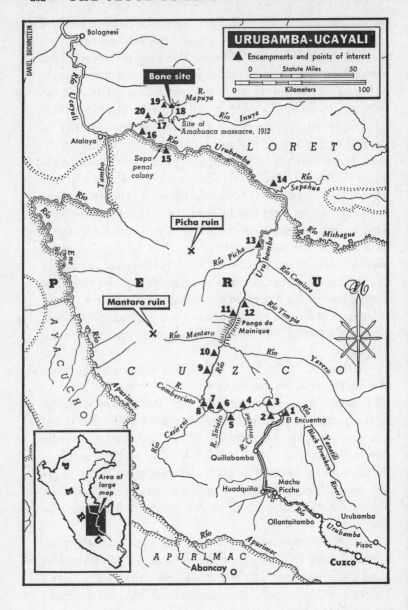

DANIEL BROWNSTEIN

URUBAMBA-UCAYALI

▲ Encampments and points of interest

0 — Statute Miles — 50
0 — Kilometers — 100

Bolognesi

Río Ucayali

Bone site

R. Mapuya

19 ▲
18 ▲
20 ▲
17 ▲
16 ▲

Río Inuya

Site of Amahuaca massacre, 1912

Atalaya

Río Tambo

15 ▲

Sepa penal colony

Río Urubamba

L O R E T O

14 ▲

Río Sepahua

Picha ruin
×

Río Mishagua

13 ▲

Urubamba

Río Picha

Río Camisea

P E R U

Río Ene

A Y A C U C H O

Mantaro ruin
×

Río Mantaro

11 ▲
12 ▲

Pongo de Mainique

Río Timpia

Río Apurimac

10 ▲
9 ▲

C U Z C O

Río

Yarero

R. Comberciato

7 ▲
8 ▲
6 ▲
5 ▲
4 ▲
3 ▲
2 ▲
1 ▲

El Encuentro

Río Casireni

R. Siriato

R. Coribene

Quillabamba

Río Yanatili (Black Drunken River)

Area of large map

P E R U

Huadquiña

Machu Picchu

Urubamba

Ollantaitambo

Río Urubamba

Pisac

Río Apurimac

A P U R I M A C

Abancay ○

Cuzco

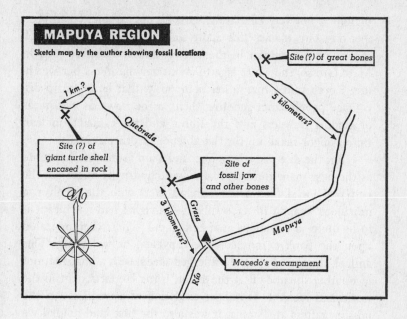

MAPUYA REGION

Sketch map by the author showing fossil locations

1 km.?

Quebrada

Site (?) of great bones

5 kilometers?

Site (?) of
giant turtle shell
encased in rock

Site of
fossil jaw
and other bones

3 kilometers?

Grasa

Mapuya

Macedo's encampment

Río

◄ KEY TO NUMBERS ON MAP OPPOSITE

1. Marquez hacienda
2. First Lugarte hacienda
3. Camp on river
4. Coribene mission
5. Sirialo mouth
6. Rodríguez hacienda
7. Second Lugarte hacienda
8. Olarte hacienda
9. Fidel Pereira hacienda
10. Pangoa
11. Camp on river
12. Timpia mouth
13. Picha mouth
14. Sepahua mouth
15. Camp on river
16. Ganadería of César Cruz
17. Camp on Inuya River
18. Victor Macedo's camp
19. Site of fossil jaw
20. Camp on river

prejudice, not very effectively, with his .44 carbine. I had been speaking out against this sport since, unlike the large black species once common in these rivers and still readily seen in Mato Grosso, the white lagarto is not only harmless but worthless; I even told Cruz, rather pompously, that he ought to discourage people from shooting them, as he now has wild ideas of guiding travelers into the Inuya, and the caimans, in lean times, might make up for the absence of other animals.

But the day was a long one, and I am as much a hypocrite as the next man, and eventually my itchy trigger finger got the better of me. I took a few offhand shots with the revolver, a ridiculous weapon for crocodilians—though I had not meant it to be quite so ridiculous as it turned out. There then appeared upon the bank a *ronsoco*—the capybara, or water pig. This animal, the size of a fat, short-legged sheep, with a huge marmot face rather squared-off at the snout, is the largest rodent in the world and looks it. With the exception of a wood rat in the mission rafters at Timpia, it was also the first land animal we had actually laid eyes on since the miniature deer below the Pongo, and Andrés missed two hasty shots at it. On this flimsy excuse, I commandeered the rifle myself. Another *ronsoco* appeared, and I contrived to knock it down with a lucky shot through the neck. It staggered to its feet and a second shot, supported by a burst of revolver fire from Andrés, put an end to it: it rolled down the bank into the water. Everybody was loudly congratulating me, not least of all myself, and meanwhile the *ronsoco* sank. Though we probed for it desperately in the current, it was never seen again.

Drunk with power, I now proceeded to cut down two crocodiles in rapid succession; with a rifle, even from a moving canoe, a crocodile is not quite a sporting shot. I then felt bad, as I had known I would in advance, and for the rest of that day did not lift a finger against them. Meanwhile, Andrés was trying his luck with the revolver, with predictable results: nevertheless, one remarkable shot, fired in anger, killed a young *lagartito* as dead as a doornail, after the first shot had missed by a distance of not less than ten feet. We are hoping, of course, for a tapir, and Andrés is talking guardedly in terms of jaguars.

We arrived at the *encuentro* of the Mapuya about three that afternoon. On the clay bank above the junction there was once an extensive rubber camp, which prospered in the days of the "black gold"; until last year a military garrison was maintained there, as a check on the wild Amahuacas farther upstream, but now the huts sink slowly beneath the jungle. These Amahuacas, the same mentioned by Cruz, live in a naked state on the upper Inuya and are said to be very treacherous; according to the *lingüisticos*, the Inuya station is presently the most precarious of their missions. The linguist there has a small band of loyal Indians, but other groups come in constantly on raiding parties, and he is unquestionably in serious danger. These same tribes, about 1910, put an end to rubber operations in this area by wiping out the camp at the Mapuya *encuentro*. More than sixty people died, according to Cruz, and only one solitary woman escaped. This was token revenge for the Indians, who had been shot down like rats throughout the selva of Peru, Brazil, and Bolivia. Someone has estimated that the number of Indians butchered in the few decades of the rubber boom exceeded all the lives lost in World War I—this figure entirely apart from the thousands who died in slavery. To this day the wild peoples of the interior rivers are considered by most South Americans as subhuman creatures, to be shot on sight—not, it should be said, that North Americans are in a very good position to bewail this matter.

The Mapuya is much smaller than the Inuya, but it is still deep enough at this season to permit good progress, and we arrived toward dark at the lumber camp of Victor Macedo, one of whose peons is the discoverer of the fossil. On the Mapuya, in late afternoon, we had seen a lovely pair of swallow-tailed kites, that most graceful of the hawks, swooping in gentle arcs over the shadowy slow stream; a few of these birds still survive in the wilderness swamps of the southern United States.

April 26. Quebrada Grasa.

Until the very last minute Andrés was skeptical about the existence of the giant bone. But there it was, sunk in the mud of the Mapuya bank, and it is almost everything Vargaray said it was: a *mandíbula* so large and heavy that it takes, if not six men, at least four strong men to lift it. Its great weight, which must exceed two hundred pounds, is less a consequence of its size than of its matter: beneath the smears of petrified clay which have adhered to it lies a solid block of petrified marble-like stone.

It appears to be the small upper jaw of an enormous animal, though of what age, and whether mammal or reptile, I am not equipped to say: we shall learn this, hopefully, in due time. It measures twenty-four inches across what was once the roof of the mouth—the corresponding distance in our own jaw might be an inch and a half—and twenty-eight inches in a line drawn from the front teeth sockets to a line drawn through the rearmost sockets on both sides. There were twenty-six teeth in all, though none remain, and the sockets are approximately round in shape, of a more or less equal size, somewhat larger than a silver dollar in diameter—in short, a formidable apparatus. On the upper side there appears to be, beneath the clay encrustations, at least one petrified nostril, as well as a large cavity behind the snout, as if the creature had ended its own life by lowering its head and charging headlong into a boulder.

Otherwise I am at a loss to describe it, so protean and amorphous is it; I have taken a photograph of César seated in the mouth, for want of any finer inspiration. César and I had a mild celebration, on *pisco* and a Peruvian vermouth called Gancia, I believe, both of which tasted excellent. We sat up very late by jungle standards, before bunking in with the peons of Macedo's camp—Macedo himself is absent—including the proud Juan Pablo, who described at some length how he found the jaw. César was attired in a handsome pair of white pajamas, surely the sole pair of pajamas which has ever found its way into the Mapuya. Really, he is a man of parts and continues to surprise me.

This morning at six I set off with Juan Pablo, another peon named Luis, and my friend Guillermo Tejo, of César's crew, to visit the original site of the *mandíbula* and determine if the rest of the animal is still visible. Andrés has given up walking for life—his ankles are still swollen from our trek in the jungle valleys—and he felt, in any case, that he would only slow us down. Though genuinely surprised and impressed by the jaw, he has no real interest in it and is most anxious that we leave here quickly, to insure his arrival in Lima five days hence. As for César, he did not pretend to an interest he did not feel, but elected to stay and savor his breakfast.

Andrés's decision turned out to be the right one, for it took us nearly an hour and a half to reach the place, and the going wasn't easy. The first half-hour or so we poled up a side creek or *quebrada* in a small canoe—the stream is nameless (the Mapuya itself cannot be located on available maps, since its region lies in those great blanks of jungle cartography which are generally labeled "unexplored") but, because of the shiny oil slicks which ooze from the mud of the bank, is called by the peons Quebrada Grasa, or Grease Creek. The slippery banks of deep mud were enough in themselves to give the place its name, and we had to ford the stream a number of times, sometimes over our waists in water.

About two miles above the Mapuya, Juan Pablo stopped at a rocky place in the stream bed. At this exact spot, he announced, he had found himself one day standing on a submerged rock and, happening to look down, discovered that he stood in something's mouth. He called out to Victor Macedo, who was nearby. Macedo was at first impatient, but came over at last and had a look. Together they managed to lever the thing to the shore.

This occurred last November. Vargaray, who lives near Atalaya, must have heard the story shortly thereafter, and he bore it with him downriver to Pucallpa, where he told it to me in the early days of January. The story was still too young to have grown very much, and was thus one of the few cases where a barroom rumor on the Amazon turned out substantially as advertised. Since November, Juan Pablo has discovered two more fossil sites, one of which contains, embedded in a rock, the petrified shell of a giant turtle, and the other a variety of enormous bones.

We located a few more bones this morning in the river bed, but whether these belonged to the possessor of the jaw would be hard to say; in any case, the great bulk of that animal was buried or missing. Since the bones were too heavy to carry back with us, I encouraged the men to leave them exactly where they were, on the theory that any horsing around we might do would only make things harder for the properly equipped expedition which might come after; I asked them to take the same precautions with the other sites as well.

We found also the skull of a modern *sajino*. Like the fossils, this was petrified, though the ivory of the tusks was still fresh and white, and it would be interesting to know what geological characteristic of this region permitted petrefaction millions of years ago as well as now; perhaps it is the oil. Finally, we found a living fossil, a sleepy baby crocodile, representing a family many millions of years old and slowly disappearing from the earth; Guillermo claims it is of the dangerous black species, and its color, unlike that of the young animals seen here and there along the rivers, is certainly black rather than bamboo. Guillermo lashed its mouth with fronds of palm, and we are taking it back with us as a mascot.

From Juan Pablo's information I was able to construct a crude diagram of the other bone sites. They are some distance from the first, more than a day's round trip, and I now very much regret having encouraged Andrés to accompany us to the Mapuya, since he is most anxious to get back for his anniversary, and we will not be able to stay here long enough to make even a cursory investigation of what may prove to be an important paleontological discovery. (It now seems to me, too, that I want very much to visit the wild Amahuaca tribes upstream; it's a pity, and infinitely frustrating, that I wasn't more decisive about this while we still had a chance to drop Andrés off at Atalaya.)

I haven't said that I've had a magnificent morning. I have. And curiously, the magnificence did not consist of finding what we were after—more poor old bones, and thus a certain scientific confirmation of the site—but lay instead in the purity of this jungle stream. Only a few woodcutters like Juan Pablo, seeking the isolated *cedro* and *caoba* trees, may ever have ascended this *quebrada*, and there is no mark of the white man's heavy hand upon it. Its still banks are laced with the tracks of tapir, capybara, and other creatures, and its clear water, running quietly on sandy shoals, sparkles with the flash of the pretty *sabalo*. In the bends the water runs beneath stone banks and is a pure, limpid green, and the trees which lend their leaf color to the water soar away in great white columns. The queer and clumsy hoatzin huffs everywhere in the lower branches, and hidden birds of unknown shape and color whistle and answer down the cool silences, in counterpoint and incredible clear harmonies. The tree frogs loose their prodigious croaks, and from a mile away resounds one of the mightiest sounds in nature, like nothing so much as an ominous moan of wind, the community howl of the *mono colorado*—the red howler monkey. In the stream itself lie the striking shells of a variety of mollusks, including a gastropod so large—the size of a very large pear—

that it is difficult to believe it is not a marine creature. (Louis Agassiz, a century ago, pointed out the marine character of the dolphins, fishes, and other aquatic fauna of the Amazon basin.) We paused to breakfast on a kind of nut, the Indian name for which has now escaped me, and I wondered why the stream itself was so much more exciting than the bones we had found in it—more exciting than the first sight of the great jaw itself the night before. And it occurred to me that, aside from its beauty—for it is precisely this inner, mysterious quality of the jungle, represented so well by this lost stream, that I have been searching for and feel I have found at last—there was an adventure here, an exploration, however timid.

It is adventure I have missed a little in the past few days, and which a visit to the wild Amahuaca tribes would restore. These days have been fun, they have even been exciting—I note here with surprise that one of the original aims of the expedition is practically accomplished—but they have lacked that element of the unknown, the unpredictable, that the ordeal of the mountain river had in abundance. We know now where we will be from one day to the next, and that we will have enough to eat: we carry our food with us, and there is plenty of it. Everything is organized, everything taken care of, and I think back on the first days of the journey with a faint regret. As so often happens, we did not comprehend, did not evaluate our experience until it was all over and gone forever from our days.

The one thing I missed this morning was a bright, early sun, not so that I could take photographs—though, dutifully, I had the damn clicking thing along—but for my own appreciation of the scene. So often, in the places which have moved me—the Pongo de Mainique is the classic example—the sun has been obscured, or rain has made photography impossible, as if the mystery of these places was better preserved in one's mind and heart than on the flat face of celluloid. If one depends on a photograph to recapture the feeling of a place, disappointment is inevitable. (On a less spiritual level, I dislike the presence of a fragile mechanism and its leather-coated accouterments swinging like goiters from my neck while I am trying to move quietly in a wild place, especially since I am also, invariably, carrying binoculars. Perhaps it has something to do with a boyhood dream of moving like an Indian, or with the fact that I take poor pictures.)

These reflections are recorded as we slide downstream on the Mapuya. We left Macedo's camp toward ten o'clock, having settled with a joyful Juan Pablo for his find; Andrés was impatient to leave, and Cruz himself was anxious to get going before Macedo reappeared, in case the latter should demand some money for himself. Juan Pablo was paid with César's money, out of the bonus he was scheduled to receive in the event we were able to obtain the bone, and Cruz was not so happy about this that he wished to pay Macedo as well. Considering the probability that the bone, monetarily, is not worth what it would cost to cart it to the slag heap—for I don't think bones have much monetary value, even to museums—Juan Pablo was handsomely rewarded, the five hundred *soles de oro* he received being equivalent to six weeks of his puny wages. Juan Pablo is a strong, modest man with a huge, enchanted smile, and I wish him joy of it.

Two hours later—we are nearing the Inuya—Cruz is clearly still in pain, but is showing his customary gallantry. We are bound downstream, moving rapidly, as we will be for the next four or five days. The sun is shining, and my gut is full of *majasz* —a fat, striped tailless agouti, shot by Guillermo on the beach last night—and the fresh heart of a *chonta* palm hacked to earth by Guillermo's deadly machete. This is not the same *chonta* from which the black Indian bows and spears are made: only the very top part of the tree, still growing, is used for food, and the wastefulness of its destruction is only exceeded by letting it stand, to rot unused in the mindless luxuriance of this unpeopled river.

April 27. Atalaya.

Now is the time of the quarter-moon, and in the jungle the changes of the moon bring rain. This morning the rain fell hard and steadily, and we hunched miserably in the canoe, passing down from the lumber camp where we had slept to the mouth of the Inuya, and from there down the windswept Urubamba to the junction of that river with the Río Tambo: these rivers flow north together as the Ucayali.

At the Tambo-Urubamba *encuentro* lies the largest jungle settlement in all the hundreds of miles of rivers between Pucallpa to the north and Puerto Maldonado far away to the southeast in Madre de Dios. This village of five hundred souls is Atalaya. Here Andrés left our humble expedition. He did not believe César's statement that the outboard canoe could go downriver to Pucallpa in two and a half days, as opposed to the four required when Andrés himself worked in this region during World War II, and all the information we could gather in Atalaya tended to support his opinion. He decided to take the chance that the little taxi plane from San Ramón could get in to Atalaya's mud strip in the next day or so, rather than risk missing the scheduled flight out of Pucallpa on the thirtieth.

As we were broke, we had to extract from Cruz the refund he still owed us on the original advance, in order to pay for Andrés's ticket. Cruz, who had been drinking a little to warm himself after the cold rains of the morning, was offended that Andrés doubted his ability to reach Pucallpa in the required time, and he now shouted angrily that he was losing his shirt on the whole operation. This anger had been building for several days. Cruz's hope had been that we would decide to go far up the Inuya to the Amahuacas, or at least spend a few days in the Mapuya, which would permit him to earn back the advance given him toward the proposed search for the Picha ruin. Unfairly, he had focused his outrage on Andrés, whose anniversary he saw as the key to his disappointment. Andrés, in turn, had mistrusted Cruz from the beginning, and their mutual dislike came out into the open at Atalaya, with neither man making any real effort to understand the position of the other. Nor was I any help, since I felt irritable myself. But the fault of the decision had been not Andrés's, but my own, a point which Cruz refused to understand. Cruz ranted to me against the whole ridiculous nature of anniversaries, as well as Andrés's single-mindedness on this subject, and since my own anniversaries mean little or nothing to me, I'm afraid I have not been as sympathetic with Andrés's need as I might have been. Like Cruz, I have been somewhat troubled by the financial aspects of the expedition. I have had no confirmation from my sponsors in New York that the Urubamba trip has been approved and, since I feel frustrated anyway, have been somewhat short with Andrés in this regard. Andrés has a low opinion of the meaning of money, which he tends to spend casually whether or not he has it, and while on theory I admire this attitude, I now permitted it, for want of anything better, to exasperate me. As a result—though Andrés and I have avoided an open dispute—the tensions between us are working in all directions and the morale of our little band has reached its nadir.

Andrés and I parted too hastily, considering what we have been through together. Cruz was impatient and sulky and shouting a lot of unnecessary orders to nobody in particular from the stern of the canoe. I last saw Andrés standing, expressionless, on the river bank in the rain, behind him the dismal huts of Atalaya squatting against the jungle wall. I much regretted my own irritation and felt sincerely sorry that he was gone, as he is an excellent and dependable companion, and his tact and good will, in combination with the august presence of a Porras Cáceres, have made the whole journey far more pleasant than it otherwise would have been. Without him, I might still be in Pangoa, and not necessarily with all parts, or any, in good working order.

Then we were off down the Ucayali, into the moody jungle afternoon, with the fossil and a cooked monkey in the bow and César brooding over his Swedish outboard in the stern; these outboards, incidentally, are vastly preferred here to the American makes, which are complicated, eccentric, and difficult to repair. What with the weather and the upsetting parting with Andrés, and the prospect of several days of César Cruz's ill humor, I was feeling a bit moody myself. I was sitting amidships, as I have been for several days, confronted with the snout of the great mud-caked fossil, and thinking how inevitable and just that an animal so patently deficient in both brains and *sang-froid* should have become extinct. My early fears that collision with a log or shoal would topple the hard-won prize for once and for all into the river ooze beneath the current were momentarily replaced by the notion that this was exactly where it belonged. While beset by this access of cheap philosophizing, I went so far as to ask myself if this rude lump, sculpted by death, did not symbolize the sterility of all our goals, and at this point my attention was caught by the profile of our faithful vassal, Alejandro, upright and rigid, with his Indian face of stone. In this instant there was a strange kinship between him and the fossil, quite apart from the fact that both are caked with mud (this is no criticism; I am caked with mud myself): Alejandro was suddenly a monolith into which, at odd moments of the day, life might be breathed and wooden, implacable motions instigated by the simple insertion of a banana.

These cross reflections subsided gradually with the nagging rain; soon a dim sun peered through the gray woollens of the sky. The Ucayali swings close beneath the foothills of the Andes, and a great flat-topped butte loomed in the west. Downriver one could see bright regions where the sun was shining, and now and then a weak ray illumined the wet canoe. Here and there lay a large white crocodile, mouth inexplicably agape, and large fish swirled at the edge of a passing shoal.

Toward twilight Cruz came forward from the stern, bearing

cans of cheese and shrimps and two large bottles of the excellent Pilsener beer. He had had a nap in the afternoon while Timo, the sole remaining member of his crew, had taken the helm, and he was a new man. This is one of the qualities I like best about Cruz, his ability to carry off disappointments with a flourish. His grand gesture—for after he had cried out at the terrible losses he was suffering, the unreal price of canned cheeses and shrimps at Atalaya made this offering a gesture— is perhaps the most Spanish of his multiple characteristics. While we talked quietly and drank, he pointed out a family of Conibo Indians on the bank—we have passed successively on this journey from Machiguenga to Piro and Amahuaca territory, and thence to Campa and Conibo—and a particularly magnificent *lupuna*, the trunk of which soared unbranched to the leafy world of its high stories.

The colors deepened with the intrusion of the light beneath the breaking gray far to the west; beneath the gray, the sky is a bright ocher. The ocher sinks to the purple of the buttes, and below the rim rest cotton tufts of valley clouds, like those seen— how very long ago it seems—on the upper Urubamba. Then the deep green of the palms, the hot-leaved *ceticos*, the glowing tassels of the *caña brava*, and beneath these the silver glitter of the river. Against this deep world of late afternoon flew large white, silent birds—the *tuyuyu*, the wood stork with its dark head and curved bill, the common and snowy egrets, and the large yellow-billed river tern, which ranges the length of Amazonas, from here to the mighty delta three thousand miles away, beyond Belém.

At sunset the gray sky turned swiftly to shreds of gold, and the gold in combination with the other colors produced the most exalted nightfall I have ever seen in the jungle. This stretch of the Ucayali is superb. The best aspects of the rain forest and broad jungle landscape are here, and downstream, beyond the western banks, the mountains in their harmonies of clouds rise one upon another; the contrasts are incomparable.

I was filled with a deep happiness and peace. With Andrés gone, the need to hurry has been removed, and though César is still muttering that we will arrive in Pucallpa by the evening of the twenty-ninth—it has become a point of honor with him—there is no emergency about it. In the past few days Andrés has been looking at his watch every other moment and declaiming the time at intervals in a military manner, though I am equipped with a watch of my own and can resort to it on those rare occasions these days when I feel the need. Under the circumstances, it seems to me a much happier arrangement that he got off in Atalaya, and I only hope that the plane was able to come in today to take him out as far as San Ramón.

Another factor not entirely displeasing is that I must now work harder at my Spanish. While Andrés was with me, and presenting our wants and ideas so much more ably than myself, I scarcely spoke. Come to think of it, I've hardly put a hundred Spanish words together since we left Machu Picchu, nearly three weeks ago. But now I must talk in *castillano* all the time and already have made noticeable progress.

We traveled an hour or two after dark, attempting to reach the settlement at Bolognesi. But the night was moonless and the river black, and eventually we struck a shoal and sheared the pin. All afternoon we had passed sections of the bank which were caving into the flood—at one point I watched a large *cetico* topple over—and now we were forced to go ashore in the dark at a spot where evil rumblings and crashes, cracks and splashes, could be heard from both upstream and down. While César struggled with the motor, I peered at the trees leaning over our heads and wondered if one was about to let go. But soon we were underway again and continued to a point not far above Bolognesi. When we stopped at last, about 7:30, there came from the river the soft puff and blowings of the river dolphins and a sweet musky perfume. I asked César what flowers these were, and he said that the smell was not of flowers but was given off by the large fruit-eating bats. Whether this is true or not, the familiar click and squeak of numerous bats filled the air over the river.

April 28. Ucayali.

On the Ucayali the renowned insects of the *selva* put in an appearance. Mosquitoes in numbers appear at night, including the *sancudo*, or malaria mosquito, and a tiny combative sand fly. I believe this insect, called *"mosquito,"* corresponds to the notorious *pium* fly of Brazil, for it causes the identical raised blood dots. Either of these creatures can bring about tropic fevers, and last night, for the first time, we were forced to use *mosquiteros*. César and myself, with Alejandro and the *boga*, Timo, shared a small porch at the *chacra* of one of Cruz's numerous contacts on the river; the little white coffin of my borrowed *mosquitero* swam with that acrid smell one finds throughout these river haciendas, and the smell was replenished throughout the night by Alejandro, who was taking his ease at my elbow. The smell cannot be entirely attributed to its main ingredient, which is sweat: it is far more insidious. Perhaps it has something to do with the yuca diet. In any case, it has of recent days permeated my hat, and I must face the fact that I am now a carrier.

We rose at four, since César still holds to his avowal that we shall dine tomorrow evening, shaved and showered, at the Gran Hotel Mercedes. I don't think he can make it, but it will be interesting to see how he saves face as, in Latin America, he is obliged to do.

We were nearly an hour in Bolognesi, while César looked into some of his lumber dealings, and we paused again a little later in the morning to talk with a friend who lives in a river boat by the bank. César is anxious that I come ashore in each of these places, asking if I wouldn't like to savor the local color, and it occurs to me that his strategy is this: if we should not make Pucallpa by Friday night, he can now say he would have made it if Don Pedro had not wished to visit Bolognesi and all the other points of interest on the river. But we shall see, and I pledge to record faithfully how this all comes out.

On we go, downriver, and today Cruz is in capital spirits. He displays our *mandíbula* to one and all, calling out that it costs five *soles* to look at it and ten to touch it. Most of the morning Timo ran the boat while César and I swilled beer. He tells me now that he has been through the Pongo, in the month of June, and that he knows the Pereiras; like the Dominicans, he has an intense admiration for the old man, without those overtones of moral disapproval with which the holy men feel bound to qualify their respect for a noted murderer and unrepentant sinner. I asked him if Epifanio was a man *de su confianza*, as the expression goes, and with a directness unusual in a Peruvian he said shortly, "No."

César wishes to come to the United States to visit me—indeed, he can talk of little else—and we seem to have recaptured the camaraderie of three months ago in Pucallpa. For some reason this was quite impossible while Andrés did most of my talking for me. It may be that César is fattening me for a kill of some sort, but I don't really think so.

In the early afternoon we stopped at a Conibo settlement near the Chesea River. My dislike of my camera grows and grows, especially when I must point the thing at Indians and other people. I wouldn't blame the Conibos in the least if they had run us out of camp in a shower of stones and arrows, but these people are less shy of the camera than the Machiguengas and Campas, and a few made me feel like the tourist I am by rushing to put on their best ceremonial dress.

The Conibos are very colorful, with intricate black face marks, blue dye on the hands, elaborate bracelets of beads and wild animal teeth, and metal ornaments in the nose; the women also wear a long pendant of metal pierced through the lower lip. Most of the men have adopted the shirts and pants of civilization, but the women cling to a kind of black embroidered wrap-around skirt, with a bright blouse which does not quite reach the navel. They usually wear rawhide thongs at the ankle, and their hair is invariably cut in bangs across the forehead. All of these characteristics the Conibos share with other tribes of the so-called Chamas—the Shipibos, who may be seen around Pucallpa, and the Cashibos, who occupy country north toward the mountains, between Pucallpa and Tingo María. Two of these tribes made quite an impression on Dr. William McGovern, an English wayfarer whose *Jungle Paths and Inca Ruins* appeared around 1928. Dr. McGovern and myself have this solitary bond, that we first approached South America by way of the Amazon on a small ship of the Booth Line.

"There are," the doctor writes, "the Konibo Indians, who kill off their aged and infirm. There are the Ungoninos, who inflict strange nameless tortures upon their girls at the age of puberty. There are the Kashibos or Vampire Indians who, like the loathesome bats, suck the blood of beast and man. . . ."

Actually, it is not the Ungoninos, as Dr. McGovern styles what may be an obscure subtribe of Machiguengas, but the Conibos who are best known for their puberty rites: the ceremony, named *pishita*, consists of the excising of the clitoris, and is performed not as a torture but in a mistaken effort at feminine hygiene. The Cashibos are not known as the Vampire Indians, though they are sometimes called the Bat People, in the same way that the Shipibos are called the Monkey People and the Conibos the Bird People. At present the Cashibos are in a degenerate state and may soon disappear; unlike the river Chamas, they have failed to adapt to civilization. Not only is their culture disappearing, but they manifest such symptoms of decline as indiscriminate exchange of mates and two husbands for each wife.

The river Chamas of today are a round-faced quiet people who consider themselves, probably correctly, superior to any jungle tribe of Peru. Their culture is rich and imaginative and includes a lovely, subtle pottery; in fact, they are the only true

artisans in the jungle. They will not work for anybody else—
though they themselves sometimes keep Campa slaves—and
the women, unlike those of many other tribes, are most reluctant
to sleep with a white, a mestizo, or even a non-Chama Indian.
Frequently, when traveling on the river, one notices Chamas
bathing along the banks: this has not been true of the other
Indians nor, for that matter, of the whites. Unlike the Campas,
Piros, and other tribal groups—and like the enduring Hopi and
Pueblo civilizations in North America—they are unrenowned
as warriors and have tended to avoid the inter-tribal attrition
which has always curtailed the numbers and the progress of the
Indians of both continents. Nor do they share the system of
the Campas and Machiguengas, among whom any property may
be utilized by him who needs or wants it most at any given
moment. As all good Americans will agree, only harm can come
of such a communistic system, which is on no account to be confused with the Christian ethic.

Later we drew to the bank again, at the large *lingüístico*
station at Caco, where we watched the Chamas prepare their
meals, mend their fish nets, dry the raw cane for their arrows,
and perform in general as Indians are said to do. Some of the
younger women struck me as very pretty, despite a red smear
about the mouth like a kind of garish lipstick, and the fine
mesh of the black face tattoos; unlike the Campa and Machiguenga women, who tend to be bow-legged and flat-hipped
when they are not fat, these girls are possessed of fine, straight
legs and tidy buttocks.

At dark, beneath another sky of silver fires, we tied up to a
balsa of huge *cedro* logs being towed slowly down the river.
Lumber is presently the chief industry of these regions, and of
all the woods the *cedro*, which is not only handsome and easily
worked but floats, is currently most in demand. Its disadvantage
is that it occurs as a solitary tree rather than in stands, and removing it from the forest, a process I watched at the encampment of Cruz's brother-in-law on the Inuya, is a laborious busi-

ness. The *cedro* has all but disappeared from the banks of the main rivers—Bates mentions that it was gathered extensively a century ago—but there are many other valuable woods here to replace it, and the caoba is already in general use.

We drifted in silence, peacefully, and the night was cold, as it often is on the rivers. From the bank, the *tarato* or *raton*, that remarkable animal I had first heard on the first night below the Pongo, was venting its loud imitation of Chinese blocks, and its cry was taken up by others farther down: it turns out that it is neither frog nor monkey, but a singular species of rodent. The red cinders of the eyes of floating crocodiles were picked up by Timo's flashlight, and bats hurried everywhere. I fell asleep at last in the bottom of the canoe, a new experience: in the past weeks, when not on the river beaches, I have laid my head on the mud floors of thatch huts, on the wood floors of Dominican missions, in coca lofts and in cacao bins. Of these, I can recommend only the river beaches, though just now I'd prefer a decent bed to any of them.

April 29. Ucayali.

César awoke just after midnight, and as the night had remained clear—the Southern Cross had climbed the sky and turned a little, and Sirius seemed to have disappeared, though this may have been my own hazy observation—we forsook the great raft and set off again on our own. It was quite cold, and I returned to my sleeping bag and lay down again in the bilges with the dead monkey. Toward three in the morning we came to the mouth of the Pachitea, where at a hacienda above the *encuentro* we routed out some peons in Cruz's employ. They prepared for us the first hot meal in days, eaten by candlelight, but nevertheless I was glad to leave the bank again, for the place was a pest hole of sand flies and *sancudos*: I can't get over how sharply the Ucayali differs from the whole length of the Urubamba in this respect. On we went, into a magnificent dawn of white river birds and early hawks and swift parrot silhouettes and jungle smell and the soft blowing of dolphins. Once again I had a feeling of huge well-being; life on the river, I felt, deserved every nice thing that has ever been said about it. I had given up cigarettes last month, while with missionaries in Brazil, but now I have taken them up again, I'm afraid, and am enjoying every puff.

César came forward, and we talked all morning. He is reading simultaneously a biography of Einstein and the collected works of Gabriela Mistral—he keeps a little suitcase full of such surprises—and he remarked in an offhand manner that he did not think Boris Pasternak deserved the Nobel Prize, or not, at least, for *El Doctor Zhivago*. We stopped at another Chama settlement—I am looking for a carved miniature canoe for a little boy at home—and there he spent an hour working skillfully on the infected foot of an old Indian. The infection, in a huge open wound, had splayed the little toe away from the rest of the swollen foot, which looked split right down the middle. To the amusement of the other Indians, César gave the man a penicillin shot in the behind, then washed the wound not quite gently with salt and water; with his customary flourish he dumped a quantity of iodine and penicillin powder over the whole works. The old man was perfectly stoic throughout a treatment so painful that I felt dizzy even as a spectator; he had a dignity that the other Shipibo men in these camps, drunk and indolent, rarely possess. And it is no coincidence that, in a society in which the women have clung to the old ways while the men have not, the former have alone retained the traditional serenity and grace.

By noon an infernal heat had risen from the sun and its reflection on the river, a heat which seemed to paralyze the jungle. We went on in silence, pausing only to take a photograph of the fossil in the bow of the canoe and an atmospheric shot of myself with the revolver on my hip: we have been using the revolver to annoy the crocodiles—in one narrow lead, yes-

terday afternoon, César, Alejandro, and myself got off thirty
rounds without doing the slightest damage—and in ordinary
circumstances this would probably be the sole function of a
revolver on these rivers, though perhaps, as Andrés says, the
possession of it tends to eliminate any more crucial need. At two
o'clock the metal roofs of Pucallpa's sheds gleamed in the misty
inferno ahead, and by four the fossil was safely ashore and in the
hands of a good carpenter, to be crated for the truck trip over
the mountains to Lima. We had reached Pucallpa in twenty-
eight hours of navigation, two less than César had promised
Andrés, and I was only relieved that I had kept my own doubts
from Cruz, or I would have had to eat my acrid hat. And, in
fact, Cruz was still brooding about Andrés when, at my elbow,
my erstwhile partner materialized: as Cruz had predicted, the
plane to San Ramón had not appeared in Atalaya, and it had
been only by the wildest chance, after two days of terrible
chagrin, that a plane of the *lingüísticos*, passing through to
Pucallpa, had appeared. Andrés would leave the next morning
on the Lima plane, weather permitting, and arrive in time for
his famous anniversary celebration in the evening.

Andrés had been certain that we were still far upriver, and
was rather put out when he learned from Fausto Lopez at the
Mercedes that I had not only checked in two hours ahead of him
but was even now standing in plain view in front of the carpenter shop down the street. He was a good sport about it and received our remarks with a smile: sheepishly he congratulated
Cruz, and, as of this evening, the two are friends again. César
was very moody when Andrés first appeared, and abruptly broke
off the plan we had made earlier, that he and his wife would have
drinks and dinner with me at the Mercedes. But later he turned
up alone—Andrés feels that Cruz is keeping his wife away, so
that the whole embarrassing business about which *encuentro*
had been meant would not rebound to Cruz's disadvantage—
and we had a quiet celebration. Whether or not Andrés is right,
I continue to like César Cruz, who has come up fast the hard

way. As Johnny Mutch, a sensible Scot who directs the lumber mill in Pucallpa, remarked to me last January, "César's all right. He's as good a man as you're apt to find around a place like this. Just don't turn your back on him too long, that's all." Mutch, incidentally, was as astonished as Andrés that we had actually found the fossil, and indeed the whole town is crowding around to see it. The local *comandante*, Juan Basurco, who was originally supposed to accompany us, appeared in town later without having heard about the fossil and, getting all his facts confused, told me excitedly about a fossil he had heard of in the Inuya which we should go and find together. I took him down the street and showed it to him.

I plan to remain here a few days to confirm certain names and other points, and to see the precious fossil safely off, with Alejandro to guard it, on one of the lumber trucks. The man I am most anxious to talk to is Wayne Snell, who is said to be out at the headquarters of the *lingüísticos*, some eight miles from town on the lake called Yarina Cocha.

May 2. Pucallpa.

On Saturday morning, just as Andrés was about to board the plane for Lima, Cruz came running up. A telegram had arrived for the police chief of Pucallpa from his confrere in Atalaya.

"Please detain a Señor César Cruz," it read—for I saw it myself later, and am paraphrasing only a little—"who appears to have removed a fossil mandible from property on the Mapuya River without consulting the owner, Victor Macedo."

Cruz's worst fears had been realized, for clearly Macedo, upon learning from Juan Pablo what had happened, had raced downriver to Atalaya and registered—despite the nice wording of the radiogram—a charge of theft. Macedo feels entitled to a share of the loot, for there was a fast-spreading and troubling rumor in Atalaya and now in Pucallpa that the fossil is worth a fortune. Having heard Juan Pablo's account, I don't feel Macedo has any claim—though Macedo and the luckless Vargaray might well argue that they had at least as much right to a fee as César Cruz. In any case, the bone has now been confiscated by the police "until the matter is clarified." In South America this phrase can usually be translated "until a satisfactory amount of money has changed hands, or more powerful influences are brought to bear." Before boarding the plane, Andrés promised to arrange for those influences in Lima, in the form of a cable from a cabinet minister which would release the local police from further responsibility and direct them to return the bone to me, but so far there has been no word. I am scheduled to fly out tomorrow, to Tingo María in the montaña, but it looks very much as if I shall have to stay.

Yesterday Macedo himself turned up in Pucallpa. Cruz ran into him on the street, and they greeted each other with their relentless Peruvian civilities, but Macedo walked off coldly without mentioning the small matter of the bone. This afternoon the three of us convened in the office of the chief of police, who was duly informed by Macedo that the poor unsuspecting Juan Pablo had delivered up a very valuable stone belonging to Macedo for the equivalent of eighty cents, having been brought previously to a state of total intoxication. Either Juan Pablo gave this story to Macedo to avoid handing over a share of the spoils, or Macedo gave this story to the police to strengthen his own claim. It doesn't much matter, though I am inclined to believe the latter. As it happens, Juan Pablo received five hundred and thirty *soles* from my own hand before touching the single draft of *pisco* handed around by Cruz to celebrate the transaction, and he had not touched a drop in the previous four hours, all of which had been spent with me in Quebrada Grasa.

But Macedo's claim as the owner of the stone was supported by the circumstance that in March he had been offered one thousand *soles* for it by the defendant, César Cruz, a point which Cruz had not seen fit to tell me until this afternoon: this shot a terrific hole in our position that Juan Pablo had always been recognized by all parties as the lawful owner, though I still believe this to be the case. Cruz now claims that he had dealt with Macedo only as the employer of Juan Pablo, not as the jaw's owner (though where this maneuver would have left poor Juan Pablo is difficult to say, unless it was up Grease Creek), and that anyway, he had informed Andrés of the offer of *mil soles.* (Andrés subsequently denied this.) César is the very picture of a man unjustly accused and complains bitterly of his plight, though in fact he is the only person to make anything out of the whole business. Macedo is also embittered. He tells me that if we had awaited his return that day everything would have worked out, but that now he is so angry with the thieving Cruz that he will not give up the bone for any price. He has a great many unkind things to say about Cruz, and Cruz, who says that everything would have been dandy if Andrés had not made us hurry, has a great many unkind things to say about Macedo. As for myself, I am mired indefinitely in the heat and mud of Pucallpa, and I have a great many unkind things to say about them both.

On Sunday, prior to the arrival of Macedo, I made my way out to Yarina Cocha, where I left with the base doctor's wife our unused supply of an excellent snake anti-venin; this anti-venin, which I had obtained for the journey in Brazil, is put up by the Butantan snake farm in São Paulo and is unobtainable in Peru. On a bluff overlooking the lake, above the doctor's house, was a cottage occupied by Wayne Snell, whose misfortune it was —considering that I took up about four hours of the poor man's Sunday—to be at home. Snell presently runs the *lingüístico* station at Camisea and another some distance above the rival Dominican operation on the Picha; it is he who for three years managed the ill-fated station at Pangoa, and I was most anxious to have his impressions of our experiences both at Pangoa and in the Pongo.

Wayne Snell is a solid, agreeable man with an attractive wife and children, and once he had brought under control an open suspicion of writers (shared with good reason, unhappily, by many honest people in the selva, where irresponsible writers rank first in the noble hierarchy of jungle liars) and a rather irritating smile of superior knowledge intended to indicate that he had my number, we got along perfectly well. The Snells were kind enough to give me lunch, and I'd like to say here how grateful I am to him for his confirmation of certain important points which would otherwise have been too hypothetical to retain in this journal.

While at the Pangoa station, Snell passed through the Pongo de Mainique three times. This is a claim few others can make, and one which probably establishes him as the leading authority on the canyon. Like Epifanio Pereira, he was anxious to assure me that an April passage would be relatively simple. Having never passed through in the dry season, I cannot dispute him. If he is correct, however, one can't help wondering why it is that the Machiguengas themselves travel it only in the dry season, and why no one, including Epifanio and Mr. Snell, has ever cared to try it in the "time of waters," when the *Happy Days* made its voyage. The reason, I think, is that Indian and white alike are awed by the speed and force of the spring torrents, and while on theory it is true that such navigational hazards as emergent rocks would increase in the summertime, so would the chances of surviving a mistake.

In Snell's opinion, anyone entering the Pongo who does not have to do so is a fool, and he feels that his own luck has run out: if he can possibly avoid it, he will not travel the Pongo ever again. He has heard that the Dominicans too have given up their occasional journeys for good.

Snell agrees with the padres that Ardiles has probably never been through the Pongo, and that Epifanio himself would not run the risk in April, though he would not hesitate to encourage others to do so, nor to order three of his Indians to go. Andrés and I had wondered from the start how Epifanio had gotten the Indians to obey, especially in the light of their subsequent terror, and I asked Snell if their fear of Pereira could account for it. Before answering, he asked who the three were. Agostino, I said, and Raul and Toribio. With the help of his wife, Snell was able to identify them in his mind. Agostino's father, he recalled, had been a Pongo *boga*, and Agostino himself might well have seen the Pongo from above. But he felt certain that none of our *bogas* had ever been through before, and thus had no real concept of what Epifanio had ordered them to do: they were as innocent as the rest of us.

Snell is less dogmatic about "sin" than most of the Protestant evangelists one meets in South America: the majority are fundamentalists who would speak of the padres and the Pereiras in the same breath. Though there is no love lost between the Catholics and Protestants, Snell referred to instances of cooperation with the Dominicans, and he did not feel obliged to condemn Fidel Pereira before remarking on the fine qualities of the old man. According to Snell, Fidel Pereira is intelligent and cultured and a man of honor in whose care Snell himself once felt quite confident in leaving his wife during a three-week absence. Though Señor Pereira is a Catholic, he has gotten along poorly with the Dominicans on the river, who not only disapprove of him but have attempted, not entirely unsuccessfully, to draw away his Machiguenga slaves. (Slavery has been outlawed in Peru for more than a century, and there is now in effect a fine law stating that no debt accumulated by an Indian which cannot be paid off by a week's labor shall be considered valid. This law, of course, is of no importance in Pangoa, and of very small importance elsewhere in the selva, where laws are difficult to enforce. The Indians themselves keep slaves and are glad to sell captives, and even their own children, to the white *patrones*; one missionary told me that in Atalaya itself perhaps one third of the population lives in what amounts to an enslaved condition.) In any case, the essential dispute between the

Pereiras and the Church concerns authority over the Machiguengas. As early as 1928 the Dominicans attempted to establish a mission at Pangoa; since they did not have Pereira's cooperation, the mission failed almost immediately. In recent years Pereira invited the *lingüísticos* to establish a station, but he soon tired of the noise of children, the occasional airplanes, and his own self-imposed obligation to extend an unceasing hospitality; also, he felt too old to be bothered with an atmosphere of religious zeal. He withdrew to his present hacienda upriver, and Epifanio, who took over Pangoa, failed to cooperate sufficiently to permit Snell to continue. Since the departure of the Snells, who managed to convert one of the Pereira daughters, Epifanio has begun to see himself in a religious light, and occasionally styles himself as an "evangelist."

The three Pereira sons holding property on the river are very different from one another. Justo, who was eleven when Jolly passed through in 1929, "gentle and refined, with manners that many European children might well be proud of," now considers himself a Machiguenga—like the rest, he is three-fourths Indian—and lives, eats, drinks, and dresses accordingly. He is harmless and considered a little dense. Alfredo, who occupies a hacienda hidden away from the main river, below Pangoa, is solitary and moody, but a gentleman like his father: the story is that he has never touched one of his Machiguenga women and that once, after a dispute with the old man, he took off downriver on a balsa and actually passed through the Pongo alone. Epifanio, the youngest son, has inherited his father's brilliance and his violence; he is a notorious drunk and trouble-maker.

In a reluctant way, Wayne Snell is sympathetic with Epifanio, whom he calls "Eppy." Epifanio is usually very pleasant—certainly this was our experience—and at one time, Snell says, he was extremely promising, but he has a streak of criminality which has grown more dominant in recent years, or ever since a disastrous liaison with a Peruvian woman much older than himself who, he told Andrés, ran away from him. His sister has told Snell that after the woman's departure Epifanio went temporarily berserk—it was in this period, apparently, that he invaded the Dominican mission at Coribene—and that since that time he has grown gradually more strange. In this regard, Snell was interested to hear my impressions of Epifanio, the curious soft smile and the feeling he gives that part of him is absent: these are new symptoms of his illness.

Snell rejected my lingering idea that Andrés had exaggerated our plight at Pangoa. As a religious man, he believes that Pangoa is a seat of the devil, beyond redemption, and that we were in trouble from the moment we stepped ashore. He related a story of his first encounter with a dangerous tribe, and how the instinct of a veteran companion that they were in serious danger had probably saved their lives. "In the jungle," he concluded, "you don't survive many mistakes. From your account, you were with a man who knows the jungle and knows what he is talking about. You were lucky. A less experienced man might have taken your side in that argument and gotten you both killed. There's no law down there, you know, and they wouldn't hesitate to throw you in the river."

Epifanio not long ago hacked a Machiguenga woman to death with a machete: Snell knows all the details of the case, in which Ardiles is somehow involved, but preferred not to go into them. The murder is common knowledge among the Indians, but to date the Pereira children have managed to keep the story from the old man, who is already sadly worried about his son. As for the police, they have shown their traditional lack of interest in what goes on down in the jungles of Pangoa.

Before I left I asked Snell if he had told me anything he did not want repeated. "No," he said, "I've been very careful. I haven't told you half of what I know." He smiled thinly. "As to Pangoa, you could write practically anything and you'd probably be right."

May 6. Pucallpa.

I have now passed a week in Pucallpa, attempting to deal with an aroused populace. The bone has become the talk of the town, almost every inhabitant of which has come to the yard outside the police station to stare at it. The misinformation heaped up by the excited reports of Pucallpa's radio station has caused me to be recognized by one and all as I stalk the streets, and I am frequently stopped and asked my opinion as to the identity of the monster. The truthful answer, that I have no idea, is entirely unsatisfactory, and I now say that it appears to be some sort of long-extinct herbivorous mammal. Depending on the alertness of my audience, this answer brings about either a blank stare or a furious nodding of the head, as if to say, Of course, of course, it's just what I suspected.

After six days of suspense a radiogram has at last arrived from Andrés, saying everything is OK, whatever that means. Things are not OK here, for the police have still heard nothing, and Macedo, who also stalks the streets, is open to neither bribe nor logic. The question of ownership is hopelessly lost in a mountain of lies and accusations, and the only hope of a change in this situation appears to be a wire from Lima stating that the bone belongs to neither Macedo nor myself but has been confiscated by the state. Meanwhile it stands mutely in its crate beneath this vulture sky, of no use to anybody.

My original plan was to take the fossil to the American Museum of Natural History in New York, since there is nobody in Peru equipped to make an exact identification. But an expert is not required to state that our unwieldy find is of considerable scientific value, and it seems unlikely that the Government of Peru, should they once claim it, will ever let it go: this is especially true since Peruvians, resenting the number of Inca and pre-Inca artifacts which have been taken from the country, are more than sensitive about "national treasures." The law on national treasures does not embrace paleontological finds, but doubtless it can be construed to do so.

I have taken photographs of the bone from every angle, but there seems to be nothing else that I can do here, if indeed there ever was: I am flying out to Tingo María tomorrow, minus the object of the expedition, with only the faint hope that matters can be straightened out in Lima. The week has passed in a sort of dream, a kind of miasma of unreality which only a jungle town could induce. Aside from the interview with Wayne Snell, the only noteworthy experience was an evening when César and myself took a jungle potion prepared by an old Indian of the town. This bitter stuff, which in color alone resembles opaque apple cider, is called variously *ayahuasca*, which is Quechua for "dead man's vine," or *soga de muerte*, which is Spanish for "vine of death." It produces hallucinations of faraway music and arrested time, a sense of several simultaneous worlds, which is quite remarkable; there is also the vague giddiness of being drunk, without the exhilaration. Toward the end a distinctly morbid state occurs, quite disagreeable. I have since identified the plant as *Banisteriopsis caapi*, a flowering liana of the Malpighiad family first described by Richard Spruce in 1853 and used as a narcotic by the Indian tribes throughout the Amazon: it is the narcotic known to the American writer William Burroughs and other admirers of its use as "yage." (In Lima I turned over a large draft of *ayahuasca* to the wandering beat poet Allen Ginsberg, who subsequently visited Pucallpa and saw the "excellent monstrous fossil." Of *ayahuasca* he wrote me fervently, "No wonder it's called *soga de muerte*.")

I have talked many times to César on the subject of the Picha ruins. He is sincerely convinced that they exist, on the basis of what he has been told by the Machiguenga at his *ganadería*. His description corresponds with that of Basagoitia, except that, according to Cruz, the ruin lies four days upriver rather than fifteen, plus a trek of several days into the jungle.

Last year, he says, two Englishmen tried to reach it but had to give up when their guide refused to go any farther.

Another man who believes completely in these ruins is Wayne Snell. Snell, incidentally, lent four of his Pangoa Indians to the Tennant expedition which discovered the ruin on the Mantaro, referred to earlier: he says that the party would not have gotten through had Fidel Pereira not approved it and passed word of his approval from tribe to wild tribe of the savage Machiguengas who inhabit the interior tributaries. Apparently there are also Machiguengas on the upper Camisea who kill on sight, and one gets the impression that civilization has reached only the outposts of some of these peoples; in many areas of Peru there remain wild rivers up which, past a certain point, no traveler dares to go. The Mantaro ruin lies about fifteen days, by canoe and foot, from the Urubamba.

Like César Cruz, Snell knows a Machiguenga who claims to have visited the Picha ruin. There is also another boy, a Machiguenga-Campa now at Yarina Cocha, who he thought might have been there too, and he talked to this boy the afternoon I was there. The boy had indeed been to the ruin, as had his father. He and Snell talked for a while in Machiguenga, and, adding this new information to what he already had heard, Snell was able to supply the following description, by far the most complete I have obtained to date.

The ruins lie at a journey of two days up a small tributary of the Picha, followed by four days on foot: this more or less corresponds to the distance estimated by Cruz's man. The Machiguengas do not like strangers prowling around in the region and avoid going there themselves, as their legend is that the place was cursed and deserted by its original chief: this may account, Snell feels, for the reluctance of the Machiguengas at the Dominican mission at the mouth of the Picha to admit any knowledge of the place.

The site itself is not a ruin in the usual sense, but a high cliff with a huge cavern: in former times a waterfall ran over the cliff and down across the cave mouth, making a natural fortress which was almost impregnable. The water course has now changed, and the cave has become accessible. A low wall surrounds the entire place, which is known to the Indians today as Shankivirintsi.

Snell hopes to reach the ruin this summer and, if he succeeds, will be the first white man ever to see Shankivirintsi. I wish him luck, but I must confess to a deep regret that Cruz was not there awaiting us at Timpia. For on the basis of all the evidence, pro and con, that I have heard, I now believe that the Picha ruin exists.

But if it served once as an excuse to enter the jungle, it can serve again. At this point I am suffering from a certain sense of failure, for not only did we miss our chance of locating Shankivirintsi but, after all this time and risk, we are also unable to leave the jungle with the bone. Still, I am leaving Pucallpa willingly, in the certainty I will be here again another time, for I have caught Andrés's jungle fever, the strong sense that something mysterious exists here which, even if located, can never quite be found.

And Alejandro. Alejandro, bowing and tugging his forelock to the last. Alejandro Condoris, beloved son, one hopes, of people named Condoris in Cuzco, though Alejandro, wandering away with us from the Rodriguez hacienda and now anxious to try his luck in Lima, gives the impression of being alone. Alejandro spent most of his meager pay on a great shining clumping pair of black shoes, for he had arrived in Pucallpa barefoot. (At one point he possessed a rude pair of sandals hewn from the defunct tire of a large truck, but these met an obscure fate somewhere on the rivers.) Besides his salary, he has been given his fare and food money and a little extra for his own diversion, should he care to make a distinction between diversion and food, and the promise from Andrés of a job in Lima. He left on a lumber truck this afternoon.

I feel bad about Alejandro, though he himself is as happy

as his mountain melancholy will ever let him be. I feel bad because, in a very trying moment on the Ucayali—Cruz lost his hold on the rope by which I was swinging myself from the canoe to a steep mud bank, and I fell ignominiously into the river, camera and all; I managed to hold the camera high, but in doing so smashed that hand hard on the snout of the great fossil—I became exasperated by his weak grasp of the situation, and I showed it. Afterward he brooded and seemed sullen. I bought some fresh bananas from the Chamas (he loves bananas and has a way of lying down next to a large bunch and quietly absorbing the lot, without ever appearing to take one up and peel it) and presented these, repentant, but still he looked distraught.

Alejandro had been longing to shoot the pistol or the rifle, and on the Inuya I had suggested to Andrés permitting him to do so, but both Andrés and César had dismissed any such idea as unheard of, and no more was said about it. On that afternoon on the Ucayali, however, I gave him the pistol to console him; he fired wildly at one crocodile, turned pale, and handed the gun back, sinking immediately into an even more impenetrable gloom. And I kept thinking how very much we had taken this slow, shambling boy for granted, as a kind of ungainly presence, as faceless and heavy and patient as one of the big duffels— this is the way such peons are treated here, and, having always had liberal pretensions, I disliked very much how easily I had fallen into this custom and become hardened to it.

At a loss, I tried to talk to him. This is not a rewarding occupation, especially when a certain language barrier is compounded by a Quechua accent, and probably I have avoided it more than I should. But anyway, we talked haltingly, reminiscing about our trip together, and immediately he came alive. I had been mistaken: the poor fellow had not been resentful of me but only despondent because he had angered me. Now it was clear to him that we were friends again, and he could scarcely contain himself, hunching forward over the rubber duffels until he was perched at my shoulder. With a frantic smile, eyes shining, he began to wring one of his hands, just as he had that afternoon in the Pongo de Mainique.

He cried out, "And the Pongo! Do you remember that time we went through the Pongo together, *señor*, do you remember how terrible it was!"

"*Sí, sí,*" I said as eagerly as I could. "*Sí, sí,* Alejandro." But I felt heavy-hearted and very small. I thought of all the interest and credit Andrés and I had received for having gone through the Pongo de Mainique in *el tiempo de agua*: Alejandro Condoris had been with us on the *Happy Days* and had received no credit whatsoever. As a peon, he was presumably not supposed to know what had befallen him, much less give himself airs.

Well, he's off to Lima, our good and faithful Alejandro, to match his wits with his loud *vivo* compatriots of the city streets. I'll remember him with fondness, and I wish him well.

EPILOGUE

SINCE RETURNING TO THE UNITED STATES, I have looked at a number of journals of South American exploration in attempts to find further information about the Urubamba and the Pongo de Mainique. Mr. Leonard Clark, as we have seen, has referred to the river as "forbidden," and while this is scarcely the case, there are few references to it in the literature of the jungle. Mr. Stratford Jolly and Mr. Julian Tennant, already mentioned, are the only writers known to me who speak about the Pongo.

The first descent of the Urubamba of which I have found record was made in the summer of 1846 by a party under the direction of a noted French naturalist, Francis de Castelnau: an account of its hardships appears in *The Valley of the Amazon*, by William Herndon and Lardner Gibbon, published in 1854. The account makes no reference to the Pongo de Mainique by this name, but an extract quoted from Castelnau's journals describes the loss of one of the party in an attempt to cross the river and portage around a dangerous waterfall—quite possibly that which lies at the head of the main rapid of the Pongo.

We found the current of exceeding rapidity; and the second cataract roared and foamed only one hundred metres below us. The Indians at every instant cast anxious glances over the distance that separated them from the danger. . . . At this moment we heard the cries behind us, and an Indian pointed with his finger to the canoe of M. Carrasco, within a few yards of us. It was struggling desperately with the violence of the current; at one instant we thought it safe, but at the next we saw that all hope was lost, and that it was hurried toward the gulf with the rapidity of an arrow. The Peruvians and the Indians threw themselves into the water; the old priest alone remained in the canoe, and we could distinctly hear him reciting the prayer for the dying until his voice was lost in the roar of the cataract. We were chilled with horror; and we hastened to the bank, where we met our companions successively struggling to the shore from the lost canoe. . . . We deeply regretted the loss of our companion, whose death was as saint-like as his life.

The photographs of the giant *mandíbula* I took to the American Museum of Natural History in New York. Dr. Charles Mook, the museum's senior authority on fossil reptiles, inspected the prints with a magnifying glass and tentatively identified the former owner of the jaw as a very large fossil crocodilian. Dr. Edwin Colbert of the museum agreed with this opinion; he estimated that the giant animal must have attained a length of at least thirty-five feet. According to Dr. Mook, it inhabited the earth at some period between five million and twenty-five million years ago. He was much interested in the discovery of this fossil, which represents a species heretofore unknown to him; he said that the museum would very much like to see it and would pay for its shipment from Peru if I could obtain permission for its export.

I have written a number of inquiries to Peru, where César Cruz has since become the defendant in a suit brought by his former friend Victor Macedo, and the ownership of the bone itself obscured for good by the mass of documents and memoranda: but for the written testimony of Mr. Allen Ginsberg, who saw it in its last known resting place, in Pucallpa, I might almost believe that the whole adventure of the jaw was the very sort of jungle hallucination against which I had been warned. "Between the outer world and the secrets of ancient South America," as Colonel Fawcett once lamented, "a veil has descended," and it now appears that the giant *mandíbula* will remain behind it, sinking slowly beneath man's detritus on the steaming banks of the Ucayali.

INDEX

FOR THE BEST IN PAPERBACKS, LOOK FOR THE

In every corner of the world, on every subject under the sun, Penguin represents quality and variety—the very best in publishing today.

For complete information about books available from Penguin—including Puffins, Penguin Classics, and Arkana—and how to order them, write to us at the appropriate address below. Please note that for copyright reasons the selection of books varies from country to country.

In the United Kingdom: Please write to *Dept. JC, Penguin Books Ltd, FREEPOST, West Drayton, Middlesex UB7 0BR*.

If you have any difficulty in obtaining a title, please send your order with the correct money, plus ten percent for postage and packaging, to *P.O. Box No. 11, West Drayton, Middlesex UB7 0BR*

In the United States: Please write to *Consumer Sales, Penguin USA, P.O. Box 999, Dept. 17109, Bergenfield, New Jersey 07621-0120.* VISA and MasterCard holders call 1-800-253-6476 to order all Penguin titles

In Canada: Please write to *Penguin Books Canada Ltd, 10 Alcorn Avenue, Suite 300, Toronto, Ontario M4V 3B2*

In Australia: Please write to *Penguin Books Australia Ltd, P.O. Box 257, Ringwood, Victoria 3134*

In New Zealand: Please write to *Penguin Books (NZ) Ltd, Private Bag 102902, North Shore Mail Centre, Auckland 10*

In India: Please write to *Penguin Books India Pvt Ltd, 706 Eros Apartments, 56 Nehru Place, New Delhi 110 019*

In the Netherlands: Please write to *Penguin Books Netherlands bv, Postbus 3507, NL-1001 AH Amsterdam*

In Germany: Please write to *Penguin Books Deutschland GmbH, Metzlerstrasse 26, 60594 Frankfurt am Main*

In Spain: Please write to *Penguin Books S. A., Bravo Murillo 19, 1° B, 28015 Madrid*

In Italy: Please write to *Penguin Italia s.r.l., Via Felice Casati 20, I-20124 Milano*

In France: Please write to *Penguin France S. A., 17 rue Lejeune, F–31000 Toulouse*

In Japan: Please write to *Penguin Books Japan, Ishikiribashi Building, 2–5–4, Suido, Bunkyo-ku, Tokyo 112*

In Greece: Please write to *Penguin Hellas Ltd, Dimocritou 3, GR–106 71 Athens*

In South Africa: Please write to *Longman Penguin Southern Africa (Pty) Ltd, Private Bag X08, Bertsham 2013*

FOR THE BEST IN PAPERBACKS, LOOK FOR THE

The Penguin Nature Classics Series
Edward Hoagland, Series Editor

☐ SELECTED JOURNALS AND OTHER WRITINGS

John James Audubon
Edited by Ben Forkner
Gathered here are Audubon's journals, letters, bird biographies, a memoir of his early years, and stories of the American frontier.
8 pp. color illustrations   *ISBN 0-14-024126-4*

☐ TRAVELS

William Bartram
Introduction by James Dickey
Bartram's exquisite travel diary, first published in 1791 and graced with his line drawings, is an account of his adventures in America's southern wilderness.
B/w line drawings throughout   *ISBN 0-14-025300-9*

☐ UNDER THE SEA WIND

Rachel L. Carson
The author of *Silent Spring* reveals the mysteries of the ocean and the dangerous, predatory ways of all marine life.
B/w line drawings throughout   *ISBN 0-14-025380-7*

☐ NORTH AMERICAN INDIANS

George Catlin
Edited and with an Introduction by Peter Matthiessen
This compilation of sketches, paintings, letters, and journal entries portrays Catlin's travels across the West and his life with various Indian tribes.
50 b/w illustrations   *ISBN 0-14-025267-3*

☐ THE JOURNALS OF LEWIS AND CLARK

Meriwether Lewis and William Clark
Edited and with an Introduction by Frank Bergon
The thrilling account of Lewis and Clark's odyssey across the uncharted wilderness of the American West.
Maps and illustrations throughout   *ISBN 0-14-025217-7*

☐ RING OF BRIGHT WATER

Gavin Maxwell
A lush portrait of Maxwell's life in the Scottish highlands—the beauty of his home, the surging sea, the mist-hung mountains, and his beloved pet otters.
12 pp. b/w photographs   *ISBN 0-14-024972-9*